Literature, Exile, Alterity

The New York Group of Ukrainian Poets

STUDIES IN RUSSIAN AND SLAVIC LITERATURES, CULTURES AND HISTORY
SERIES EDITOR: LAZAR FLEISHMAN (STANFORD UNIVERSITY)

ACADEMIC
STUDIES
PRESS

Literature, Exile, Alterity

The New York Group of Ukrainian Poets

MARIA G. REWAKOWICZ

This publication was made possible in part by the financial support of the Shevchenko Scientific Society, USA, from the Dr. Olha Mosiuk Fund.

НАУКОВЕ ТОВАРИСТВО ІМ. ШЕВЧЕНКА

SHEVCHENKO SCIENTIFIC SOCIETY, INC.

ISBN 978-1-61811-403-7 (hardback)

ISBN 978-1-61811-777-9 (paperback)

ISBN 978-1-61811-404-4 (electronic)

Book design by Ivan Grave
On the cover: "The New York Group,"
    by Jurij Solovij

Published by Academic Studies Press in 2014, paperback 2018
28 Montfern Avenue
Brighton, MA 02135, USA
press@academicstudiespress.com
www.academicstudiespress.com

Acknowledgments

This study reflects more than a decade of work on various aspects of the New York Group's evolution and creativity. It would not have been possible without the generous support and advice of many people—colleagues and friends alike. I would like to express my heartfelt gratitude to Maxim Tarnawsky, George G. Grabowicz, Larissa M. L. Zaleska Onyshkevych, Myroslava Znayenko, Marian J. Rubchak, Bohdan Rubchak, Bohdan Boychuk, Halyna Hryn, Tamara Hundorova, and Vasyl Makhno for their inspiration and continuous assistance. A special thanks is due to Tanya Chebotarev, Curator of the Bakhmeteff Archive at Columbia University in New York City, and Sofiia Sliusar, Curator at the Central State Museum-Archive of Literature and Art in Kyiv, Ukraine. Finally, I would like to thank the Ukrainian Research Institute at Harvard University for offering me a five-month Shklar Fellowship in the spring of 2003, which allowed me to rethink and refine my initial conceptualization of the New York Group, as well as the Shevchenko Scientific Society for its many years of unwavering financial support.

Early versions of three chapters in this study were previously published as journal articles and I am grateful to the editors for reprint permissions.

Chapter 3: "Periphery versus Centre: The New York Group's Poetics of Exile" appeared in *Canadian Slavonic Papers* 45.3-4 (Sept.-Dec. 2003): 441-57; chapter 5: "(Post)Modernist Masks: The Aesthetics of Play in the Poetry of Emma Andiievska and Bohdan Rubchak" was published in the *Journal of Ukrainian Studies* 27.1-2 (Summer-Winter 2002): 183-93; and chapter 6: "From Spain with Love, or, Is There a 'Spanish School' in Ukrainian Literature?" in the *Toronto Slavic Quarterly* 2 (Fall 2002), and is available online at: http://www.utoronto.ca/slavic/tsq/02/rewakowicz.html.

I dedicate this book to the memory of Danylo Husar Struk, whose untimely passing left a void in the Ukrainian scholarly community and whose encouragement and mentorship I cherish to this day.

Contents

Note on Transliteration and Translation

For the most part I use the Library of Congress system of transliteration in the body of this book, but with a few exceptions. The proper names of the poets of the New York Group are given in the form they themselves adopted in their respective countries of residence—thus Boychuk instead of Boichuk, Andijewska instead of Andiievs'ka. Moreover, the soft sign (ь) is omitted in proper names and the adjectival ending –s'kyi in Ukrainian surnames is rendered by –sky; therefore Kostetsky instead of Kostets'kyi. However, I preserve the Library of Congress system of transliteration without any modification in the footnotes and Selected Bibliography. Unless otherwise indicated, all translations are my own, as are any errors or misinterpretations.

Preface

The phenomenon of the New York Group comprises two generations of Ukrainian émigré poets residing, despite the group's name, on three continents (North America, South America, and Europe). New York City, however, has always constituted a seminal point of reference and its name signified an innovative approach to Ukrainian poetry. The significance of the city of New York is not just symbolic; this is indeed the place where in the mid-1950s the group originated, imbuing the postwar Ukrainian literary émigré milieu with avant-garde spirit and fresh designs. The poets eagerly experimented with poetic forms, privileging vers libre and metaphor, and embraced artistic and philosophical trends that were fashionable at the time, such as surrealism and existentialism. By the early 1960s, all seven founding members of the New York Group (Bohdan Boychuk, Yuriy Tarnawsky, Zhenia Vasylkivska, Bohdan Rubchak, Patricia Kylyna, Emma Andijewska, and Vira Vovk) had published at least one poetry collection; in fact, a majority had by then two or even three books to their credit. At that early stage, the poetic output of the group's members formed a genuine aesthetic alternative to socialist realism, which was still prevalent in Ukraine of the 1950s under the communist regime.

While the label "New York Group" commonly refers to the seven poets
named above, the group's membership also includes five poets who joined
the original contingent a decade or more later. These "fellow travelers" (Yuriy
Kolomyiets, Oleh Kowerko, Marco Carynnyk, Roman Babowal, and Maria
Rewakowicz) betray the same inclination toward formal experimentation and
display continuity in the realm of thematic preferences. Added to the univer-
sally poetic themes of love and death are the motifs of the erotic, the city,
alienation, and malaise. The preferable modes of expression are highly subjec-
tive, intellectual, and often playful and ironic. But what really unites the
founding members with their younger counterparts is a common desire to
express themselves freely in their native tongue. Despite a few cases of bilin-
gualism (Tarnawsky, Babowal, Kylyna, Carynnyk), Ukrainian by and large
remains the main and preferable medium for poetic expression among the
group's members. As much as the overall conceptualization of the New York
Group warrants the analysis of all twelve poets, this book of essays will focus
on the founding members only.[1] There are two main reasons for my choice;
first, the latecomers did not discursively participate in the formation of the
group, and second, the poetry analyzed here is primarily from the group's most
active period—that is, the second half of the 1950s and throughout the
1960s—in which Kolomyiets, Kowerko, Carynnyk and Babowal were only
marginally involved. With that in mind, my goal is to underscore those traits in
poetic idiom and aesthetic outlook that justify the existence of the New York
Group as a definable and coherent entity in the history of Ukrainian literature.

I intend to examine the group's activity and output from a theoretical
standpoint that is cognizant of power and transgression, exile and liminality,
and, finally, alterity or "otherness." The group's understanding of and relation
to modernism and postmodernism will also be discussed, as will be its prefer-
ence for such philosophical and aesthetic trends as existentialism and
surrealism. While this scheme necessarily points to a methodological

---

1   In fact, all major anthologies of the group's poetic output published thus far include
     selections from all twelve members. Cf. O. H. Astaf'iev and A. O. Dnistrovyi, eds., *Poety
     N'iu-Iorks'koi hrupy: Antolohiia* (Kharkiv: Ranok, 2003); Mariia Revakovych, ed., *Pivstolittia
     napivtyshi: Antolohiia poezii N'iu-Iorks'koi hrupy* (Kyiv: Fakt, 2005); Mariia Revakovych
     and Vasyl' Gabor, eds., *N'iu-Iorks'ka hrupa: Antolohiia poezii, prozy ta eseistyky* (Lviv:
     Piramida, 2012).

pluralism, it sets the stage for my own synthesis of literary politics, social history, and close textual analysis.

In Chapter 1, I situate the poets against the background of Ukrainian and Western modernisms and elucidate the New York Group's general aesthetic orientations. The group's version of modernism betrays hybrid qualities, mainly because it subsumes elements of both the historical avant-garde and high modernism. Moreover, the New York poets are typical late modernists in the sense that their proclaimed affinity with modernist aesthetics is self-consciously fashioned and underscored. They aspire to be part of an international community of writers and artists who place high value on formal experimentation and the individual search for personal values.[2] However, even though their claim to formal newness holds in the context of Ukrainian literature, the poets of the New York Group have not managed to secure for themselves wide recognition in their adopted countries, despite appearing in translation in numerous literary magazines.

Chapter 2 places the group's emergence and activity within a clearly defined social and political context. This contextualization is presented as a series of distinct discourses which foreground the poets' interactions not only with their predecessors and contemporaries, but also among themselves. I make use of archival material and refer to a number of letters the individual members sent to each other and to their literary mentors in order to show how much energy and thought the group devoted to gaining recognition and power. Asserting their distinct voice and presence was of utmost importance to them. Their beginnings were not chaotic but strategically designed to win over both the émigré reading public and the émigré critics of the older generation.

In Chapter 3, I introduce the concept of exile as one possible way to interpret the New York Group's poetic output. I argue that even though these poets do not fit the typical paradigm of exile writers, they nonetheless display exilic sensibility in their work. This sensibility manifests itself not only in feelings of alienation and "otherness" but also in the desire to make the experience of exile as universal as possible. The motifs of homelessness, uprootedness, and love for the native land, if occasionally present, are immediately cleansed of any local

---

2   As I will indicate below, their involvement in many translation projects underscores this
     desire to be part of the modernist community of poets.

reference. In this chapter I also discuss the group's situatedness vis-à-vis Ukraine, on the one hand, and vis-à-vis its periphery, the émigré milieu, on the other. The poets' creative position was literally betwixt and between two powerful structures: the communist regime of Ukraine and the politicized émigré majority, which had a hard time accepting such atypical exile postures as pure aestheticizing and formal playfulness.

Chapters 4 and 5 assess the group's poetic output from the perspective of two dominant trends in twentieth-century arts and literature, namely modernism and postmodernism. Chapter 4 analyzes the poets' surrealist turn and traces modernist and postmodernist characteristics in their writings, arguing in the process that in the "vocal"[3] period, modernism prevailed. The poets' insistence on the autonomy of art, their hostility to mass culture, and their fetishization of newness and individualism indeed place them directly in the middle of the modernist camp. Chapter 5 focuses specifically on the aesthetics of play in the poetry of Emma Andijewska and Bohdan Rubchak. Despite the fact that both these poets toy with the ludic and employ some typically postmodern techniques such as intertextuality, irony, and fragmentation, they remain modernists at heart. This is also the case as far as Yuriy Tarnawsky is concerned, even though in his late poetry he assumes a somewhat postmodernist posture.

In Chapter 4, I also introduce the concept of liminality, which entails transitional or ambiguous states.[4] Liminality seems to be equally applicable to the questions of poetic shifts within the modernism–postmodernism paradigm and to the exilic condition into which the poets of the New York Group were thrown by the necessity of historical circumstances. Giuseppe Mazzotta in *Dante, Poet of the Desert*, for example, views both exile and poetry as naturally liminal states.[5] In the case of the New York Group of poets, I contend that in spite of their émigré status (which necessarily entails a considerable degree of marginalization), they were able to transcend their periphery by pushing the aesthetic boundaries of Ukrainian literature.

---

3   This is my own designation for the period stretching roughly from 1956 to 1971.

4   I am using the concept of liminality in the sense given to it by Victor Turner. See his *The Ritual Process: Structure and Anti-Structure* (Chicago: Aldine, 1969), 94-96.

5   Giuseppe Mazzotta, *Dante, Poet of the Desert: History and Allegory in the Divine Comedy* (Princeton: Princeton University Press, 1979), 107-46.

The following two chapters, 6 and 7, approach the group's oeuvre from thematic perspectives. Without doubt, eroticism, with its existential subtext, and "Spanishness" are two themes that have proven seminal and pervasive for the New York Group. What I also view as important to point out is that inherent in each of these themes is the multiplicity of signification. Erotica, for example, was not only used to stir controversy by debunking sexual taboos and promoting transgressions or alterity, but also to convey an existentialist credo, including the need for freedom and responsibility for each individual choice. The emergence of the "Spanish School" phenomenon, on the other hand, happens to be the poets' guise for deeply felt and espoused internationalism.

While the "Spanish bug" affected only a handful of the group's members,[6] Eros has proven to be universally inspiring, although it manifested itself differently in each poet. In fact, Chapter 8 discusses various representations of the erotic, at the same time tying them to the condition of exile. In many ways, this chapter returns to some of the concerns introduced in Chapter 3, expanding them by comparing the exilic condition to the state of being in love. Both constitute liminal states, and both imply lack and desire to possess something that is valuable, yet absent. I am also trying to convey in this chapter the idea that the dynamic between Eros and exile is capable of exposing all the inconsistencies in the process of reconfiguring the topoi of identification. Self-proclaimed cosmopolitanism, for example, can be the mask of an exile in distress. Or, escape into the poetic craft (the veneration of ars poetica) can help to alleviate the sense of not belonging. Thematizing difference (linguistic and territorial), as well as estrangement and separation through the passage of time, lie at the heart of the group's poetic output and clearly elucidate its exilic sensibility.

Chapter 9 is devoted exclusively to the oeuvre of Patricia Nell Warren (Kylyna).[7] Her rendezvous with Ukrainian literature is truly remarkable considering that she, unlike the other members in the group, volunteered to be exiled. She did not need to accept such a condition, and yet she did, learning

---

6   I am referring here mainly to the poetry of Tarnawsky, Kylyna, and Boychuk. These poets as well as Vovk and Vasylkivska learned the language and spent considerable time and energy translating the works of modernist and contemporary Spanish authors.

7   Kylyna is a pseudonym of Patricia Nell Warren, an American born in the state of Montana, who married Yuriy Tarnawsky in 1957.

Ukrainian well enough to express herself in that language poetically. I argue that all her transformations, those of a Ukrainian poet and of an American gay writer and activist, can best be explained by the concept of alterity, especially as conceived and proposed by the French philosopher Emmanuel Levinas. To him, alterity is the most radical gesture of ethical responsibility in the face of the Other. In Warren's case, I make an exception and discuss not only her poetry but also some of her English-language fiction. This decision stems from the necessity to underscore the simple fact that her Ukrainian poetry on the one hand, and her fiction in native English on the other, display a remarkable continuity and inextricably complement each other.

In the concluding Chapter 10, I ponder why the city of New York, so emblematic and essential to the group's image, has been so scarcely thematized in the poets' oeuvre. I contrast the approach to the New York themes found in the poetry of Tarnawsky and Boychuk with that of their predecessors (Vadym Lesych, Iurii Kosach) and, most importantly, with that of their much younger colleague, Vasyl Makhno, a Ukrainian poet who settled in New York in 2000. While the group's reluctance to explicitly refer to New York can be partially explained by the fact that their attention was turned mostly to their own subjectivity (quite in line with a modernist premise), the absence of poems with urban motifs, referring specifically to the metropolis in which they lived and worked, is rather glaring. In this respect, Makhno's emphasis on the concrete and the local comes as a stark contrast to the group's practice, underscores his postmodern inclinations for the particular rather than the universal, and, finally, outlines a new path forward for Ukrainian poetry outside Ukraine's borders.

Before I embark on the story of the New York Group, however, it is fitting to begin by telling the life stories of its members, all the more so because their biographies have considerably impacted their poetry. Furthermore, they all represent a generation that not only experienced the horrors of war but also lived through an enormously dynamic and even transformative period of history. The postwar decades in America witnessed the proliferation of artistic styles and movements that necessarily found their expression and cultivation in the creative endeavors of young émigré poets.

Bohdan Boychuk's organizational skills contributed to the impression (sometimes upheld even by his colleagues) of his being the unnamed leader of the group, a label he has neither disputed nor defended. Born in 1927 in the village of Bertnyky in Western Ukraine, he was old enough to be directly affected by the dread of World War II, and suffered forceful deportation to Germany for hard labor by the Nazis at the age of sixteen. He completed his high school education in a Displaced Persons' Camp in Aschaffenburg, Germany, and immigrated to the United States in 1949.

Eager to establish himself in his adopted homeland and taste its everyday comforts, he enrolled in City College of New York, and in the mid-1950s graduated with a Bachelor's degree in electronic engineering. By a twist of fate, his college education was interrupted by a military draft and the subsequent discovery of a serious illness, which prevented him from serving in the Korean War. Diagnosed with tuberculosis, he spent three years recovering at Stony Wold Sanatorium in upstate New York. Upon his return to the city in 1953, he resumed his studies at CUNY and three years later finished his college education. In 1957, Boychuk's first poetry collection, *Chas boliu* (The Time of Pain), came out, marking the beginning of an émigré literary career. The two professional roles he assumed ran perfectly parallel lives and seemingly never interfered with each other. He retired from his engineering job in 1992 and since then has devoted himself to literature full-time. In 2000 he moved to Kyiv, Ukraine, and in the past decade he has divided his residence between Kyiv and Glen Spey in the Catskills in upstate New York.

Boychuk's poetic oeuvre, viewed from the angle of its philosophical underpinnings, exhibits a remarkable degree of unity and continuity, despite the fact that his eleven collections to date span half a century. He is an existential poet with a strong metaphysical bent, placing supreme emphasis on the individual—his thoughts, fears and desires—as well as on the individual's relationship to society, the universe, and God. The anguish caused by human mortality and his frustrated attempts to rise above the historicity imposed by time is counterbalanced in Boychuk's poetry by the energy drawn from creativity and physical love. The poet embraces and identifies with the pain that life brings as it unfolds, because it alone allows the fullness of experience and construes the identity of each individual.

Bohdan Boychuk and Yuriy Tarnawsky met in 1953, and from the very start engaged in organizing a variety of forums for their literary production: ad hoc café gatherings, literary evenings, and the bulletin "Students'ke slovo"

(The Student Word), an addendum to the daily newspaper *Svoboda*. Born in 1934 in Turka, a small town in Western Ukraine, Tarnawsky was luckier in some ways than his older colleague. Like Boychuk, he finished his high school education in Germany, but unlike him, arrived in the United States in 1952 not alone, but with his father and siblings, an older sister and a younger brother. Tarnawsky's family settled in Newark, and he graduated from Newark College of Engineering with a degree in electronic engineering. He subsequently worked for IBM until his retirement in 1992, settling permanently in White Plains, New York. Perhaps it was the computers' communicative potential that prompted him to expand his education. In the mid-seventies he returned to school to study semantics, and in 1982 earned a PhD in linguistics from New York University. In the mid-nineties, he taught Ukrainian literature for three years as an adjunct professor at Columbia University in the department of Slavic languages and literatures. In the past decade he has shifted his focus from writing poetry in Ukrainian to writing experimental prose in English. His most recent publication is a collection of mininovels titled *The Placebo Effect Trilogy* (2013), consisting of *Like Blood in Water*, *The Future of Giraffes*, and *View of Delft*.

By general consensus, Tarnawsky is considered the most radical and experimentally daring poet among the members of the New York Group. A fervent proponent of vers libre in poetry, he practices what he preaches. The author of ten books of poetry in Ukrainian, the last of which, *Ikh nemaie* (They Do Not Exist, 1999), was published in Kyiv, Tarnawsky delights in formal and genre diversity: lyrical miniatures, stanzaic poems, prose poems, and even poems constructed as questionnaires. His poetic oeuvre displays an incessant search for novel formal solutions in order to channel his vision as accurately as possible. Tarnawsky's poems evince a certain sense of mathematical precision, especially in the realm of poetic language. His images tend to be word efficient, concrete, and calculated, yet spontaneous at the same time. The poet exhibits a real talent for mixing the ordinary with the unusual, for perceiving the similarity in the dissimilar.

The initial core of the group, consisting of Boychuk and Tarnawsky, soon expanded to include Zhenia Vasylkivska and Bohdan Rubchak, the latter residing in Chicago at the time. Vasylkivska, born in 1929 in Kovel in the Volhynia region of Western Ukraine, emigrated with her family first to Austria in 1944, and then in 1951 to the United States, settling in New York City. She delayed her poetic debut until 1959, but by the mid-1950s had become active in editing and translating, especially from French, Spanish, and English into Ukrainian, and occasionally also from Ukrainian into English. A PhD candidate in French literature at Columbia University at the time of the group's inception, she was highly respected by her male counterparts and encouraged to share her considerable literary and language expertise. After receiving her degree, she moved south and settled in Washington, DC, got married, and by the mid-1960s disengaged completely from things literary, abandoning active participation in Ukrainian émigré culture. She worked at the Library of Congress for a few years, but after she earned a Master's degree in political science she was hired by the U.S. government as a political consultant, specializing in the issues of nuclear arms.

Korotki viddali (Short Distances, 1959), Vasylkivska's only book of poetry, foregrounds the elusive, the veiled, the oneiric. Avoiding confessional directness, she filters her poetic vision through dense, opaque metaphors that are nonetheless fresh and not without a dose of surprise. The emotions of the lyrical heroine—never overexposed but always intensely felt—are imperceptibly interwoven into the voluble world of nature, a world in which poetry and nature seamlessly conflate. Slight as her poetic output is, it manages to unveil an idiolect that is both mature and youthfully promising, with a deeply felt responsibility for the written word and an almost childlike delight in the freedom of expressive possibilities.

Bohdan Rubchak's connection with the New York Group turned out to be more steady and significant, even though, unlike Vasylkivska, he did not reside in New York at the time the group was consolidating, but rather visited New York on a regular basis. Discursively and creatively, through correspondence and publications, he was very much in the center of all the major efforts undertaken by the group. Born in 1935 in Kalush, Western Ukraine, he was barely a teenager when he arrived in America in 1948, together with his mother. His early proclivity for things philological eventually resulted in a full-fledged literary and scholarly career. He graduated with a PhD in comparative literature from Rutgers University in 1977. After almost a decade of living on the East Coast, he returned to Chicago in 1973 and took a teaching position at the University of Illinois. He worked as a professor in the department of

Slavic languages and literatures until his retirement in 2005. Currently, he resides in Boonton, New Jersey.

The author of six books of poetry, Rubchak defies hasty compartmentalization. On the surface, he easily strikes us as a traditionalist, the least experimental member of the group, especially in the way he approaches poetic language and forms, but what is often missed is that behind his refined intellectualism and poetic craftsmanship lies a strikingly innovative incorporation of the implied reader into the structure of his texts. Rubchak appears to be the only poet of the New York Group who displays a penchant for a playful dialogue with the reader. His early poems clearly betray an existentialist bias and foreground the motif of dichotomy between nature and the city, but his more mature oeuvre favors intellectual, referential, and distanced or rational treatment of the subject matter over the guarded spontaneity and lyrical directness of his early poems. Interestingly, Rubchak's poetry bears no reference to American reality; by and large it basks in the universal rather than in the particular and the local.

When Patricia Kylyna published her debut collection *Trahediia dzhmeliv* (A Tragedy of Bees, 1960), it was greeted by her colleagues as well as by the critics with much awe and enthusiasm. Born Patricia Nell Warren in 1936 in the state of Montana, she embraced alterity as a guiding force in her creative endeavors quite early on. Her Ukrainian turn came as a result of events of a personal nature. While still a student of medieval studies at the Manhattanville College in Purchase, New York, she met the young Ukrainian poet Yuriy Tarnawsky in 1956, and a year later they were married. Kylyna mastered the Ukrainian language within a remarkably short period of time and published three books of poetry, using Ukrainian as her only medium of poetic expression. Her rendezvous with Ukrainian literature spanned approximately sixteen years, from 1957 to 1973, during which time she also worked professionally as an editor for *Reader's Digest*. By the late 1960s, Kylyna's interest was increasingly shifting from writing poetry in Ukrainian to writing fiction in her native English. In 1973, she divorced Tarnawsky and declared herself a lesbian. Since then she has devoted herself exclusively to prose in her native English. The author of eight novels, the best known of which is *The Front Runner* (1974), a gay love story, she currently resides in Glendale, California, and co-owns a media company, Wildcat International.

Kylyna's poetic oeuvre conveys existentialist anguish, at the same time underscoring a surrealist sensibility. She is an intellectual poet and often incorporates Hellenic, Arabic, Spanish, and American native mythic sources, deliberately spicing up her lyricism with dramatic and narrative elements. In her mature poems, Kylyna experiments with poetic forms—lyrical miniatures, sonnets, long poems—and ventures into new themes, the most interesting of which are her poetic descriptions of Spanish cities.

The year in which Kylyna began to learn Ukrainian, 1957, also saw the arrival of Emma Andijewska from Munich, Germany, and the beginnings of her association with the group. By then she was a well-known young poet—her debut collection *Poezii* (Poems) came out in 1951—whose thirst for novelty and experiment earned wide critical acclaim. Born in 1931 in Donetsk, Andijewska is the only poet among the founding members of the group who comes from Eastern Ukraine. During the war her family managed to settle in Germany, and this is the country she has adopted as her second homeland, even though at various times she has taken temporary residence in New York City and Paris. She currently lives in Munich and, in addition to writing, devotes much of her time to painting, for which she has gained considerable international recognition.

Andijewska's almost three-year residence in New York coincided with the most dynamic period in the group's existence. It is arguable that her best poetic work comes from those years, and her knowledge of the riches and nuances of the Ukrainian language has been phenomenal and much admired by her colleagues, who many a time were criticized for insufficient mastery of the language. In 1959, Andijewska married Ivan Koshelivets, a Ukrainian émigré literary critic, and shortly after that they both returned to Munich.

An enormously prolific poet and writer, Andijewska has authored twenty-eight books of poetry, three novels, and numerous works of short fiction. The hermeticism of her poetry, at times intriguing and bewildering, invites many interpretations. This is most likely why her output has triggered a variety of responses, some positive and some negative. The poet herself never reacted in public to the criticism about her, never attempted to explicate her particular approach, and made no effort to dispel the charges of elitism. The perceived difficulty of Andijewska's poetry stems from the way she approaches poetic language. Language, to her, constitutes the material out of which a new reality must be built; it is never simply a tool that enables her to inform or mirror something already in existence. The mystery of existence sparks the dance of words for Andijewska and simultaneously instigates the desire to go beyond them into the unknown and primordial.

Vira Vovk's affiliation with the New York Group came about comparatively late, at a point when she was already deeply involved in literary matters of the Ukrainian émigré community. By the time she became acquainted with most of the group's members in 1959, she had authored three collections of poetry and three books of short fiction. Perhaps that is why she has always guarded her independent stance and preferred to speak of her association with the group in terms of a friendly cooperation rather than in terms of outright membership. However, her creative peer exchanges with the poets of the group left a mark on the development of her poetic idiom.

Born in 1926 in Boryspil, Western Ukraine, Vira Vovk (a pen name of Vira Selianska) left her homeland while still in her teens, joining her parents as they fled the Soviet occupation of Lviv. The family settled in Dresden, Germany, where Vovk received her high school diploma and witnessed the death of her father during the relentless bombing by Allied troops in the final stages of the war with the Nazis. After the war, she completed her undergraduate education, attending universities in Tübingen and Munich, but did not stay in Germany. In 1949, she immigrated to Brazil, where she continued her studies, earning a doctorate in comparative literature at the Catholic University in Rio de Janeiro. For many years, until her retirement, she taught at the Federal University in Rio. In addition to seventeen collections of poetry, she has also published numerous books of prose, drama, and translations.

Vovk's poetry focuses on positive aspects of human reality such as friendship, charity, love, and ultimately faith in God. A religious undercurrent remains strong throughout her entire oeuvre and stands in sharp contrast to the skeptical (if not atheistic) existentialist posture of her colleagues. Thematically and formally, Vovk's poetry is dynamic, diversified, and constantly searching. Her poetic world is not insulated from surrounding reality; the mythic and the contemporary coexist and are of comparable importance. Feminine (and occasionally feminist) concerns also captivate her imagination: whether it is a woman-lover, a woman-poet, or a woman as mother, the poet identifies herself with every womanly hypostasis, at the same time ascribing to her originary qualities, a dimension in which causality dissolves. Within the context of the New York Group's output, this particular imprint is Vovk's alone.

Critics often contend that literature is an open concept, an activity always in process, an entity that has no permanent essence or canon. While canons indeed often come and go, there are always certain junctures and events in the historical development of any literature which resist erasure no matter how open and unstable the concept of literature itself is. This book is an attempt to show that the phenomenon and poetry of the New York Group constitutes an example of one such juncture in the history of Ukrainian literature.

CHAPTER 1

Introduction: New Land, New Poetry

One can only imagine what a teenager or young adult might have felt after two weeks of sailing through the Atlantic, seeing the approaching shores of a new continent and discerning on the horizon the contours of a new city. Was it excitement, confusion, fear, or perhaps a plain bewilderment at the enormous adjustments to be made in the host country? Displacement brings uncertainty but it also opens up many new opportunities. Émigrés often look nostalgically back to the past and the country of their origin, but they can also embrace their new home and immerse themselves in the culture of the new land. The Ukrainian poets of the New York Group clearly chose the latter, quite possibly because arriving in North America at a relatively early age made it easier for them to adjust.

The poetry produced by the members of the New York Group cannot be fully appreciated without examining the group's affinities with intellectual and cultural developments in the West, including its relation to the modernist and avant-garde movements, partly transplanted from Europe and flourishing in the United States shortly after the Second World War. In fact, the interplay between modernism's perpetual thirst for newness, on the one hand, and the avant-garde's rebellious spirit, on the other, figures quite prominently in the poetic oeuvre of the group. In the context of Ukrainian literature, the poetry of the New York Group constitutes a synthesizing, and at the same time somewhat hybrid phase in the history of Ukrainian modernism. It is hybrid in the sense that it incorporates the elements of both international "high" modernism and the historical avant-garde, mainly surrealism. However, modernism has always been an important signpost for these poets, and it would be difficult to appreciate their output without understanding what it actually meant for them. One thing is certain—at the time that they entered literature, that is, the mid-1950s, modernism was no longer the vanguard but already considered a new establishment, and New York was its capital. In the context of international modernism, the New York Group was a latecomer, but within the confines of Ukrainian literature it definitely represented a new wave of modernist aesthetics and proposed novel poetic experiments.

Discussions of literary modernism have remained very much national or regional in character, often to the point that the same term may denote completely different concepts.[1] Yet there is a general agreement that the modernist movements and the debates they generated are the products of an era characterized by internationalism and ever-increasing artistic migrations. Malcolm Bradbury and James McFarlane put it succinctly: "No single nation ever owned Modernism, even though many of the multiform movements of which it was made did have national dimensions and origins in specific regions of European culture."[2]

In the Anglo-American tradition, the term "modernism" is predominantly associated with the writings of such authors as Ezra Pound, T.S. Eliot, James Joyce, Virginia Woolf, Wallace Stevens, and Gertrude Stein, most of whom had their literary debuts in the period following World War I. Their works display a high degree of technical innovation, which, in terms of form and language, stands in sharp contrast to the literary production of the preceding

---

1   Spanish literature is especially a case in point, where *modernismo* (roughly a Hispanic variant of French Symbolism) refers to literature written in the last decade of the nineteenth century, and *postmodernismo* refers to literature written before World War I, 1905-1914. See Matei Calinescu, *Five Faces of Modernity: Modernism, Avant-Garde, Decadence, Kitsch, Postmodernism* (Durham: Duke University Press, 1987), 77.

2   Malcolm Bradbury and James McFarlene, eds., *Modernism, 1890-1930* (Harmondsworth: Penguin, 1991), 13.

era. The concept of "high modernism," which is often applied to the writings of the aforementioned authors, is also extended to include literary figures whose medium of expression was not necessarily English. The modernist canon also embraces such writers and poets as, for example, Thomas Mann, Franz Kafka, R. M. Rilke, Marcel Proust, and André Gide. This kind of "high," metaphysical modernism, as Tamara Hundorova puts it, is simply missing in Ukrainian literature.[3]

The period around the First World War in the Continental-European tradition is characterized by the presence of a wide range of avant-garde movements rather than by a canon of individual writers. Such movements as Expressionism in Germany, Futurism in Italy and Imperial Russia, and Dada and Surrealism in Switzerland and France bring about the question of the interrelationship between modernism and the avant-garde. While there are critics who see the avant-garde as a concept subordinate to modernism or as its prominent feature,[4] there are also those who want to draw a firm line between these two artistic approaches, seeing the avant-garde as a more radical form of artistic negation, reflected especially in its daring experimentation and in opposition to art as an institution.[5] Within the latter frame of reference, the term

---

3   See her "Dekadans i postmodernism: pytannia movy," *Svito-vyd* 1 (1995): 66.

4   Cf. Astradur Eysteinsson, *The Concept of Modernism* (Ithaca: Oxford University Press, 1990); Peter Nicholls, *Modernisms: A Literary Guide* (Los Angeles: University of California Press, 1995); M. H. Abrams, *A Glossary of Literary Terms*, 4th ed. (New York: Holt, Rinehart and Winston, 1981), 110.

5   The most notable proponent of such a divide is Peter Bürger. In his book *Theory of the Avant-garde*, he insists on separating the European avant-garde of the 1920s from aestheticism (and one can assume from "high" modernism as well) on the basis of the avant-garde's goal to undermine, attack, and alter the bourgeois institution of art and its ideology of autonomy. In other words, changing artistic and literary modes of representation (something that experimentation is supposedly all about) was insufficient—one had to also attempt to reintegrate art and life to be considered truly "avant-garde." However, as Bürger himself recognized, the avant-gardists failed to achieve their ultimate goal of dissolving the borders between life and art, and the question of aesthetic autonomy remained as much of an issue for them as for the modernists. (An excellent critique of Bürger's work is included in Richard Murphy's *Theorizing the Avant-Garde: Modernism, Expressionism, and the Problem of Postmodernity* [Cambridge: Cambridge University Press, 1998], 26-48.) The other critics who also advocate drawing a line between the avant-garde and modernism base their stand more on the grounds of the avant-garde's artistic extremism and rebellious spirit rather than on issues related to the autonomy and institution of art. See, for example, Charles Russell, *Poets, Prophets, and Revolutionaries: The Literary Avant-garde from Rimbaud through Postmodernism* (New York: Oxford University Press, 1985); Matei Calinescu, *Five Faces of*

"modernism" is understood more along the lines of the Germanic literary tradition, in which modernism is a concept applied to the literary activities of the 1880s and 1890s, a period characterized by a proliferation of manifestoes and "modern" magazines all in the spirit of some kind of hybrid synthesis between romanticism and naturalism.[6]

The era of *fin de siècle* in the Anglo-American context corresponds to aestheticism and decadence (the writings of Oscar Wilde are the best representation of this movement in English literature) and to symbolism in France (with Charles Baudalaire as a point of origin and source of inspiration). The French symbolists (poets Mallarmé, Verlaine, Rimbaud, Laforgue) exerted an enormous influence upon the development of modernism in general, but there is no agreement on whether the movement itself is a constituent part of the modernist trends, or if it stands out as a completely separate phenomenon. René Wellek, for example, identifies symbolism with modernism and sets it off from the new avant-garde movements after 1914.[7] The problem with this approach is that it sometimes creates paradoxical situations. In Ukrainian literature, symbolism is almost nonexistent or (at most) poorly represented prior to 1917. Hence, following Wellek's interpretation, one could make a logical conclusion that it is impossible to speak of Ukrainian modernism before 1914. Bohdan Rubchak, for instance, consistently refers to the writers of "Moloda muza" (The Young Muse) and "Ukrains'ka khata" (The Ukrainian House) (the only two modernist groupings before World War I) as pre-symbolists. In those few instances when he does use the term "modernist" in reference to their writings, he puts it in quotation marks.[8]

Modernity; Richard Kostelanetz, ed., *The Avant-garde Tradition in Literature* (Buffalo, NY: Prometheus, 1982). Lastly, it is important to point out that there are also scholars who conflate the avant-garde and modernism, and make the latter subordinate to the former. Renato Poggioli's concept of the avant-garde, for example, is so extensive that it really corresponds to what others designate as modernism. See his *The Theory of the Avant-garde* (Cambridge, MA: Harvard University Press, 1968). John Weightman's *The Concept of the Avant-garde: Explorations in Modernism* (London: Alcove, 1973) clearly follows Poggioli's line of conceptualization.

6   See Bradbury and McFarlene, *Modernism, 1890-1930*, 105-19.

7   See his "The Term and Concept of Symbolism in Literary History," in *Discriminations: Further Concepts of Criticism* (New Haven: Yale University Press, 1970), 119.

8   Taking into account that the members of the New York Group (and Rubchak, of course, is one of them) have always regarded themselves as the only genuine modernists in Ukrainian literature, this approach is quite symptomatic. One can certainly infer from this practice that

Until very recently, modernism in the context of Ukrainian literature had a rather narrow connotation: a pre-revolutionary period from roughly the mid-1890s to 1914, which found its most vocal representation in the activities and writings of two literary groupings, namely Moloda muza in Western Ukraine and *Ukrains'ka khata* in Kyiv (the latter also being the title of the modernist journal published there in the years 1909-1914). This traditional (if not outdated) conceptualization of Ukrainian modernism is broadened occasionally to include other writers and poets (e.g., Olha Kobylianska, Mykola Vorony, Ahatanhel Krymsky, Mykhailo Kotsiubynsky, Vasyl Stefanyk, Volodymyr Vynnychenko, and Hnat Khotkevych) who did not belong either to Moloda muza or to the circle of Ukrains'ka khata, but whose works nonetheless reflected the new literary vogue: pursuit of the beautiful, denial of utilitarianism, devotion to aesthetic individualism, and emphasis on psychology and mood.[9]

The renewed interest in modernism has brought to the surface many inconsistencies that are inherent to this term. A series of articles published in *Harvard Ukrainian Studies* 15 (1991) under the general heading "Discussion: Ukrainian Modernism" (245-88)[10] is a case in point. Both Oleh Ilnytzkyj and Maxim Tarnawsky include in their considerations authors and works from the post-revolutionary period, and thus they seem to question the validity of the traditional approach to Ukrainian modernism, i.e., seeing it as a period designator for *fin de siécle* literary production. On the other hand, O. Ilnytzkyj insists on excluding futurism from the modernist movements, even though he makes a reference to Bradbury and McFarlene (who certainly view futurism as an integral part of modernism) and mentions the tendency to

---

he considers the pre-revolutionary literary production but a prelude to modernism. See Bohdan Rubchak, "Probnyi let," in *Ostap Luts'kyi—Molodomuzets'*, ed. George S. N. Luckyj (New York: Slovo, 1968), 9-43.

9 See, for example, George S. N. Luckyj, *Ukrainian Literature in the Twentieth Century: A Reader's Guide* (Toronto: University of Toronto Press, 1992), 3-22. See also George G. Grabowicz, "Commentary: Exorcising Ukrainian Modernism," *Harvard Ukrainian Studies* 15 (1991): 281-82.

10 The articles included there are Danylo Husar Struk, "The Journal *Svit*: A Barometer of Modernism"; Oleh S. Ilnytzkyj, "The Modernist Ideology and Mykola Khvyl'ovyi"; and Maxim Tarnawsky, "Modernism in Ukrainian Prose."

include futurism under the term "modernism" which prevails in the West.[11] Ilnytzkyj sees symbolism and impressionism as essentially modernist trends, but not futurism and neoclassicism.[12] Yet the inclusion of symbolism alongside futurism under the term "modernism," for example, does not seem to pose a problem for scholars in Russian literature.[13]

In light of the above discussions, the importance of the appearance in the late 1990s of Solomiia Pavlychko's monograph,[14] *Dyskurs modernizmu v ukrains'kii literaturi* (The Discourse of Modernism in Ukrainian Literature), cannot be overestimated. This is the first systematic attempt to juxtapose and outline various Ukrainian modernist movements as distinct phases (rather than separate literary phenomena) in the development of Ukrainian modernism throughout most of the twentieth century. Pavlychko differentiates four main "waves" of modernism in Ukrainian literature: the first encompasses the period of *fin de siècle* and the 1900s (characterized by her as anti-populist and bent toward aestheticism[15]); the second refers to the avant-garde movements of the 1920s; the third involves the activity and discourse of MUR;[16] and the fourth incorporates the phenomenon of the New York Group. While her

---

11 See his response in the forum "Discussion: Ukrainian Modernism," *Harvard Ukrainian Studies* 15 (1991): 286-87.

12 This is the stance that O. Ilnytzkyj also expounds in the following papers: "Ukrainian Symbolism and the Problem of Modernism," *Canadian Slavonic Papers* 34 (1992): 113-30; and *"Ukrains'ka khata* and the Paradoxes of Ukrainian Modernism," *Journal of Ukrainian Studies* 19.2 (1994): 5-30.

13 See Victor Terras, ed., *Handbook of Russian Literature* (New Haven: Yale University Press, 1985), 284, and George Gibian and H.W. Tjalsma, eds., *Russian Modernism: Culture and the Avant-Garde, 1900-1930* (Ithaca: Cornell University Press, 1976).

14 The first edition was published in 1997; the second, revised and expanded, in 1999.

15 To be exact, one should mention that Pavlychko for some reason separates these two contiguous periods (designating the 1900s as "the second wave") even though they are clearly aesthetically and ideologically continuous (especially if contrasted with the trends of the 1920s) and are presented as such in her monograph.

16 The abbreviation MUR stands for Mystets'kyi ukrains'kyi rukh (The Artistic Ukrainian Movement) and refers to an artistic-literary organization that emerged in the DP camps shortly after the Second World War. Its main objectives were the consolidation of artistic resources, the establishment of a publishing house, and the creation of a forum for literary dialogues among émigré writers. See Danylo Husar Struk, "Organizational Aspects of DP Literary Activity," in *The Refugee Experience: Ukrainian Displaced Persons after World War II*, ed. Wsewolod W. Isajiw, Yury Boshyk, and Roman Senkus (Edmonton: CIUS Press, 1992), 224-25.

account is not without notable shortcomings,[17] it is nonetheless significant not only because of her unorthodox periodization of Ukrainian modernism, but also because of the reaction it triggered among some members of the New York Group. I am referring here to the extensive review written by Yuriy Tarnawsky, followed by the response from Bohdan Boychuk, both published in *Krytyka*, the preeminent intellectual journal coming out in Kyiv.[18] It seems that Pavlychko's publication handed them (directly in the case of Tarnawsky and indirectly in the case of Boychuk) an opportunity to articulate their own understandings of the issues surrounding modernism in general, and its Ukrainian manifestation in particular.

Tarnawsky's review-essay, "Temna storona misiatsia" (The Dark Side of the Moon), is structured around two main considerations: the first is evaluative (his assessment of Pavlychko's book, parts 1-3) and the second conceptual (in other words, his own view on the issue, parts 4-6). Tarnawsky's major critical objections vis-à-vis *Dyskurs modernizmu* center on three areas: its exclusion of analysis of even most representative works of literature produced during the periods investigated;[19] its inconsistent use of some key definitions (e.g.,

---

17 Among them, the most conspicuous is her deliberate disregard of actual poetic and prose texts produced at the time. Her analysis of modernism in Ukrainian literature concentrates instead on the process alone and the debates that these texts evoked in critical writings. Also questionable is her inclusion of the MUR period as a credible representative of the modernist discourse in Ukrainian literature. The two figures that she relies on heavily in the section on MUR, namely Viktor Petrov-Domontovych and Ihor Kostetsky, constitute exceptions rather than the mainstream trends (by and large conservative) advocated by this organization. For example, Domontovych's works, published in the West shortly after the war, were to a large extent written in the late 1920s and arguably belong to a different phase of Ukrainian modernism. Kostetsky's modernism, on the other hand, and especially his formal experiments in the realm of drama, from the very beginning did not quite fit the utilitarian and nationalist (disguised as aesthetic under the concocted phrase "velyka literatura" [a great literature]) concerns of the MUR's main ideologues, Iurii Sherekh and Ulas Samchuk.

18 See Iurii Tarnavs'kyi, "Temna storona misiatsia," *Krytyka* 4.7-8 (2000): 4-10; and Bohdan Boichuk, "Zatemnena storona misiatsia," *Krytyka* 4.10 (2000): 27-28.

19 Interestingly, this particular objection was taken up by Eleonora Solovei in her "Shche trokhy pro misiachni zatemnennia" (Still More on Lunar Eclipses), yet another *Krytyka* contribution to the debate surrounding *Dyskurs modernizmu*. Solovei vigorously defended Pavlychko's approach against the charges brought forth both by Tarnawsky and Boychuk by pointing out that "хочеться заперечити проти того, в чому Тарнавський і Бойчук одностайні: що книжці Павличко бракує текстового аналізу творів. Досить дивна вимога до праці суто теоретичної, яка охоплює дуже широке коло явищ, за визнанням

modernism, populism, the avant-garde, Europeanization);[20] and finally its too-selective (if not incomplete) presentation of the modernist canon in Ukrainian literature of the twentieth century.[21] But he apparently does not question the validity of Pavlychko's rationale for expanding the application of the term "modernism" to include (in addition to the period of *fin de siècle*) the literary processes of the 1920s, late 1940s, and mid-1950s through the early 1970s.

Far more engaging than the criticism directed toward Pavlychko's account, however, is Tarnawsky's own conceptualization of the development of modernism in Ukrainian literature. Not surprisingly he starts with a definition:

Тарнавського, "практично все, що діялося в українській літературі" протягом мало не цілого століття. Саме тому авторка й обрала один конкретний наскрізний "сюжет": теоретичну саморефлексію українського модернізму періоду його становлення та розвитку, а також полеміку довкола нього як невіддільний дискурсивний складник" (27) (... one wants to contest that with which both Tarnawsky and Boychuk agree, i.e., the charge that Pavlychko's book lacks textual analysis of actual works. It is a strange requirement for a purely theoretical account, an account which encompasses a wide circle of phenomena, according to Tarnawsky himself, "practically everything that happened in Ukrainian literature" during almost an entire century. That is why the author selected one transparent "plot": a theoretical self-reflection of Ukrainian modernism in its inception and development as well as the polemics it stirred, all constituting its inseparable discursive element.)

20 The latter, Tarnawsky admits, is not defined, but one can infer from context that Pavlychko understands it as a movement (mostly conservative) that strove to refashion Ukrainian literature according to the European models. The inconsistencies Tarnawsky refers to stem mostly from Pavlychko's hesitant stance vis-à-vis the opposition of modernism to the avant-garde. On the one hand, she seems to follow the Anglo-American tradition and treats the avant-garde movement as an integral part of the twentieth-century modernist project; on the other, in the Ukrainian context she clearly dissociates futurism from modernism. Thus, according to Tarnawsky, she does not uphold her own definition of modernism as a movement born of conflict, denial, and destruction of the old, antecedent, and traditional (the attributes typical to futurism as well). The definition of modernism proposed by Pavlychko to a large extent follows Jürgen Habermas's reasoning as presented in his essay "Modernity—An Incomplete Project." See Hal Foster, ed., *Anti-Aesthetic: Essays on Postmodern Culture* (Port Townsend, WA: Bay, 1983), also published as "Modernity versus Postmodernity," *New German Critique* 22 (1981): 3-14.

21 The most conspicuous omissions, according to Tarnawsky, are the experimental fiction of Osyp Turiansky, Leonid Skrypnyk, and Maik Iohansen; and the poetry of Bohdan Ihor Antonych, Vasyl Khmeliuk, and the Kyiv School (Mykola Vorobiov, Vasyl Holoborodko, Viktor Kordun, and Mykhailo Hryhoriv).

Модернізм, отже, я окреслю як літературну (мистецьку) творчість, яка характеризується глибокими особистими потребами, радикальною новизною і тем, і форм, зокрема й мови, з потребою руйнувати попереднє. Наслідком цього є майже універсальна елітарність модерної літератури (мистецтва).[22]

Thus I will define modernism as a literary (artistic) creative output, characterized by the deep personal needs, by the radical novelty of themes and forms, and of language in particular, an output compelled to destroy everything preceding. An almost universal elitism of modern literature (art) is a consequence of all that.

He further states that he does not intend to contrast modernism and the avant-garde, clearly considering the latter (quite in line with the practice of Anglo-American critics and literary scholars) an integral part of modernism. Therefore, he expounds the view of modernism as an umbrella concept for a series of movements that began with symbolism (with Baudelaire necessarily providing the starting point of reference), and proceeds with decadence, neoromanticism, expressionism, and surrealism. Tarnawsky also considers it essential to differentiate two trends within modernism itself; the first one he calls "innovative," and the second he calls "established." It is not particularly clear for what purpose he introduces this particular classification, but from the subsequent outline of his own version of the modernist canon in Ukrainian literature, it becomes obvious that he favors formal experimentation rather than philosophical outlook and/or aesthetic posture as a defining criterion in determining the extent of the modernist attributes of a given text.[23]

This proclivity to judge a work of literature or art as truly "modernist" almost solely on the basis of its formal innovation becomes particularly pronounced in his assessment of the individual members of the New York Group. While he attempts to make a case for the group's radical modernism, he simultaneously admits that some poets (mainly Bohdan Rubchak) have notably retreated from modernist positions back to more traditional ones.

---

22 *Temna storona misiatsia*, 6.

23 But as Boychuk succinctly noted in his response, Tarnawsky is not entirely consistent here. The poet Volodymyr Svidzinsky is especially a case in point. Tarnawsky considers him a modernist, but bases his evaluation on Svidzinsky's philosophical bent toward irrationalism rather than his poetics, which favored traditional forms ("Zatemnena storona misiatsia," 28).

Again, Tarnawsky pinpoints the shift by foregrounding the formal aspects. On the other hand, when he summarizes the accomplishments of the New York Group, he mainly refers to the aesthetic and philosophical underpinnings of the poetry of its members:

> Оригінальним у творчості групи є екзистенціалістична поезія. В англомовній чи іспаномовній поезії, наприклад, або в російській, такої немає. Вона дещо схожа на повоєнну польську поезію, але контакту з нею не мала ніякого, витворилася сама. Оригінальним є згаданий вище асоціативний стиль, що ототожнюється з сюрреалізмом. Може, було б корисно назвати його сюрреалізмом українським. Ще оригінальним для української літератури є у творчості групи звільнена від традицій романтизму та, в декого з членів, із лещат лінґвістичного пуризму, мова.[24]

> The existentialist poetry is original in the group's output. There is no such in English or Spanish poetry, or, for that matter, in Russian as well. It has some affinity with the postwar Polish poetry, but there was no direct contact between them, and it evolved on its own. The aforementioned associative style, often identified with surrealism, is also unique to the group. Perhaps, it would be useful to call it Ukrainian surrealism. Another original contribution to Ukrainian literature can be found in the group's poetic language, free of romantic tradition and, among some members, linguistic purism.

Notwithstanding Tarnawsky's case for boosting the group's standing in Ukrainian literature, Bohdan Boychuk's response to his essay is not particularly approving. Boychuk does not argue with Tarnawsky as far as Pavlychko's book is concerned. He agrees with his criticism in that regard. However, he objects to his colleague's own inconsistencies (both in theory and praxis). Boychuk questions the validity of Tarnawsky's rationale for conflating modernism and the avant-garde, noting that the latter is an ahistorical concept applicable as much to the 1920s as to any other historical period in the modern era. He also expands Tarnawsky's definition of modernism by adding three more characteristics: intellectualism, a return to the sources of the past (tradition), and individualism of style. Moreover, he states that the attributes of modernism proposed by Tarnawsky are conceivable, but certainly not universal or binding. This is clearly done in order to undermine his colleague's

---

24 "Temna storona misiatsia," 9.

version of the modernist canon in Ukrainian literature. Tarnawsky's dismissing of such unquestionably modernist poets as Pavlo Tychyna, Bohdan Ihor Antonych, and Mykola Bazhan, according to Boychuk, is troublesome and problematic to say the least. Boychuk concludes his criticism by saying that both the definition of modernism and its practical application, as presented by Tarnawsky, are narrow and reflect but a very personal perspective based solely on personal taste.

What comes to light through their polemics is that both discuss Ukrainian modernism in the context of overall twentieth-century international artistic trends and movements, firmly believing in the soundness of such an approach. Both see the activity of the New York Group as inextricably intertwined with artistic developments in the West. They diverge on the issue of defining modernism vis-à-vis the avant-garde (Tarnawsky adhering to the Anglo-American tradition; Boychuk sticking more to the continental stand[25]), but do not question the suitability of considering Ukrainian modernism as a series of discontinuous phenomena with an underlying continuous strife against mediocrity and utilitarian restrictions in the realm of creative endeavors.

My own approach to modernism agrees in general outlines with that of Solomiia Pavlychko, although her emphasis on discursive rather than literary production foregrounds a different emphasis in the whole debate. In order to place the New York Group's output and activity, I am inclined to use the term "modernism" in a broader sense, i.e. as a concept that encompasses a variety of trends and movements which, in Ukrainian literature, began in the mid-1890s with neoromanticism, aestheticism, and decadence (early modernism), then peaked after 1917 with symbolism, futurism, neoclassicism, and constructivism (modernism proper and the avant-garde) before dying out in the early 1930s because of the implementation of socialist

---

25 Though, admittedly, Boychuk does not follow nor makes any reference to Bürger's understanding of the historical avant-garde. He contemplates the avant-garde as "the radical destruction of an existing order" ("радикальна руйнація наявного" ["Zatemnena storona misiatsia," 27]) and agrees more with Eugène Ionesco's concept of the avant-garde man as "the opponent of an existing system" (Quoted in Calinescu, 119). Therefore, the avant-garde, according to Boychuk, can conceivably exist in any period. On the other hand, he also betrays some inconsistencies in the modernism vs. avant-garde debate by stating (in reference to Mykhail Semenko) that an avant-gardist can be, but does not have to be, a modernist ("Zatemnena storona misiatsia," 27). Thus it seems that he (like Tarnawsky) conflates modernism with the avant-garde, at least as far as the 1920s are concerned.

realism and the accompanying Stalinist purges and resurging again in the 1950s and 1960s with surrealism and existentialism (late modernism).[26] The two groupings most representative of the latter are the New York Group and the Kyiv School of poets.

Despite the variety of styles these movements represent, they do share certain common traits, namely antitraditionalism (which can manifest itself either ideologically as a certain mode of aesthetic consciousness or formally as technical innovation, or as both), elitism, preoccupation with human (time) consciousness, and, finally, strongly individual and subjective representations of reality. Arguably, the major achievement of modernism lies in its apotheosis of subjectivity and subversion of the authority of tradition. Yet it is also possible to use this argument against the suitability of placing neoromanticism and neoclassicism under the same "umbrella" concept. However, these two trends reflect the general dichotomy that exists in modernist aesthetics. Astradur Eysteinsson characterizes this dichotomy as follows:

> On the one hand, it seems that modernism is built on highly subjective premises: by directing its attention so predominantly toward individual or subjective experience, it elevates the ego in proportion to a diminishing awareness of objective or coherent outside reality.... On the other hand, modernism is often held to draw its legitimacy primarily from writing based on highly antisubjectivist or impersonal poetics. T. S. Eliot was one of the adamant spokesmen of a neoclassical reaction against romantic-personal poetry...[27]

But he finds a way to reconcile these two different tendencies by stating: "What the modernist poetics of impersonality and that of extreme subjectivity have in common (and this outweighs whatever may separate them) is a revolt against traditional relation of the subject to the outside world."[28] While modernism

---

26 An interesting characterization of late modernism that Fredric Jameson pointed to in his lecture "Modernity, Modernism, Late Modernism," presented at the University of Toronto on 20 March 2001, is the fact that all late modernists—that is, those who came to prominence after World War II—are self-consciously modernist, which was certainly not the case with the authors of the interwar period. Characterizing late modernists, Art Berman came to a similar conclusion, though he put it differently: "Young artists sense that they have arrived toward the end of celebration. Modernism can no longer be created, it can only be joined." See his *Preface to Modernism* (Urbana, IL: University of Illinois Press, 1994), 82.

27 *The Concept of Modernism*, 27.

28 Ibid., 28.

may have eroded the authority of tradition, it has certainly kept the authority of the subject, i.e., the individual "I." This "I," whether expressed through the poetics of impersonality or subjectivity, still retains certain metaphysical attributes (a quality which is by and large missing in highly parodic and surface-oriented postmodernist discourse).

The significance of early modernism in Ukrainian literature cannot be overlooked, mostly because it introduced a radical shift in the realm of aesthetic thinking (the concepts of art's autonomy and freedom of artistic expression were revolutionary in the context of Ukrainian *fin de siècle* period, still dominated by a populist ideology). However, this period was not particularly revolutionary (with a very few exceptions, such as Vasyl Stefanyk and Mykhailo Kotsiubynsky) in the realm of artistic innovation, which was more characteristic of the post-revolutionary era (poetic form and language, although coming from entirely different angles, was as important to Mykhail Semenko, the futurist, as it was to Mykola Zerov, the neoclassicist). In comparison to their turn-of-the-century colleagues, the modernists of the 1920s were more radical and consistent in carrying out their aesthetic platform: antitraditionalism, cosmopolitanism, and formal novelty. What distinguishes the poets of the New York Group from their avant-garde colleagues of the 1920s is the reluctance of the former to express their political views poetically. Both groupings shared the criticism of caving in to foreign influences and were often labeled "un-Ukrainian" in their approach to art.

Literary production prior to 1914, characterized first and foremost by an attempt on the part of a young generation of writers to bring down the populist ideology and to distance itself from ethnographic realism, is uneven and torn between two loyalties: whether to serve Art and nothing else, or to serve the *narod* (the people) in its struggle for statehood. The modernists of the 1920s believed that the latter goal had been achieved and that they could finally taste the real freedom of artistic expression. They soon realized, however, that to a large extent the problems faced by early modernists were still with them, except it was now the Soviet proletarian ideology rather than pre-revolutionary populism that they had to wrestle with.[29] Notwithstanding the fact that at least in the beginning quite a few of them embraced the

---

29 Although it can easily be argued that in terms of their aesthetic reification, these two phenomena conflated rather seamlessly under the Communist reality.

revolutionary postulates of the Communist regime, this period witnessed an enormous explosion of real talent. The diversity of styles and the degree of experimentation (not only in literature but also in cinema, theatre, and the arts)[30] were very much on par with similar avant-garde developments in Russia and in the West. However, it all came to a standstill with the Stalinist purges of the early 1930s. Thus, it can be argued that the first writers who successfully disengaged themselves from any utilitarian or political concerns were the late modernists of the 1950s and 1960s, mainly the poets of the New York Group. They focused almost exclusively on experimentation with poetic form and language, and on projecting a highly subjective vision of the world. The individualistic approach to art, the autonomous role of language, and the emphasis on the universal were taken for granted.

As much as the founding members of the group embraced their exilic situatedness as stimulating rather than halting, and turned to Western literary sources for inspiration, by choosing the Ukrainian language as the main (if not exclusive) medium of artistic expression they necessarily and also quite consciously cultivated a link with the literary past of their own country. Their indebtedness to this native line of tradition assumed two hypostases: the first, "confrontational," refers to the sphere of discourse and ideology (manifested as a decisive rejection of traditionalist approaches to poetry, formal and aesthetic, represented by the majority of older generation émigré poets), and the second, "inspirational,"[31] less obvious and more indirect, points to the writers' actual influences (not always readily admitted by the poets themselves) in the sphere of creative activity. This "confrontational" streak in the New York Group's attitude toward the poetic production of its immediate émigré predecessors, mainly the poets of the so-called Prague School[32] and those literati who had witnessed their debuts in the Displaced Persons' camps in the second half

---

30 Cf. *Modernism in Kyiv*, ed. Irena R. Makaryk and Virlana Tkacz (Toronto: University of Toronto Press, 2010).

31 Both designations are mine.

32 This label refers to the group of poets, namely Iurii Darahan, Evhen Malaniuk, Oleh Olzhych, Oleksa Stefanovych, Oksana Liaturynska, Natalia Livytska-Kholodna, and Olena Teliha, who began their literary careers in Prague in the 1920s. Some of them (e.g. Malaniuk, Teliha, and Livytska-Kholodna) moved later to Warsaw, Poland. They are also known as *visnykivtsi*, for they were actively contributing to the journal *Vistnyk* (Herald), published in Lviv under the editorial direction of Dmytro Dontsov.

of the 1940s under the auspices of MUR,[33] revealed itself in the desire to open up new possibilities for Ukrainian poetry by bringing forth texts qualitatively different and formally experimental. This stance stood in sharp contrast to what the Prague School (or MUR) had to offer poetically in the 1920s, 1930s, and 1940s. The poetry of the Prague School was patriotic and very much committed to the cause of Ukrainian independence; thus it was full of heroic pathos, though, strange as it might seem, it was not entirely devoid of merits on a purely artistic plane.[34] This is how Mykola Ilnytsky characterizes the Prague School in his outline of twentieth-century Ukrainian poetry:

> The worldview, which became the basis for the poetry of this group, was historiosophy. It derives from the very status of these people, who, having lost the battle for their homeland's independence, found themselves in a foreign country. This is the source for the motifs of distress, of omens taken from the revived imagery of pagan Kyivan Rus, of anxious premonitions, and at the same time, of strong-willed, even voluntaristic principles; it is also the source for the thirst for action, for a cursing of their homeland and the glorifying of it at the same time, for faith in its rebirth.[35]

The postwar reality left no illusions for the younger generation of émigré poets. Poetry for them was inconceivable as an expressive platform to be used in fighting for a national cause. They saw an utmost futility in such voluntaristic tendencies.

There can be no doubt that the modernism espoused by the poets of the New York Group was of Western provenance. Yet that does not mean that there were no Ukrainian poets who provided at least some inspiration for the individual members of the group. The imagery of Bohdan Ihor Antonych had an unquestionable impact on the poetry of Bohdan Rubchak, Emma Andijewska, and Vira Vovk. The earthy, expressive, elemental quality of Todos Osmachka's poetic vision reverberates in the early poetry of Bohdan Boychuk. Zhenia

---

33 For example, the poets Leonid Poltava, Yar Slavutych, Borys Oleksandriv, Ihor Kachurovsky, and Ostap Tarnawsky all represented the traditionalist line in poetic craft.

34 They wrote good traditional poetry and possessed considerable talent, as later Bohdan Boychuk would sum up in his criticism on the Prague circle. See his "Dekil'ka dumok pro N'iu-Iorks'ku hrupu i dekil'ka zadnikh dumok," *Suchasnist'* 1 (1979): 22.

35 Mykola Il'nyts'kyi, "At the Crossroads of the Century," trans. Olesia Shchur, in *A Hundred Years of Youth: A Bilingual Anthology of the 20th Century Ukrainian Poetry*, ed. Olha Luchuk and Michael M. Naydan (Lviv: Litopys, 2000), 66.

Vasylkivska, Andijewska, and Vovk also substantially drew from the riches of Ukrainian folklore. However, the most significant sources of inspiration came from the West.

The group's initial fascination with the modernist poetic world found its reflection in the realm of translation. The scope and number of poets translated into Ukrainian from Spanish, French, English, German, and Portuguese is indeed impressive. Among the group's most active translators are Yuriy Tarnawsky (cf. his renditions of Federico García Lorca, Pablo Neruda, Georg Trakl, Ezra Pound, and Samuel Beckett), Vira Vovk (García Lorca, Neruda, Fernando Pessoa, Paul Celan, and a number of lesser-known Brazilian poets), Bohdan Boychuk (e.e. cummings, Juan Ramón Jiménez, and Beckett), Zhenia Vasylkivska (García Lorca, Paul Eluard, Henri Michaux, and Jacques Prevert), and Patricia Kylyna (García Lorca and Miguel Hernandez).[36] It is therefore no wonder that these endeavors resulted in an intimate knowledge of the work of the prominent representatives of the modernist canon and left some traces of poetic influence on the emerging poets of the New York Group. Federico García Lorca, for example, unmistakably affected the poetry of Patricia Kylyna and Zhenia Vasylkivska. Pablo Neruda, on the other hand, had a marked impact on the beginnings of Tarnawsky's poetic endeavors. Bohdan Rubchak and Bohdan Boychuk, as their early poetry attests, were both devoted readers of Anglo-American high modernists, most notably e.e. cummings, T. S. Eliot, and Ezra Pound.[37] Emma Andijewska's metaphoric ambiguities and the exploitation of the formal and aural properties of verse align her noticeably with the hermetic oeuvre of Stéphan Mallarmé. On the other hand, some measure of indebtedness to Velemir Khlebnikov's experiments with word formation and sound association, alluded to on more than one occasion,[38] makes her the only poet in the group who displays a trace of the Russian influence.

---

36 The only two poets in the group not particularly inclined toward the art of translation were Bohdan Rubchak and Emma Andijewska.

37 The title of Boychuk's second book (which the poet later disowned) *Zemlia bula pustoshnia* (The Land Was a Wasteland, 1959) clearly evokes, though in no parodic terms, Eliot's famous poem "The Waste Land."

38 Cf. Iurii Lavrinenko, *Zrub i parosty: Literaturno-krytychni statti, esei, refleksii* (Munich: Suchanist', 1971), 262; Danylo Husar Struk, "Emma Andiievs'ka: 'vershyvannia—virshuvannia'," *Smoloskyp* 19.5 (1967): 7; Emanuil Rais, "Poeziia Emmy Andiievs'koi,"

The above name-dropping is not intended to create an impression of bondage and lack of originality among the poets of the New York Group, but rather to indicate that the signposts for their poetic beginnings were decisively outside the sphere of contemporary Ukrainian literature of the 1940s and early 1950s. At the same time, continuity with the native line of tradition (however weak and less conspicuous) was also preserved. As each individual member of the group evolved as a poet, the foreign influences gradually dissipated or became uniquely amalgamated with the poet's innate elements. Understandably, as each poetic voice matured, stylistic diversification followed. What unites the New York Group poets, however, is their conspicuous worship of metaphor. More than a mere trope, metaphor constitutes to all of them the very essence of poetic reality. Regardless of the manner of its practical application (whether lavish and ambiguous as with Andijewska, or skeletal and concrete as with Tarnawsky), the primacy ascribed to the use of metaphor remains invariable for all the members. Their understanding of metaphor's role is in line with Art Berman's characterization: "In modernism, artistic intent is transferred from narrative, conceptual, and didactic poetry to poetry as visual metaphor.... Metaphor is not simply poetic ornament but corresponds to essence."[39] The associative, often surrealistic way of conveying poetic visions, initially combined with unmistakable existentialist underpinnings, makes the New York Group's contribution to Ukrainian literature unique and new. No wonder, therefore, that in late 1958, thinking of the right title for their new literary magazine, the poets settled on *Novi poezii* (New Poetry).

Suchasnist' 2 (1963): 44; Bohdan Rubchak, "Homes as Shells: Ukrainian Émigré Poetry," in *New Soil—Old Roots: The Ukrainian Experience in Canada*, ed. Jaroslav Rozumnyj (Winnipeg: Ukrainian Academy of Arts and Sciences in Canada, 1983), 117.

39   See his *Preface to Modernism*, 269.

CHAPTER 2

Discursive Practices: Poetry as Power

"**P**oetry is knowledge, salvation, power, abandonment,"[1] declares Octavio Paz in his book of essays *The Bow and the Lyre*. To understand the phenomenon of the New York Group is to keep in mind that for its members, poetry was not only an aesthetic proposition but also an ideological statement. Theirs was an ideology of freedom, and to advocate their position they used poetry as a tool to gain recognition, to assert their literary presence, and to acquire some power within the limited confines of the Ukrainian émigré milieu of the 1950s. While not keen to theorize their stand, the members of the group engendered a series of distinct discourses, which at first aimed at affirming their voice and securing venues for their literary production, then at gaining readers, and finally at affecting their legacy once Ukraine became an independent state.

The concept of discourse, as I use it here, refers to a system of regular dispersion of statements (both private and public) reified in actions, which, in turn, impact power relations among various groups, institutions, and networks. In other words, a discourse thus understood comes across as a force able to

---

1   Octavio Paz, *The Bow and the Lyre: The Poem, the Poetic Revelation, Poetry and History*, trans. Ruth L.C. Simms (Austin: University of Texas Press, 1973), [3].

influence or even change situations, conditions, circumstances, etc.[2] Putting aside for the moment the New York Group's aesthetic propositions, in this chapter I want to trace the chronology and significance of its discursive practices from the mid-1950s through the 1990s, as revealed by individual letters and published statements in various periodicals. The poets' involvement in the émigré literary process will provide a necessary context for a subsequent analysis of their oeuvre.

Researching the archival material of the New York Group in the Bakhmeteff Archive at Columbia University, I came to the following conclusion: the impulse to form a group arose not so much from a well-defined aesthetic platform but from practical, if not pragmatic, considerations. Notwithstanding the fact that the poets under scrutiny were all young and relatively inexperienced, they quickly realized that a coherent assemblage constituted a convenient vehicle to affirm their literary presence and that it would give them an opportunity to shape paradigms of Ukrainian literature outside Ukraine. For example, Melanie Pytlowany in her 1977 article insisted that "the genesis of the New York Group was somewhat spontaneous and anarchic,"[3] but what I found in the letters of the group's most active members, namely Bohdan Boychuk, Yuriy Tarnawsky, and Bohdan Rubchak, not only contradicts this statement but, more importantly, also underscores how strategically thought-out the group's beginnings were. Here is, for instance, an excerpt from Rubchak's letter to Tarnawsky, dated 25 November 1955:

> We, the young Ukrainian writers, must keep together, must unite in indissoluble friendship, because individually we shall vanish without a trace. I hope you have realized the precariousness of our situation. Ten, fifteen more years of émigré existence, and no one would be writing in Ukrainian. Ukrainian culture undergoes an awful crisis nowadays, and it's truly faced with, forgive my cliché, the last "to be or not to be." Vlyzko, Khvylovy, M. Kulish and other wonderful people gave their lives for it. We do not dare put it down.

---

2   This is very much in line with Michel Foucault's conceptualization of discursive formations. The exercise of power, according to Foucault, is "a way in which certain actions modify others," or, to put it differently, it is "a mode of action upon the actions of others." See his "The Subject and Power," in Hubert L. Dreyfus and Paul Rabinow, *Michel Foucault: Beyond Structuralism and Hermeneutics*, 2nd ed. (Chicago: University of Chicago Press, 1983), 219 and 221, respectively.

3   Melanie Pytlowany, "Continuity and Innovation in the Poetry of the New York Group," *Journal of Ukrainian Graduate Studies* 2.1 (1977): 4.

Our task is to rescue it. You've certainly noticed that our "older" cultural activists do not display any interest in us, and no one gives a damn about our work (I'm saying this in general and my use of "our" is impersonal). We've got to form our own circle of critics, our own publications, even our own publishing houses. We must join in some kind of a formal organization, then we shall have the power.[4]

This passage aptly underscores several dilemmas facing young poets. First, they recognized that the questions of power should be formulated in terms of tactics and strategy; second, it became clear to them that the recognition they yearned for would not dawn on them gracefully on its own, but required an effort and struggle on their part (forming a group, for example, would represent one of the strategies for achieving such an end); finally, they evinced a strong sense of responsibility, onerous as it might be, for the very existence and continuation of Ukrainian literature. One cannot but notice that this sense of responsibility Rubchak refers to reverberates with the atmosphere and concerns of the DP literary period, mainly the propositions advocated by MUR.[5] Yet the prescriptive tone, so typical of all the MUR programmatic statements, is noticeably absent here. The young poets saw themselves as

---

4   Letter to Iurii Tarnavs'kyi, 25 Nov. 1955. Iurii Tarnavs'kyi Papers, Rare Books and Manuscript Library, Columbia University, New York. The original text reads: "Ми молоді українські письменники, мусимо держатися <u>разом</u>, ми мусимо з'єднатися нерозривним перстнем дружби, бо одинцем пропадемо безслідно. Маю надію, що Ви усвідомили безнадійність нашої ситуації. Коли ми ще поживемо на еміграції десять—п'ятнадцять років, у нас взагалі не буде ніхто писати українською мовою. Українська культура переживає тепер <u>страшну</u> кризу і вона справді стоїть перед, вибачте трафаретний вислів, останнім "бути чи не бути". Влизько, Хвильовий, М. Куліш і інші прекрасні люди згинули за неї, ми не сміємо її занапастити. Наше завдання—врятувати її. Напевно завважуєте, наші "старші" культурні діячі зовсім не цікавляться нами, ніхто й не плюне в наш бік (говорю загально і не особисто вживаю слова "наші"). Ми мусимо виробити собі власну плеяду критиків, власні публікації, навіть власні видавництва. Ми мусимо об'єднатися в якусь формальну організацію, тоді в нас буде й сила." The underlinings are Rubchak's.

5   This is a period when, according to George Grabowicz, "the two fundamental premises that Ukrainian artists, specifically writers, have a moral duty to their nation, an obligation to bend all their efforts to the overarching national cause of Ukrainian independence, and that their task is to be effected through art that is of the highest quality, are more than plain." See his "Great Literature," in *The Refugee Experience: Ukrainian Displaced Persons after World War II*, ed. Wsevolod W. Isajiw, Yury Boshyk, and Roman Senkus (Edmonton: CIUS Press, 1992), 250.

champions of freedom who resisted large organizational structures and direc-
tives that such structures as a rule entail.

The power issue raised by Rubchak in the letter quoted above found a
sympathetic ear in Tarnawsky. His letters to Rubchak attest that the idea of
having a group as a force promoting new venues in Ukrainian poetry was
viewed as essential: "Старайтеся переїхати в N.Y. [New York] Тут веселіше—
будемо працювати разом, треба творити свою школу, ми мусимо дати
поштовх укр. літературі, а особливо поезії! Мусимо промостити шлях
молодшим!"[6] ("Try to move to N.Y. It's more cheerful here. We'll work together,
we must create our own school, we have to give a nudge to Ukrainian literature,
and especially to poetry! We've got to pave the road for a younger generation!")
Tarnawsky also viewed the group as a force offsetting the stifling atmosphere
of the Ukrainian émigré literary process: "Я просто задихаюся від нашого
мистецького повітря; часами здається, що навіть атомова бомба не
зворушила б його; – а воно воняє. Час нам братися до праці, ми мусимо
разом, спільно робити, творити, боротись, мусимо розбудувати якусь
плятформу, на якій можна будувати майбутнє!"[7] ("I'm simply suffocating
from our artistic air; sometimes it seems to me that even the atom bomb would
not be able to shake it—it stinks. It's about time for us to get to work, we must
together, jointly push matters, create, fight, must build some kind of platform,
which may facilitate the future!") These letters manifest the fact that the forma-
tion of the group with its attendant institutions, namely a publishing venture
and the publication of a periodical, had been thoroughly discussed early on.

Poetry and power became inextricably intertwined in the initial stages
of the New York Group. There can be no doubt that the more avant-garde,
"transgressive" character was found in the poetry produced, the more visible
or controversial it became. An increase in visibility brought about more atten-
tion and thereby laid the foundation for more power. This power, in turn,
backed up by the net-like forces inherent in the group, was used to secure
more weight for the poetry brought forth, often regardless of its actual
aesthetic or historical merit.[8] Therefore the concerns behind the formation

---

6   Letter to Bohdan Rubchak, 27 Aug. 1956. Bohdan Rubchak Papers, Private Collection.
7   Letter to Bohdan Rubchak, 10 Sept. 1956. Bohdan Rubchak Papers, Private Collection.
8   Zhenia Vasylkivska is a case in point. Notwithstanding the first-rate quality of her poetry, her
     overall contribution, spanning less than ten years, is certainly rather marginal (she produced

of the group were by and large pragmatic rather than programmatic, although this does not imply that the poets were free of goals and commitments.

These private discussions produced a desired effect. The first issue of the New York Group's yearly almanac *Novi poezii* came out in 1959, and its publishing venture was thus established. This event marked an important new phase in the development of the group. Not only did it underscore the gains made in the realm of group cohesiveness, it also revealed and substantiated the poets' viewpoint concerning the group's role in the émigré literary process. To that end, it made public what had been already heavily discussed informally either in correspondence or in café gatherings as early as 1955.

The following introductory editorial note opened the first issue of the almanac:

> Our émigré literary life has found itself sloping downward since 1949.... On the other hand, literature in Ukraine has been in decline ever since Tychyna and Bazhan became silent, Khvylovy and Kulish perished, and literary life had been stamped with socialist realism, the very essence of which is not only to deny but simply to kill any individual creative effort. ...
>
> The persistence of such reality increases the sense of artistic responsibility among the individuals representing the young literary generation....
>
> That is why the New York Group, already well-known in literary circles, decided not only to vigorously keep up its creative endeavors, but also to enliven and deepen the literary process.[9]

Though the New York Group of poets denied ever writing any manifestoes, this editorial statement, issued in the name of all the members of the group,[10]

---

only one book of poems, *Korotki viddali*), and without the support that the network of the group provides her name would have disappeared a long time ago. However, her being one of the initiators of the group perpetuates her literary existence.

9   The original text reads: "Починаючи з 1949 року, еміграційне літературне життя опинилося на похилій вниз.... З другого боку, література на Україні була вже на похилій ще від часу, коли замовкли Тичина і Бажан, коли загинули Хвильовий і Куліш, а на літературному житті випалено штамп соціялістичного реалізму, що в самому принципі не тільки заперечує, а просто вбиває всяку індивідуальну творчість.... Наявність такої дійсності посилює в людей молодої літературної ґенерації почуття мистецької відповідальности.... Тож відома вже в літературному житті Нью-Йоркська Група вирішила не тільки інтенсивніше продовжувати свої творчі намагання, але й вплинути на оживлення та поглиблення літературного процесу" (5-6).

10 The first issue of *Novi poezii* included (in the order of appearance): Bohdan Rubchak, Zhenia Vasylkivska, Bohdan Boychuk, Yuriy Tarnawsky, Patricia Kylyna, and Emma Andijewska.

comes relatively close. Moreover, it not only stressed the role of the group in rejuvenating the literary process outside of Ukraine, but also unequivocally declared the group's aesthetic credo:

> ... Creative work of each individuality calls for an absolute freedom of expression, such work is a world of its own and knows only its own, totally subjective, laws of life and death. Each artist acutely feels the demands of his/her own inner world, and, having no other choice, s/he must creatively manifest it to the fullest. In other words, s/he must freely express herself (himself) in the native tongue.[11]

From the very beginning, guarding the sovereignty of artistic creativity had become of utmost importance to the young poets, in stark contrast to the controlled and prescribed formulas propounded by MUR. One such formula that was particularly opposed and outright rejected by the New York Group was the notion of a "national-organic" style, introduced by Iurii Sherekh (a pseudonym of George Shevelov), the main proponent and theoretician of MUR. The idea that one can a priori arbitrate the content and direction of a creative process was unacceptable and abhorrent to the poets of the New York Group. The only concession to the national cause (and not necessarily style—itself a highly problematic concept) that they could come up with was the fact that they retained the language. Rather than adopting the language of a new homeland (English, in the majority of cases), they chose Ukrainian as the main medium of artistic expression.

The poets' early discursive practices primarily engaged their MUR predecessors. The most interesting exchanges happened between the group and Sherekh, on the one hand, and Ihor Kostetsky, on the other. To be precise, however, there was never any direct public dialogue between Sherekh and the New York Group, the most likely reason being that the group, with its extremely cosmopolitan attitude, Western orientation, and poetically (but not necessarily discursively) apolitical stance, struck at the very heart of Sherekh's thesis and made his concept of a "national style" if not obsolete,

---

11 The original text reads: "... творчість кожної індивідуальности вимагає повної зовнішньої свободи вияву, вона є окремий світ і знає власні закони життя і смерти—вкрай суб'єктивні. Кожний мистець дуже різко відчуває вимоги свого внутрішнього світу і, не маючи іншого вибору, мусить дати йому повний творчий вияв. Іншими словами, мусить вільно висловити себе своєю мовою." (6)

then surely inapplicable.[12] The idea that a writer (or a poet) ought to self-consciously work on the national character of her/his oeuvre or that s/he should somehow strive to express artistically the essence of a national spirit seemed incomprehensible to the young poets, and triggered a reaction in the form of almost obsessive emphasis on the freedom of creative process. Sherekh, on his part, pointedly ignored the poets' literary debuts and preferred to greet the group's endeavors with silence. When in 1964 he finally did react to the poetry of one member of the group, Tarnawsky, he did so in order to undermine Tarnawsky's (and thereby the group's) claims of being truly modernist and innovative. Sherekh's reaction came as a presentation at a symposium on "Tradition and Innovation," held during the second meeting of the "Slovo" Ukrainian Writers' Association in Exile. The subsequent article, "Troie proshchan' i pro te, shcho take istoriia literatury" (Three Farewells and What the History of Literature is All About), was published four years later in the almanac *Slovo* (Word). In this article, the critic compares three poems (all dealing with the theme of a parting between a man and a woman) from three different literary periods by three different poets, Levko Borovykovsky (1806-1889), Olena Pchilka (1849-1930), and Yuriy Tarnawsky (b. 1934). The fact that there are thematic similarities between Borovykovsky's poem and Tarnawsky's in and of itself proves nothing. Obviously, Tarnawsky's innovative approach in this particular poem pertains to the formal rather than the thematic sphere. But, it seems, Sherekh's goal was to undermine the influence and recognition the poets had managed to usurp thus far.

Another theoretical construct that sprang from the MUR's activity, which was less of a "red flag" for the young poets, was the concept of "a great literature" (*velyka literatura*). This notion refers to MUR's recommendation that Ukrainian writers should strive to achieve excellence in their oeuvre so that their collective effort would subsequently alleviate the seeming provincialism of Ukrainian literature.[13] This is not to say that the New York Group agreed

---

12 It is to Sherekh's credit that he admitted the dubiousness of this concept later on. See his book of essays *Tretia storozha* (Baltimore: Smoloskyp, 1991), 388.

13 In his insightful analysis of this phenomenon, Grabowicz points out that "the central *stated* issues of *velyka literatura* ("Europe" vs. provincialism, quality vs. populism, a sense of "mission" and of optimism for the future of Ukrainian literature) and the more thoughtful programmatic statements of MUR (the articles of Sherekh and Kosach) had Khvyliovy as their touchstones" (259). In other words, the polemics engendered by MUR to a large extent

with the reasoning and remedies proposed by MUR to alleviate the seeming "provincialism" of Ukrainian literature, but the attitudes the poets assumed in this area were somewhat less defined, more likely because they refused to formulate the problem in such terms in the first place. They did not give any sign that they themselves suffered from any form of inferiority complex, and they were not against high-caliber texts per se. What the poets did oppose is the notion that this process can be somehow controlled and micromanaged by a series of postulates coming from the organization.

Unlike Iurii Sherekh, Ihor Kostetsky, a maverick initiator-activist of MUR,[14] wholeheartedly embraced the New York Group's youthful initiatives, often advising its members to guard their independence at all costs and to be watchful of all sorts of "doctrinaires" (undoubtedly referring to the organization he himself represented not so long before):

> I am deeply convinced that the most important thing for you now is not to listen to the advice of any doctrinaires, not to pay any attention to them at all. To put it differently—at all costs do not allow yourselves to be pigeon-holed by those who think that they know everything and that they are the sole spokesmen of all that was, is, and will be. I do not point out their names, because I never say or do anything behind someone else's back (my polemical disputes are always public and under my own name), but let this circumstance give you an opportunity to place under the notion of "doctrinaire" all those that you yourself feel belong to that category.[15]

---

resembled the essence and the mode of the debates in Ukraine during the artistically turbulent 1920s.

14 Danylo Husar Struk lists six people as initial founders of MUR: I. Bahriany, V. Domontovych, Iu. Kosach, I. Kostetsky, I. Maistrenko, and Iu. Sherekh. See Struk, "Organizational Aspects of DP Literary Activity" in *The Refugee Experience: Ukrainian Displaced Persons after World War II* (Edmonton: CIUS Press, 1992), 223-39.

15 Letter to Bohdan Boichuk, 11 Nov. 1956. Bohdan Boichuk Papers, Rare Book and Manuscript Library, Columbia University, New York. The original text reads: "Моїм глибоким переконанням, найголовніше для Вас тепер—ні в якому разі не слухатися порад жадних доктринерів, взагалі на них не зважати. Інакше кажучи—за всяку ціну не дати себе вкласти на якусь поличку в систематизаційних вправах тих, які гадають, що вони все знають і що вони є єдиними речниками всього, що було, є, і буде. Не називаю їхніх імен, бо ніколи не роблю нічого поза очі (з полемікою виступаю тільки прилюдно і під власним прізвищем), але нехай саме ця обставина й дає Вам можливість підставляти під поняття "доктринера" тих, кого Ви самі відчуваєте як таких."

Clearly, by 1956, Kostetsky had no desire to be associated with the MUR's overly dogmatic past. Instead, he quite swiftly aligned himself with the emerging group and had high hopes for a fruitful cooperation with the young poets, whether in the sphere of criticism or that of translation.[16] In a way, such a turn was rather natural for Kostetsky, considering that his own modernist, quite experimental texts challenged, to a large extent, MUR's rhetoric. Taking into account that even in the DP period, the cultivation of the writer's individuality and freedom was the prime issue for Kostetsky, his estrangement and subsequent disengagement from the organizational web does not come as a surprise.

In the debates of MUR on how best to achieve the goal of *velyka literatura*, Sherekh and Kostetsky stood on opposite ends. The first advocated the previously mentioned "national-organic" style, with its notorious motto "to the sources of Ukrainian national culture"[17]; the second unequivocally championed an orientation to the West. This orientation constituted the basis for the initial mutual respect and cooperation between Kostetsky and the poets of the New York Group. Yet, following his own advice, the poets eventually spurned his ambitions of becoming a mentor to them. Like any true avant-garde, they simply resisted any authority and guidance, even from an ally. Kostetsky's friendly counsel to ignore hostile critics was, in a way, falling on deaf ears, because the poets were already doing precisely that. In a 1963 letter written to Tarnawsky, Kostetsky, somewhat disappointed and defensive in tone, reiterated his position regarding the need to construct the theoretical discourse around the group, de facto questioning the poets' insistence on speaking out through poetry alone:

> Don't you think that it would be considerably more interesting if at least one of you, the members of the group, formulated what is in your opinion a modern literature? Wouldn't it be more convincing for you to debate in the present situation? Wouldn't the "urbanites" secure then more advantageous positions, pushing the "villagers" [populists] back to the shadow of the past? In fact, it was I, no one else, who some three years ago, in a letter to Boychuk

---

16 Publishing *Selected Works of Garcia Lorca* in Ukrainian translation in 1958 was one of the first successful collaborations between Kostetsky and the poets of the New York Group. Three poets contributed their translations to this edition: Zhenia Vasylkivska, Yuriy Tarnawsky, and Bohdan Boychuk.

17 See Iurii Sherekh, "V oboroni velykykh," *MUR Zbirnyk* 2 (1946): 12.

or, perhaps, even to you, insisted that someone from your ranks turned to theory and criticism. How come no one did? How come you don't have your own critics, your own thought-out positions, your own detailed theory, which you could use in your fight with the old-fashioned?[18]

Kostetsky's treatment of the group as a uniform entity rather than a circle of individual poets triggered Tarnawsky's protest: "Коли говорите про Н.Й. групу, говорите про людей, які не творять ніякої єдности. Ми не маємо ніяких обов'язків ні відносно себе, ні відносно зовнішнього світу. Я не бачу ніякої причини чому котрийсь із нас мав би писати якісь там маніфести чи оправдання своїх смаків."[19] ("When you speak about the New York Group, you speak about the people, who do not form any unity. We do not have any obligations vis-à-vis ourselves, or vis-à-vis the world. I do not see any reason why any one of us ought to write any manifestoes or apologies for his or her own taste.") There is some dishonesty in this statement, because Tarnawsky has always displayed concerns about the well-being of the group, and has been its most outspoken proponent, but in the context of Kostetsky's ruminations one almost feels that the poet wanted to distance himself from the critic's position and implicit demands. The correspondence between them cooled substantially following this exchange. Kostetsky, on his part, replaced his initial euphoric generosity toward the young poets with more and more biting criticism. His series of reviews in *Ukraina i svit* (Ukraine and the World, 1963-65) is a case in point. Therein he calls Vasylkivska a "light-minded poet" (Rev. of *Novi poezii*, 111), underscores Boychuk's lack of mastery in stress (ibid.), accuses the group's translation endeavors of being too literal (112), and finally concludes:

18 Letter to Iurii Tarnavs'kyi, 29 Mar. 1963. Iurii Tarnavs'kyi Papers, Rare Books and Manuscript Library, Columbia University, New York. The original text reads: "Чи не гадаєте Ви, що було б куди цікавіше, якби принаймні хтось один з Вас членоподільно сформулював, що таке—на Вашу думку—модерна література? Хіба не було б тоді ще більше переконливо Вам виступати у сучасній ситуації? Хіба не здобули б тоді великоміські більше вигідних позицій, відсуваючи селюхів у тінь минулого? А саме я, до речі, ніхто інший, років зо три тому, чи то у листі до Бойчука, чи то навіть і до Вас, наполегливо пропонував, щоб саме хтось із Ваших лав удався до теорії і до критики. Чому не вдалися? Чому нема у Вас власних критиків, власних осмислених позицій, власної деталізованої теорії, якою можна б було бити по застарілих?"

19 Letter to Ihor Kostets'kyi, 9 June 1963. Iurii Tarnavs'kyi Papers, Rare Books and Manuscript Library, Columbia University, New York.

> At present the New York Group does not have much to offer other than poems about death which do or do not give birth to a new life, and poems with a confusing overflow of metaphors which one cannot remember and which, on the whole, do not bind in any way, because it would be so easy to compete with them by making up hundreds alike while sipping coffee.[20]

He could not express his disappointment in the young poets more forcefully than that. But despite the disagreements about the direction the New York Group was supposed to assume, Kostetsky's contacts with some members of the group continued (e.g., Boychuk, Vovk), and joint projects were undertaken.[21] Among the founders of MUR, Kostetsky was the only one who engaged in a lively exchange with the poets of the New York Group, be it on the level of personal or professional interaction.

In comparison to MUR, the group's attitude toward the poets of the Prague School was considerably more respectful and constructive, notwithstanding the fact that aesthetically and ideologically these two groups could not be farther apart. Romantic voluntarism, deeply rooted nationalism, and a belief that literature should play a pivotal role in the regeneration of Ukrainian statehood were not the watchwords the poets of the New York Group would accept as their own. However, this kind of "national" style was respected mainly because it was considered genuine, truly "organic"—that is, coming from the inner imperatives and not from the prescribed dogmatic and rhetorical postulates. The poetry of the Prague School was embraced because it managed somehow to exude such an explicitly nationally *engagé* attitude without sacrificing the high standards of poetic craft or universal humanist concerns.

By and large, the discursive exchanges between the New York Group and the Prague School were minimal. The only two New York poets who came up with critical and/or editorial responses to the legacy of the Prague School

---

20   Letter to Ihor Kostets'kyi, 9 June 1963. Iurii Tarnavs'kyi Papers, Rare Books and Manuscript Library, Columbia University, New York.

21   Ihor Kostets'kyi, "Rev. of *Korotki viddali*," *Ukraina i svit* 25-27 (1963-65): 115. The original text reads: "Нью-Йоркська група як на нинішній день не має багато чим похвалитися крім віршів про смерть, яка породжує або не породжує нове життя, і віршів з вакханалією метафор, які не запам'ятовуються, які взагалі ні до чого не зобов'язують, тому що їх на змагання без труду можна вигадувати сотнями за чашкою кави."

were Bohdan Boychuk and Bohdan Rubchak.[22] Conversely, the poets of the New York Group received even less attention and critical treatment from their older colleagues. Oksana Liaturynska's extensive essay-review of Emma Andijewska's second book of poetry *Narodzhennia idola* (Birth of an Idol, 1958) is an exception, rather than the rule. The "fathers/sons" complex, conspicuously present in the group's dealings with MUR, is absent when it comes to its rapport with the Prague School. That perhaps explains why, at the level of non-poetic discourses, the rebelliousness of the young poets against the colleagues from the School was muted. However, at the level of poetry itself, the poets of the New York Group went to great lengths to emphasize the differences by opening up their doors to formal experimentation and by rooting out any traces of the integral nationalism and voluntarism espoused by the Prague School.

The publication of the first issue of *Novi poezii* in 1959 not only marked the beginnings of a new chapter in the history of the group, but also constituted a consummation of approximately five years of intensive work directed toward the solidification of power relations within the existing literary structures. Bold as they were, the poets would not have managed to establish themselves so quickly were it not for the support they received from such key figures as Iurii Lavrinenko, Vasyl Barka, Vadym Lesych, and the previously discussed Kostetsky. Lavrinenko, a co-editor of *Ukrains'ka Literaturna Hazeta* (*ULH* hereafter)—a prestigious literary forum in the 1950s—was particularly instrumental in the poetic debuts of Tarnawsky, Boychuk, and Rubchak. He encouraged the publication of their first poetry collections: Tarnawsky's *Zhyttia v misti* (Life in the City, 1956), Rubchak's *Kaminnyi sad* (Stone Orchard, 1956), and Boychuk's *Chas boliu* (Time of Pain, 1957). He also invited their contributions (both poetic and critical) to *ULH*, and reviewed and analyzed profusely new poetry sent to him by the members of the group. His criticism was generous, insightful, and very prolific.

---

22 That could very much be connected with their work on the anthology of émigré poetry *Koordynaty* (Coordinates, 1969). The fact remains, however, that Boychuk, in addition to writing a couple of articles on Malaniuk and the Prague School, also compiled and edited *Zibrani tvory* (Collective Works) by Oleksa Stefanovych (Toronto: Ievshan-Zillia, 1975). Bohdan Rubchak, on the other hand, contributed a very extensive introduction to Natalia Livytska-Kholodna's collected poems, entitled *Poezii—Stari i novi* (Poems—Old and New), published in 1986.

When Lavrinenko, however, declined to review the first issue of *Novi poezii*, Rubchak complained about it in his letter to Boychuk:

> Well, our journal is still not being reviewed. They stubbornly ignore us—systematically and consistently. An idea comes to mind: what would happen if we ignored them and all began to write in English? What would they do then? The idiots do not even fancy that they cannot afford to ignore us—they simply do not have much of a choice here. But what can you do?[23]

While Rubchak's observation about an unavoidable immanent interdependency between the two literary generations is quite accurate, his charge about the lack of critical response at that time does not reflect the true state of affairs. In fact, the first years of the group's activity, roughly the period from 1955 to 1961, evoked a considerable resonance. True, not all the accounts were favorably disposed, but in terms of publicity it is almost irrelevant whether the response was constructive or hostile, for either contributes to strengthening visibility and gaining power. Operating within the nexus of such manifold interactions greatly accelerated the maturation process of the New York Group and allowed Rubchak to question the need for its continuation as early as 1962, barely six years after the publication of his debut collection *Kaminnyi sad*:

> As you see, our émigré literature deteriorates more and more. The breeze of the New York Group has fallen and no one has done anything spectacular lately.... Yes, the formative period of the New York Group is a thing of the past, as are for that matter youthful exuberance, novelty, the poems in *ULH* and irresponsible youth. Now each of us has developed his/her own literary image, each of us now signifies something to intelligent Ukrainians, each has become an individual writer in his/her own right. Only now the real struggle begins, i.e. the consolidation and strengthening of all that which we undertook, fought for and envisaged. Overwhelmed by nostalgia, I browsed through some issues of *ULH*. Our beginnings—excepting no one—were much more interesting than our immediate reality these days....

---

23 Letter to Bohdan Boichuk, 4 Aug. 1959. Bohdan Boichuk Papers, Rare Book and Manuscript Library, Columbia University, New York. The original text reads: "А рецензії на журнал таки немає. Уперто ігнорують нас—систематично і послідовно. Насувається думка: що буде, коли ми зігноруємо їх і всі почнемо писати по-англійськи? Що вони зроблять тоді? Ідіоти не уявляють, що вони просто не можуть собі позволити на те, щоб нас ігнорувати—вони аж такого широкого вибору не мають. Але що зробиш?"

Please share your thoughts not as much on the New York Group (it hardly exists any more, for its need has withered) but on the fate of its individual members.[24]

Rubchak's comment about the group's dissipation proved to be considerably premature. But his generally dismissive tone was somewhat justified, especially in the sense that by 1962 the group had reached its apex, and all the consolidation of force relations within and without had occurred by then. In 1957, Emma Andijewska arrived in New York from Munich, and for the next few years she entertained the "New Yorkers" with her colorful personality.[25] In 1959 and 1960, Zhenia Vasylkivska and Patricia Kylyna had their respective book debuts. At the end of 1959, Vira Vovk came to New York from Brazil and acquainted herself with the other members of the group. Thus the second issue of *Novi poezii*, published in 1960, included the poetry of all seven original members of the group. In 1961, *ULH* merged with *Suchasna Ukraina* (Contemporary Ukraine) to form a monthly *Suchasnist'* (Contemporaneity). Ivan Koshelivets (by then Andijewska's husband) became its first editor and invited Bohdan Boychuk to the editorial board, asking him to be responsible for providing literary texts from the United States. Thus the New York Group secured for its own literary production a key émigré publication.

The formative period of the New York Group was thus completed. It was all about forming power relations and gaining the support of the influential émigré critics and poets of the older generation. The following decade, the

---

24 Letter to Iurii Tarnavs'kyi, 25 Sept. 1962. Iurii Tarnavs'kyi Papers, Rare Book and Manuscript Library, Columbia University, New York. The original text reads: "Як бачиш, наша література на еміґрації щораз більше підупадає. Прошумів легенький вітер Нью-Йоркської групи, і ніхто більше нічого "спектакулярного" не робить.... Так. Формативний період НЙГ пройшов, а з ним молодече захоплення, новизна, вірші в УЛГ і безвідповідальна молодість. Тепер кожний з нас виробив собі літературне обличчя, кожний з нас вже тепер щось значить для інтеліґентних українців, кожний вже є в повному розумінні цього слова індивідуальним письменником. Аж тепер починається фактична боротьба—закріплення, утривалення всього того, що ми почали, за що боролись і на що сподівались. Сповнений ностальгією, прочитав я деякі річники УЛГ. Наші початки—всіх без вийнятку—були далеко цікавіші, ніж безпосередня наша літературна сучасність.... Напиши свої думки не так про НЙГ (вона вже майже не існує, бо потреба її перецвіла), але про дальшу долю її індивідуальних членів."

25 Emma Andijewska had her poetic debut in 1951, considerably ahead of most other poets in the group. However, her second book *Narodzhennia idola* (1958) came out while she lived in New York.

1960s, was about winning over the reading public, especially in light of the competition coming from the wave of new literary voices from Soviet Ukraine, the so-called *shistdesiatnyky* (the generation of the sixties).

It was in the journal *Suchasnist'*, in several issues of its 1962 volume, that the émigré audience had a chance to acquaint itself with works of some *shistdesiatnyky*, specifically Ivan Drach, Mykola Vinhranovsky, Ievhen Hutsalo, and Valerii Shevchuk. This series of publications marked the beginning of a new era for the New York Group of poets, one that opened up alternative avenues for an average émigré reader, thereby forcing the group to contend for attention even more vigorously. For that matter, the 1962 issue of *Novi poezii* presented an expanded list of contributors. In addition to the regular members of the group, Vasyl Barka and Vadym Lesych were both invited to submit selections of their poetry. These two poets were highly respected in literary circles, and their participation in the group's activity was of considerable import. Even more significant was the fact that this participation and support, unlike that of Kostetsky or Lavrinenko, appeared to be coming to the members of the group with no strings attached. Lavrinenko, for example, in his letter to Bohdan Rubchak, outlined a few projects he hoped the group would undertake:

> I thought that your group would collect the best there is. That it would compile an anthology of Ukrainian poetry in English translation (of modern poetry, beginning with Tychyna), an anthology of prose, that it would translate three plays of M. Kulish. Furthermore, you and Zhenia, having graduated from universities with degrees in literature, could write two monographs, one on poetry, the other one on prose and drama. Then we would secure necessary funds and export it. I thought that kind of work would create a climate ... as indispensable for your own original poetic production as air is.[26]

None of the projects suggested by Lavrinenko has ever been realized. Thus the fact that neither Lesych nor Barka seemed to be harboring any intention to

---

26 Letter to Bohdan Rubchak, 20 June 1958. Bohdan Rubchak Papers, Rare Book and Manuscript Library, Columbia University, New York. The original text reads: "Думалось мені, ваша група збере все найкраще. Підготує антологію української поезії в англійських перекладах (модерної поезії, від Тичини починаючи), прози, переклаɅе три драми М. Куліша. Далі: Ви і Женя, як літературознавці за університетською освітою, напишете дві монографії—одна про поезію, друга про прозу й драму. Тоді зберемо фонд—і пустимо на експорт. Думалося, що така робота дала б Вам той клімат,... який Вам як повітря потрібен для вашої поетичної оригінальної творчости."

use the poets as instruments for their own hidden agendas was not without significance. Barka profusely praised *Novi poezii* for its remarkably high standards:

> Again about "Novi poezii": the journal is so beautifully, so exemplarily edited, on such an international level, that I could not or cannot have any objections, all the more because it includes the poets (you, Tarnawsky, Vasylkivska, Andijewska) who, I hope, will present the main force in the future of Ukrainian poetry.[27]

But that did not prevent him from giving his comments for improvement:

> Naturally, one could and should expand the journal "Novi poezii." I think that especially interesting would be (very short) essays on poetry—original and in translation—at least in general outlines, written by poets themselves and by others as well. Also, [you should have included] a section on poetic drama. Still more: a concise index of special news in the realm of poetry written in many languages (a two-line annotation); it [would not hurt] to commemorate the dates of great poets from the world's past: pages with a miniature note and a new, contemporary translation on one or two pages.[28]

This particular advice was never implemented, not necessarily because the poets of the New York Group did not appreciate Barka's input, or because they themselves did not contemplate such improvements, but because it was already hard for them (mostly for Boychuk and Tarnawsky, since they alone were carrying the lion's share of editorial, publishing, and distributing duties) to

---

27 Letter to Bohdan Boichuk, 26 Dec. 1961. Bohdan Boichuk Papers, Rare Book and Manuscript Library, Columbia University, New York. The original text reads: "Ще про "Нові поезії": журнал так чудово редаґований, на рівні міжнароднього, взірцево редаґований, що я і не міг і не можу мати жодного застереження, тим більше, що друкуються в ньому поети (Ви, Тарнавський, Васильківська, Андієвська), на яких я поклав всі надії як на головні сили майбутньости української поезії."

28 Letter to Bohdan Boichuk, 6 Dec. 1961. Bohdan Boichuk Papers, Rare Book and Manuscript Library, Columbia University, New York. The original text reads: "Звичайно ж, журнал "Нові поезії" можна і треба розширювати. Зокрема, я гадаю, дуже цікаві були б (дуже короткі) есеї—ориґінальні і перекладні, хоч би в найголовніших фраґментах, про поезію, написані самими поетами і не тільки ними. Також розділи з поетичних драм. А ще—короткий показник особливих новинок з поезії ріжними мовами (анотація в двох рядках): слід би відзначати і дати великих поетів чужоземного минулого: сторінки з мініятюрною нотаткою і новим, сучасним перекладом на одну сторінку, чи дві." (Barka's underlinings.)

maintain the publication even in the form originally conceived, narrow as it was. The cooperation of individual members, much to Boychuk's disappointment, was also not always easily forthcoming. The 1962 issue of *Novi poezii* saw the last contribution of Zhenia Vasylkivska, thereby marking her irrevocable exit from literature and from the group as well. This first crack in the group's cohesiveness may not have become much of an issue if it had not come about at a juncture when mustering all of their power turned out to be crucial, especially in light of the growing fascination with the literary and non-literary processes in Ukraine, both among the émigré readers and the critics. To be exact, the poets of the New York Group were also at first very enthusiastic about the new literary wave in Ukraine, but the true dialogue they were hoping for never materialized, mainly because of political and aesthetic divergences. But in 1962 the perspective was still different. Rubchak, in a letter to Tarnawsky, bemoaning the group's idleness, underscored the importance of contacts with the young poets in Ukraine:

> Your name has completely disappeared from print. Vasylkivska also does not publish anything. Andijewska revels in literary scandals. I don't do anything important. Boychuk alone works on a book of poems. (What's going on with Vasylkivska? We've got to write to her.) And we are much needed nowadays. Not so much for the émigré milieu (although for it too!) as for the young poets in Ukraine, whose wonderful work we've got to support with our own work. Only then can a continuous process of new Ukrainian literature be born.[29]

Beginning in the mid-1960s, the poets' letters projected a sense of growing dissatisfaction. They complained of stagnation and erosion of power, but their self-criticism was still constructive, instigating the need for transformation and adjustment to the new reality. Boychuk's letter to Tarnawsky (who was in Spain with his wife Patricia Kylyna at the time) aptly illustrates the situation:

---

29 Letter to Iurii Tarnavs'kyi, 25 Sept. 1962. Iurii Tarnavs'kyi Papers, Columbia University, New York. The original texts reads: "Твоє прізвище цілком зникло з журналів. Васильківська також не друкує нічого. Андієвська робить репутацію літературними скандалами. Я нічого серйозного не роблю. Один Бойчук приготовляє збірку. (Як справа з Васильківською? Треба до неї написати.) А ми тепер дуже потрібні. Не так еміграції (а їй ми також потрібні!), як молодим поетам в Україні, що їхню прекрасну працю ми мусимо підтримати своєю працею тут. І тоді може народитися якийсь тяглий процес нової української літератури."

Your comments on "Novi poezii" no. 6 are apt. We have all locked ourselves in ivory towers, and only from time to time drop a book or a poem from there; we have not been able to create a process and establish a critical exchange of thoughts—and it looks like our work is gone downhill. I think we've got to do something. Koshelivets and Kostetsky prefer riding on the wave of *shistdesiatnyky* and this is how they are making a name for themselves. They use us only to patch holes. So, more likely, we shall not be able to hold to "Suchasnist'" much longer. We've got to think of something. I have a plan to establish a kind of book club: each of us would donate to the original stock 30 books of each publication, and we would offer this to our members. Then we could publish at least 2-4 issues of "Novi poezii" a year, and one or two books of individual authors. We should expand "Novi poezii" to include prose and criticism, and art—and take action to gain more subscribers. Only in this way shall we be able to create a lively atmosphere, a publishing house and our own journal. We should also take into consideration our relation to the Kyiv poets and Ukrainian literature over there. Moreover, we should bring forward concrete demands and take over the initiative with regards to literature and art. But we'll talk about all these things once you come back, because it is impossible to realize such imposing plans on my own. Besides we must find a way to publish our works in English. So come back and we shall then have some kind of an atmosphere. I have in mind an administrator who would take charge in this matter. We shall open a branch in Chicago, which would publicize our publications in the West.[30]

---

30 Letter to Iurii Tarnavs'kyi, 10 May 1965. Iurii Tarnavs'kyi Papers, Columbia University, New York. The original text reads: "Твої завваги до "Н.П." [Нові поезії] ч. 6 правильні. Ми всі замкнулися в вежах слонової кости, і тільки час-від-часу висунемо звідти збірочку чи вірша; не зуміли створити процесу і критичної вимiни думок,—і, виглядає наша творчість іде вниз. Думаю, нам треба буде щось робити. Кошелівець з Костецьким пересілись на коня шестидесятників і роблять собі на тому "ім'я". Нас вживають тільки, щоб запихати діри. Тож з "Сучасністю", мабуть, довго не витримаємо. Треба щось думати. Я маю в пляні своєрідний клюб книжки, кожний з нас дав би в початковий фонд клюбу 30 книжок кожного видання, це ми поручили б до вибору для наших членів, і тоді видавали б щорічно хоч 2-4 числа "Нових поезій" і одну чи дві книжки окремих авторів. "Нові поезії" треба було б поширити на прозу і критику, і малярство—і повести акцію за передплатниками. Так ми створимо живу атмосферу, видавництво і свій журнал. Також треба буде подумати про співвідношення до київських поетів та української літератури там. Ми повинні поставити конкретні вимоги і перебрати ініціятиву відносин в літературі й малярстві. Але про це треба буде говорити, як Ви повернете назад, бо мені самому неможливо проводити такі широкі пляни. Крім того треба буде пропихати свої твори в англійській мові. Отож приїжджайте і будемо робити якесь життя. Маю вже на приміті адміністратора, що вестиме це діло. В Чікаґо створимо свою філію, яка пропихатиме наші видання на Заході."

This extensive excerpt, despite its gloomy beginning, is not lacking in enthusiasm. It evinces a strong resolve (at least on Boychuk's part) to make a difference; it radiates a determination to regain control over the literary process. It also alludes to Boychuk's personal difficulties in professional cooperation with Ivan Koshelivets, the editor-in-chief of *Suchasnist'*. A year earlier Boychuk wrote to Rubchak:

> I want to talk to you about "Suchasnist'"—Koshelivets and I have not been communicating with each other for four months now.... So it looks like it will be difficult for us to cooperate any further. It would be a pity to break up with the journal, because there is nothing else. If it came to my resignation, perhaps you could take over this task. I would collaborate with you either as an author or coworker, and this way we could still publish something in Proloh[31] from time to time.[32]

Suchasnist' no longer appeared to be in the group's steadfast grip, hence the call for the expansion of *Novi poezii*. But this expansion and the plan to establish a book club, outlined by Boychuk in his letter to Tarnawsky, never materialized. What did happen in 1965, however, is that the group itself experienced an expansion. The no. 7 issue of *Novi poezii* included samples of poetry by Marco Carynnyk, Oleh Kowerko, and Iurii (George) Kolomyiets. Unfortunately for them, the timing of their debuts was not particularly propitious for gaining recognition, because it coincided with the wave of "cultural exchange mania" among the Ukrainian émigré community.[33]

Rubchak's reaction to the realities of this situation was rather bitter, more so than Boychuk's:

> What are your thoughts on the future of our group? Everything seems to fall apart. Well, there are reasons for that. Everybody's eyes turned to Ukraine

---

31 Proloh was a publishing house responsible for issuing *Suchasnist'*.

32 Letter to Bohdan Rubchak, 20 Sept. 1964. Bohdan Rubchak Papers, Rare Book and Manuscript Library, Columbia University, New York. The original text reads: "Я хотів з Тобою поговорити про "Сучасність"—ми з Кошелівцем мовчимо вже 4 місяці.... Тож виглядає, що нам буде тяжко далі співпрацювати. А шкода було б нам зривати з журналом, бо нічого іншого нема. Якщо б мені прийшлося зірвати, може Ти міг би взяти на себе це діло, я б з Тобою, як автор чи співробітник співпрацював, і так можна було б час-від-часу щось видавати через Пролог."

33 This cultural exchange in the mid-1960s was de facto rather limited and one-sided, i.e., involving meetings of a handful of Soviet Ukrainian poets and writers with the émigré communities in Canada and the United States.

and we've become completely forgotten. They buried us and that's it. Sometimes I ask myself if it makes sense at all to carry on writing in Ukrainian… An artificial death has been imposed on us. Koshelivets, Kostetsky and Lavrinenko came to the conclusion one day that the New York Group has not warranted its tasks, that it is finished and nothing will come out of it, and began to play up to the poets in Ukraine.

All this hurts not as much us as those who have just started. The fate of Kolomyiets, Carynnyk, Kowerko is not enviable at all…. They have absolutely nothing to lean on. In theory one could say that after all it is all about one national Ukrainian literature, that both Kowerko and Kalynets represent the same roots. Actually it is the truth. But in practical terms the whole thing looks quite different. Kalynets has at his disposal 40 million readers plus an émigré audience. Kowerko does not have anyone, because even that mere handful of émigré readers who should take notice of him, gravitate toward Ukraine with their tongues put out. It turns out we should stop writing at all and also actively support the poets in Ukraine. Because even those few crumbs of attention that we were privileged with before, now we've lost it to the homeland.[34]

Rubchak's reflections, pessimistic and resigned as they were, did not paralyze the group's activity, and the struggle to expropriate control over the literary discourse continued. For example, in 1966 the group somewhat ostentatiously celebrated its decade of existence by guest-editing a special issue of the magazine *Terem*,[35] and publishing there not only their poetic texts but also an article,

---

34 Letter to Bohdan Boichuk, 10 Apr. 1965. Bohdan Boichuk Papers, Rare Book and Manuscript Library, Columbia University, New York. The original text reads: "Що думаєш про майбутнє нашої групи? Все чомусь розлітається. Та й є причини. Очі всіх звернені на Україну, і про нас забули цілком. Похоронили та й все. Я часом запитую себе, чи взагалі варто продовжувати писати по-українському…. Нам просто створено штучну смерть. Кошелівець та Костецький та Лавріненко рішили одного дня, що НЙГ не виправдала своїх завдань, що вона скінчена та що нічого з неї не буде, і почали бавитись поетами на Україні.

Все це шкодить не так нам, як тим, що щойно починають. Незавидна доля Коломійця, Царинника, Коверка…. Вони вже цілком не мають на що опертись. В теорії можна б говорити, що все це кінець-кінців загально-національна, українська література, що і Коверко, і Калинець—одне. Це зрештою правда. Але практично справа виглядає трохи інакше. Калинець має за собою 40 мільйонів читачів плюс еміґрацію. Коверко не має нікого, бо та горстка еміґрантів, що мусіла б ним піклуватись, з висолопленими язиками тягнеться до України. Виходить, що нам треба перестати писати взагалі, а активно підтримувати поетів в Україні. Бо навіть крихітку тієї уваги, що її ми мали на еміґрації, ми втратили в користь материка."

35 *Terem*, an irregular illustrated cultural serial publication, was published from 1962 to 1975 in Detroit by the Institute of Ukrainian Culture, and has been published since 1979 in Warren, Michigan, by the Association for the Advancement of Ukrainian Culture.

authored by Boychuk, "Iak i poshcho narodylasia N'iu-Iorks'ka hrupa: Do bil'sh mensh desiatylittia" (How and Why the New York Group Was Born: Celebrating More or Less the Tenth Anniversary). In the fall of the same year also Ivan Drach and Dmytro Pavlychko, the leading *shistdesiatnyky*, came to New York as part of an official delegation to the United Nations, and a historic meeting between them and the New York Group took place.[36]

This encounter spurred hopes for a genuine exchange and cooperation on both sides. Drach and Pavlychko envisioned joint publishing endeavors, promising the New York poets publication of their individual poetry collections and a group anthology. There were also plans made for reciprocal visits of the New York Group of poets to Kyiv. However, since the *shistdesiatnyky* were unable to secure official invitations for them, the diaspora poets refused to go to Ukraine as mere tourists (Vira Vovk being the sole exception in this regard). Neither Drach nor Pavlychko were powerful enough to convince the authorities of the communist regime that such collaboration could be advantageous to all concerned. On the other hand, they were both too much "of the system" to pursue (in any manner) something unsanctioned by the regime. However, following their return to Ukraine they did organize a poetry reading in the quarters of the Union of Ukrainian Writers and introduced the New York Group to the Kyivan public. This is how Drach describes this literary evening, which took place on 9 March 1967, in his letter to Boychuk:

> We had an evening at the Union and Dmytro and I talked about the New York Group, read poems. There were many questions—people are interested in the life of emigrants. Dmytro talked more about the writers, and I about the artists: Hutsaliuk, Hnizdovsky, Zubar, and, naturally, Arkhipenko.[37]

At the same time, Drach explains the difficulties with publishing émigré books but remains optimistic about the cooperation. However, toward the end of the

---

36 The poets that participated in this meeting were: Bohdan Boychuk, Bohdan Rubchak, Patricia Kylyna, and Yuriy Tarnawsky.

37 Letter to Bohdan Boichuk, 5 Apr. 1967. Bohdan Boichuk Papers, Rare Book and Manuscript Library, Columbia University, New York. The original text reads: "Мали вечір у Спілці з Дмитром, говорили про Нью-Йоркську групу, читали вірші. Було багато запитань – люди цікавляться життям еміграції. Дмитро більше говорив про письменників, я про художників—про Гуцалюка, Гніздовського, Зубаря і, звичайно, про Архипенка."

1960s, the contacts between *shistdesiatnyky* and the poets of the New York Group, friendly as they were on a purely personal level, slowly dissipated.

By the early 1970s, it became clear that the group was gradually disintegrating. The last issue of *Novi poezii* came out in 1971, and it lacked contributions from Emma Andijewska, Vira Vovk, and Zhenia Vasylkivska. While the latter had left the group much earlier, in 1962, Andijewska and Vovk, already geographically situated on the periphery (Emma in Munich and Vira in Rio de Janeiro), denied their association with the group, though they did so for different reasons and used different forums. Andijewska announced her exit from the group privately, in a letter to Boychuk; Vovk used *Suchasnist'* to declare the same.[38]

Andijewska's refusal to have her poetry published in *Novi poezii* stemmed from the affair surrounding the resignation of Ivan Koshelivets as the editor-in-chief of *Suchasnist'*. The general impression at the time was that this was a forced resignation, that Koshelivets had been coerced to leave the post. However, as he explained in a letter to Boychuk some thirty years later, he left his position voluntarily, not wanting to bend to the political pressure exerted on him by the institution responsible for publishing the journal. The fact that *Suchasnist'* in its brief announcement about the staff changes did not reflect this event accurately was especially upsetting to Koshelivets's wife, Emma Andijewska, and in her letters to Boychuk she demanded from him an official protest in this matter by removing his name from the editorial board of the journal:

> … I have done a great deal of thinking about this disgraceful affair with "Suchasnist'" and this is my conclusion: if you continue to be an editor with "Suchasnist'" (and this is your business, for God's sake don't think that I want to influence you!) without expressing your protest against the article in the January issue of "Suchasnist'," then I am no longer a member of the New York Group, because it's a matter of principles: a public violation of human dignity.[39]

---

38 Neither Andijewska nor Vovk were consistent in the matter, however. While they both publicly emphasized that they did not belong to the group, they did not refuse to participate in the interview about the group that was conducted by Ivan Fizer. See his "Interv'iu z chlenamy N'iu-Iorks'koi hrupy," *Suchasnist'* 10 (1988): 11-38.

39 Letter to Bohdan Boichuk, 3 Feb. 1967. Bohdan Boichuk Papers, Rare Book and Manuscript Library, Columbia University, New York. The original text reads: "… я ще раз передумала всю цю ганебну історію з "Суч.", і прийшла до висновку: якщо Ти далі будеш редактором "Сучасности" (а це Твоя справа, і Бога ради, не подумай, що я будь як хочу на Тебе

To Boychuk, however, retaining the journal in the group's control and not losing it to the politically oriented forces was more important than the public manifestation of his loyalty to Andijewska and Koshelivets. Ultimately, his position in this matter was justified, but initially there was a lot of confusion as to what course of action to take and what the group's stand as a whole should be.

An ideological divergence between Vira Vovk and the group (manifested publicly especially as her polemics with Bohdan Boychuk, carried out in *Suchasnist'*) emerged as a result of her accounts published in *Suchasnist'* of the several trips she made to Ukraine between 1965 and 1970. At issue was a difference in understanding of the expediency of such literary contacts. To Vovk, the possibility of interaction with Ukrainian poets and writers on a purely personal level took precedence over ideological differences; to Boychuk such a stand lacked principles, especially since her public appearances were obviously monitored and staged by the representatives of the communist regime.[40] Despite this polemic, she continued to correspond with the individual members of the group, but she declined to contribute her poetry to the last issue of *Novi poezii* and also publicly declared her independence:

> Regardless of the nature of our disputes—ideological or comradely—I am tied to the New York Group because of my work, which has already brought forth a good harvest. Personally, I do not consider myself a member of this group, because I myself constitute an autocratic "Rio-de-Janeiro Group" with autonomy of thought and taste. Obviously neither the friendship nor the unquestionable merits of the New York Group are thereby denied.[41]

To make the female desertion complete, Kylyna left the group in 1973, shortly after she divorced Tarnawsky. The same year, Boychuk resigned from the editorial board of *Suchasnist'*, referring to his lack of time due to a variety of pending projects. Thus, by the end of 1973 the group had seemingly ceased

---

впливати!), не запротестувавши проти статті у січневому числі "Сучасности", то я перестаю бути членом Нью-Йоркської групи, бо тут ідеться про принциповість: публічне потоптання людської гідности."

40 See Bohdan Boichuk, "Pro reliatyvnu absoliutnist' i navpaky," *Suchasnist'* 5 (1970): 45-53.

41 Vira Vovk, "Pro tekhnolohichnyi i metafizychnyi kshtalt myslennia," *Suchasnist'* no. 12 (1970): 81. The original text reads: "З Нью-Йоркською групою, які не були б між нами ідеологічні чи товариські спори, в'яже мене праця, яка вже принесла досить доброго овочу. Особисто я не вважаю себе членом цієї групи, бо вважаю себе самовладною "групою Ріо-де-Жанейро", з автономією думки і смаку; воно аж ніяк не заперечує дружби і повного визнання всіх безперечних заслуг, що їх має Нью-Йоркська група."

to exist as an active and cohesive entity. Yet the power gained during the vocal period (1955-1972) did not dissipate right away, and it was skillfully used by the male core of the group to secure its poetic legacy. Even though the 1970s were somewhat inactive, the New York Group reemerged again in the second half of the 1980s and especially during the 1990s, when the quarterly *Svito-vyd* was published.[42]

To talk about the legacy of the New York Group in its non-poetic contributions is to talk first of all about a variety of discourses engendered throughout the many years of its active involvement in literature. In the 1990s, the most conspicuous, though not necessarily most acknowledged, contribution of the group lay in stimulating the discourse around the Kyiv School[43] by foregrounding the mutual aesthetic affinity and by providing the platform (*Svito-vyd*) for manifesting these kinds of considerations.[44] It was also important for the New York Group to resist its comparison to the *shistdesiatnyky*, and it appeared that the alignment with the Kyiv School helped to undermine such comparisons. But, even though the discourses they produced allow speaking of the group as a single cohesive entity, it is poetry alone that determines its members' true legacy. The poetry of the New York Group, imbued with drive and originality, has offered the readers novel perspectives, which, difficult as they might have been, moved the reading public onto planes previously unknown.

---

42 *Svito-vyd* (1990-1999), a quarterly of literature and the arts, began as a joint venture between the New York Group and the Writers' Union of Ukraine. It was the first literary forum published in New York and Kyiv that brought together writers and poets living in the diaspora and Ukraine.

43 Also called the *postshistdesiatnyky* generation, a core of which consists of poets Vasyl Holoborodko, Mykhailo Hryhoriv, Viktor Kordun, and Mykola Vorobiov.

44 The second issue, of 1996, was devoted to the New York Group and was soon followed by the issue commemorating the achievements of the Kyiv School (*Svito-vyd*, no. 1-2, 1997).

CHAPTER 3

Periphery versus Center:
The Poetics of Exile

The phenomenon of the New York Group constitutes a compelling case for studying various dimensions of the exilic sensibility, including its experiential, psychological, and political aspects. By the early 1960s, the label "New York Group" stood for an innovative approach to Ukrainian poetry and referred to the oeuvres of Emma Andijewska, Bohdan Boychuk, Patricia Kylyna, Bohdan Rubchak, Yuriy Tarnawsky, Zhenia Vasylkivska, and Vira Vovk. With the exception of Kylyna, these poets experienced war and displacement as children, and immigrated primarily to the United States[1] as teenagers or young adults. This relatively early emigration may explain why the group embraced its exilic condition as something stimulating rather than stifling—and turned to Western literary sources for inspiration. Understandably, their poetic personae were formed in the West. Yet, by choosing the Ukrainian language as their main—if not exclusive—medium for artistic expression, they cultivated a link with the literary past of their own country and, by doing so, necessarily placed themselves outside the

---

1   See Maria G. Rewakowicz, "Introducing Ukrainian Émigré Poets of the New York Group," *Toronto Slavic Quarterly* 1.3 (2003). Available at http://www.utoronto.ca/slavic/tsq/03/ rewakowicz.html.

mainstream cultural space of their adopted homelands. Forced to negotiate linguistic, transnational, and transcultural issues in their creative endeavors, the poets unavoidably thrust themselves into liminal positions.

According to Victor Turner, the liminal condition is "necessarily ambiguous" because it eludes and slips through "the network of classifications that normally locate states and positions in cultural space."[2] In this chapter, I refer to liminality in order to delineate the New York Group's exilic location and to designate the spatial relationship between a center (Ukraine) and its periphery (émigré milieu), the dynamics of which define the very condition of exile. I also want to indicate the shifting, if not reversible, character of the center-periphery dichotomy, especially as it pertains to the issues of literary production.

Exiles are necessarily considered marginal personae because they take up a position of "ex-centricity" (using Linda Hutcheon's coinage)[3] vis-à-vis their respective countries of origin and a position of eccentricity in relation to their adopted homelands. Politically and socially, they are cut off from their roots. Consequently, their impact on the center is, by and large, negligible. Nevertheless, in the sphere of culture this impotence becomes less pronounced; it can even be transformed into a source of power. It is precisely in the province of aesthetic creativity that the center-periphery assignation looses its fixity and stability. It is here, given the right set of circumstances, that the paradoxical reversals I already alluded to are not only conceivable but realizable. When a center happens to be in the grip of totalitarianism, and artistic freedom is severely curtailed, then the exiled writer or poet has a unique opportunity to present a viable alternative.

Using the poetics of exile as a methodological tool, I analyze here the nature and significance of one such alternative, namely the one put forward by the New York Group. I shall argue that the members of this group, despite their émigré status, were able to transcend their periphery by defining and pushing the aesthetic boundaries of Ukrainian literature. It is also my view that their oeuvre evinces the exilic sensibility, even though the poets themselves for the most part shunned the thematization of exile. I will identify a handful of poems

---

2   Victor Turner, *The Ritual Process: Structure and Anti-Structure* (Chicago: Aldine, 1969), 95.
3   Linda Hutcheon, *A Poetics of Postmodernism: History, Theory, Fiction* (New York: Routledge, 1988), 41.

that reflect the issues of exilic "otherness" in order to underscore the ambivalent (liminal) nature of the poets' creative situatedness.

Exile, strictly speaking, refers to a forced separation from one's native land, without possibility of return. The notion covers both the moment of expulsion and the condition of life immediately following banishment. By the same token, an exile is a person who cannot return home without facing death or imprisonment for acts allegedly committed against the governing regime. Such characterization has definite political overtones, and one might even see some merit in the statement that "exile is a political rather than an artistic concept."[4] But recently, the practical application of the term "exile" has widened considerably. Edward Said, for example, without undermining the causal underpinnings of exilic existence, focuses on its experiential and psychological aspects, seeing in exile "the perilous territory of not-belonging."[5] However, Said concentrates not only on exile's miseries, but on its advantages as well: "Most people are principally aware of one culture, one setting, one home; exiles are aware of at least two, and this plurality of vision gives rise to an awareness that—to borrow a phrase from music—is *contrapuntal*."[6] Another obvious advantage of exile (which Said does not speak of) is the attainment of artistic freedom. But no matter what the advantage, the condition of exile always involves a certain ambiguity, a feeling of discomfort, and a liminal existence. Said ends his reflections by saying: "Exile is life led outside habitual order. It is nomadic, decentered, contrapuntal; but no sooner does one get accustomed to it than its unsettling force erupts anew."[7]

My own approach to the concept of exile can be formulated in two propositions, designated respectively as "psychological" and "linguistic." First, exile must denote either geographical or psychological displacement—the distinctions are not particularly relevant in my case—that leads to a sense of "otherness" (alterity). Second, and here I agree with Joseph Brodsky, it is necessarily "a linguistic event" in which "an exiled writer is thrust, or retreats, into his mother tongue."[8] The differentiation often made between an exile and an

---

4   John Glad, ed., *Literature in Exile* (Durham, NC: Duke University Press, 1990), viii-ix.
5   Edward Said, "Reflections on Exile," *Granta* 13 (1984): 162.
6   Ibid., 172.
7   Ibid.
8   Joseph Brodsky, "The Condition We Call Exile," *Altogether Elsewhere: Writers on Exile*, ed. Marc Robinson (Boston: Faber, 1994), 10.

émigré—with the former referring to a person who is compelled to leave the homeland for fear of persecution but bent on returning when circumstances allow, and the latter implying someone who has no intention of returning— seems less important to me. I conflate these two designations, simply because in the case of the New York Group both seem applicable.[9]

The seven founding members of the group all conform to the characterization of exile given above. They have all retained the mother tongue as their main medium of expression, all experienced some kind of displacement; and— referring solely to their literary situation—none of them managed (or was even willing) to transcend the condition of "otherness" in their respective countries of residence. Patricia Kylyna's case, of course, is unique among the poets of the New York Group. Hers is the case of linguistic self-exile. Being American, she consciously chose the status of the Other in her own country, virtually celebrating her alterity:

> Я, чужинка, розумію тільки по-водяному,
> по-часовому;
> бачу те, що вже бачила, що ніколи не бачила.
> Те, що далеко, від мене далеко.[10]

> I am a foreigner, I understand only in watery,
> in temporal terms;
> I see that which I've already seen, that which I've never seen.
> That which is far, far away from me.

Kylyna's case spurs Rubchak to reevaluate the meaning of home: "Her commitment to Ukrainian literature proves that home is not always a geographic location: home can be language and culture alone, with their own rigorous territorial imperatives. The value of the 'soil' often tends to be overestimated."[11]

---

9   That also seems to be the stand of Bohdan Rubchak in his essay "Homes as Shells: Ukrainian Émigré Poetry," in *New Soil—Old Roots: The Ukrainian Experience in Canada*, ed. Jaroslav Rozumnyj, 87-123.

10 Patrytsiia Kylyna [Patricia Nell Warren], *Trahediia dzhmeliv* (New York: NIH, 1960), 10.

11 Rubchak, "Homes as Shells," 119.

Interestingly, despite the obvious disadvantages that any poet or writer faces in exile, the members of the group accepted their condition not as a curse but rather as an opportunity to expand the aesthetic boundaries of Ukrainian literature. They were eager to incorporate Western artistic accomplishments into their own vocabularies, eager to synthesize poetically their experiences from two different worlds. It is this Western orientation and general openness to new ideas that prevented them from succumbing to the typically exilic modes of writing in which feelings of nostalgia, estrangement, or terminal loss dominate. Said's remark about exile as "the unhealable rift forced between a human being and a native place"[12] is evidently refuted by the group's posture and experience. If anything, the poets in question were actively involved in healing and thus bridging the rift Said mentions.

Not surprisingly, exilic displacement is rarely thematized by the New York poets and the motifs of uprootedness, homelessness, and love for the native soil do not figure prominently in their works. The few poems that do take up such motifs necessarily place them in a broader context. It is as if the experience of exile must be cleansed of any local reference. When Bohdan Boychuk contemplates the loss of home in his poem, not only does the piece have a universal quality, but the very idea of home is questioned and undermined:

> *Десь суть була,*
> *осталися одгадки,*
> *десь дім стояв,*
> *та як його знайти?*

> Мій шлях
> неждано вихознув
> з-під ніг,
> піском розлився
> в безконечність.

> Я йшов
> і по коліна груз

---

12   Said, "Reflections on Exile," 159.

в темноті.
На грані світляних років
являвся часом день,
і час від часу зірка
падала комусь
в долоні.

Так:
десь дім стояв,
      а, може, не стояв;
була десь ціль,
      а, може, не було.
Я йшов кудись
і знав:
мій шлях—нікуди;
я йшов і знав:
мій хід—життя.[13]

There was an essence somewhere,
    only puzzles are left,
home stood somewhere,
    but how to find it?

My path
suddenly slipped
from underneath my feet,
dissipated like dust
into infinity.

I walked
and sank up to my knees
into darkness.

---

13 Bohdan Boichuk, *Virshi vybrani i peredostanni* (New York: Suchasnist', 1983), 9. This is a
    revised, more compact, version of the poem, which originally appeared in his *Chas boliu*
    (New York: Slovo, 1957).

On the edge of light years
daylight appeared sometimes,
and from time to time the star
was falling into someone's
hands.

Yes:
home stood somewhere,
           and, perhaps, did not;
the goal was somewhere,
           and, perhaps, was not.
I went somewhere
and knew:
my path leads nowhere;
I went and knew:
my steps are life.

This urge to establish the universals underlying personal experiences, according to Andrew Gurr, lies at the heart of exilic sensibility. He states: "The more individual the record, the more compulsive is the need to assert its general validity. We might well ponder how much this urge to claim universality is a reflex response to exile."[14] As Boychuk's poem above attests, it is indeed very much the case. Even his love for his lost homeland is expressed universally and abstractly:

та я устами хочу доторкнути ран,
і чорну тугу видушити з серця
на твої спечалені долоні,
а так навіки розчинитися
у лоні чорнозему
і прорости травою твого тіла,

країно чорного життя.[15]

---

14   Andrew Gurr, *Writers in Exile: The Identity of Home in Modern Literature* (Brighton: Harvester, 1981), 22.

15   Boichuk, *Chas boliu*, 30.

and I want to touch your wounds with my lips
and squeeze black longing out of my heart
onto your hands,
and afterwards to dissolve forever
in the womb of your black soil
and become your body's grass,

oh, the country of black life.

Zhenia Vasylkivska's approach in this regard is even more abstract and detached from reality than Boychuk's. Turning to her native country, she ponders:

Так, ми тебе збираєм, бо ти розбилась,
як вітер між шпильками блудних сосон.
І, все таки, ти—вітер. Ти торкаєш
солоні груди моря—і воно хвилює;
ти падаєш прозорим подихом на мутну сіль—
і оживають її таємні м'язи—
і на струнких долонях
приносиш свіжий місяць.[16]

So, we gather you, because you shattered
like a wind in-between the needles of haggard pines.
And you, after all, are the wind. You touch
salty breasts of the sea—and it waves;
you fall with a sheer breath onto the muddy salt—
and its mysterious muscles revive—
and in the slim hands
you bring fresh moon.

The native land she addresses in her long poem "Bat'kivshchyna" (Father-land), from which the above excerpt was taken, hardly contains any concrete

---

16 Zhenia Vasylkivska, *Korotki viddali* (New York: Slovo, 1959), 36.

reference to the reality and territory known as Ukraine. What we have here is Vasylkivska's attempt to construct an imaginary home, confined to and defined by her poetic imagination. In many respects her case is not singular. As a rule, the younger the émigré generation, the more it loses its identification with the homeland. Because Vasylkivska does not use direct recollections as the basis for her creativity, she avoids nostalgic sentimentality in the re-creation of home.

The uprooted temperament exhibits itself most vividly in literary texts that convey the anxieties of alienation. This type of alienation in the instance of the New York Group cannot be easily distinguished from the existentialist variety. In fact, for the majority of these poets, alienation is both a metaphysical condition and a psychological response to the world. Consider Bohdan Rubchak's poem "Zrada anhela" (The Angel's Betrayal):

Втомились плечі від незручних крил,
таких, як на старих девероритах.
В куточках уст—усмішка сибарита,
і на сандалях—тротуарів пил.

За те, що землю взяв за небосхил,
земля забрала завеликі мита:
Єдина справжність міту вже закрита,
і уявити лет немає сил.

Та хоч привабив світ ночей гостинцем,
хоч прикував тебе речей тягар—
останешся ніяковим чужинцем:

ясніють у очах знаки незмиті,
і заважають крила, і пече
сліпучий спогад першої блакиті.[17]

The shoulders got tired of uncomfortable wings,
like the ones on old woodcuts.
In the corners of his mouth—a sybarite's smile,
and on sandals the pavement's dust.

---

17   Bohdan Rubchak, *Promenysta zrada* (New York: V-vo N'iu-Iorks'koi hrupy, 1960), 11.

Because he took the earth for the sky,
the earth took tolls too high:
the myth's only truth is already closed,
and there's no strength to imagine the flight.

And even though the world of nights coaxed you with a gift,
and the weight of things chained you down—
you'd remain an awkward stranger:

unwashed signs beam in the eyes,
and the wings are in the way, and the blinding
memory of that first azure burns.

Here Rubchak not only underscores his sense of "otherness" and eccentricity—presumably caused by displacement, symbolized as "uncomfortable wings"—he also alludes to metaphysical exhaustion ("there's no strength to imagine the flight"). The vanity of material comfort cannot actually be enjoyed by the poet because "the wings" (his strangeness) and "the blinding memory of that first azure" (i.e., recollections of his place of origin) are experienced as obstacles. To put it differently, an angel (an artist? an exile?) will never feel at home with humans (ordinary people? foreign population?); ultimately, the very reality of his displacement amounts to a betrayal.

In his other collection, *Divchyni bez krainy* (For a Girl without a Country), Rubchak also takes up the theme of homelessness. Despite the strife and obstacles inherent in such a condition, he ends this poem on a positive note, asserting that, for those who seek it, home is attainable:

> Дівчино без дороги,
> мандрівнице без дому,
> захмарені болем
> наші полудні бліді,
> що ж розкажеш про нас
> по мандруванні довгому,
> коли ввійдеш струнка,
> у свій опромінений дім?[18]

---

18 Bohdan Rubchak, *Divchyni bez krainy* (New York: V-vo N'iu-Iorks'koi hrupy, 1963), 5.

> Oh, girl without a road,
>
> oh, wayfarer without home,
>
> clouded with the pain
>
> are our pale afternoons,
>
> what will you relate about us
>
> after long wandering,
>
> when you'll enter, slender as ever,
>
> your radiant home?

As is obvious in this poem, the "radiant home" may very well be poetry itself, visited by the Muse. In other words, Rubchak's home acquires a symbolic dimension and simply points to creativity. Some twenty years later, he says, "In the end, every true poet forever seeks his own house of language which becomes for him, in Heidegger's words, 'the house of Being.'"[19]

It should be emphasized that neither Rubchak nor the Group as a whole betrays any obsession with "home"; none of the poets reveal nostalgia for a lost paradise. Rubchak merely plays with the notions of "home" and "belonging," foregrounding their destabilizing possibilities. In his article "Homes as Shells" he writes:

> [The poets of the New York Group] have too many reservations and ask too many hopeless questions. In fact, they have to make reservations in order to survive, as if their imagined Ukrainian past were not so much a permanent home as a temporary abode, a hotel. At the same time, their older colleagues frequently treat them as transient guests in the Ukrainian domain. Never having been fed by the energies of the Ukrainian soil long or thoroughly enough, this generation of poets is torn between two quasi-homes, two temporary homes: one for temporary living, the other for temporary dreaming.
>
> It is no wonder, therefore, that ... these poets have chosen poetry itself as their home. They also had to make another choice, one which their older colleagues were spared: not only did they choose to make poetry their home, but they also chose to make *Ukrainian* poetry their home. This last choice was perhaps the most agonizing of all. Ukraine is, for these younger poets, not an existential necessity but something of a posited concept, in which they have elected to believe and which they have elected to follow.[20]

---

19 Rubchak, "Homes as Shells," 121.
20 Ibid., 114.

Rubchak's observations hint at the paradoxical situation in which these poets found themselves. On the one hand, they used poetry in order to neutralize or alleviate the feeling of alienation that naturally comes with exile; on the other hand, by choosing Ukrainian as their language of expression, they perpetuated exilic "otherness." No matter how cosmopolitan or assimilated they were, the issue of language would always thrust them back into eccentricity and ex-centricity.

The extent to which the notion of home is contingent and elective is illustrated by Yuriy Tarnawsky's poem "Zapovit" (Testament):

> Коли помру, то спаліть
> моє тіло, як заборонену, чи ненавиджену книжку,
> і зберіть увесь попіл, щоб ні одна молекуля із мене
> не залишилася на місці, де я згорів.
>
> І йдіть до Сантандеру, до скелі, висуненої найдальше
> в море,
> і чекайте на сильний вітер із півдня,
> і киньте цей попіл в сторону моря, хай сірим
> прапором
> він залопоче хоч кілька секунд над синьою водою.
>
> І після цього вже ніколи
> не думайте про мене і не вимовляйте мого імени,
> щоб його букви, як струпи, не тріскали,
> і не кривавила ця рана, що під ними, яка ніколи
> не загоїться.[21]

When I die, burn
my body like a forbidden or hated book,
and gather all the ashes, so not one of my molecules
is left in the place where I was cremated.

---

21 Iurii Tarnavs'kyi, *Poezii pro nishcho i inshi poezii na tsiu samu temu: Poezii 1955-1970* (New York: V-vo N'iu-Iorks'koi hrupy, 1970), 307.

> And go to Santander, to the rock protruding far
> into the sea,
> and wait for a strong wind from the south,
> and throw the ashes towards the sea, let them flap
> like a grey flag for a few seconds over the blue water.
>
> And afterwards never ever
> think about me and do not pronounce my name,
> so its letters would not crack like scabs
> and the wound beneath, which will never heal,
> does not bleed.

The desire to spread his ashes over the sea in Santander, the Spanish city where Tarnawsky lived on and off in the 1960s and early 1970s, undoubtedly invokes Taras Shevchenko's poem "Zapovit," written almost one hundred years earlier. Shevchenko also spent most of his adult life outside Ukraine, but wanted to be buried in his native country. Tarnawsky's alter ego, unlike Shevchenko's, does not wish to be buried in Ukraine. His ostentatious statement clearly cuts through clichés associated with the oeuvre of exiled writers. It denies nostalgia, questions the necessity of homecoming, and defiantly celebrates uprootedness. Yet Tarnawsky's pronounced cosmopolitanism is in fact a mask, a consciously chosen pose, behind which there is an exiled person who deeply cares about the fate of his native land. For example, in one of his poems he addresses Russia, Ukraine's colonizer, with such contempt that it cannot but invoke Shevchenko's own passions:

> Країно, що страждаєш на комплекс материнства
> і обмотуєш інші нації колючим дротом своєї
> любови,
> хіба не знайдеться серед твоїх синів
> хоч один, який сказав би: «Залиши їх, мамо!»[22]

---

22 Ibid., 314.

Oh country, you suffer from the maternity complex
and wrap other nations with barbed wire of your love,
how come not one among your sons
comes forward and says: "Please, leave them alone, oh mother!"

Tarnawsky's schizophrenic response to his liminal situatedness is quite in line with the exilic sensibility. This simultaneous belonging and not-belonging to two different geographical and psychological territories engenders poetry that is necessarily contradictory and polyphonic.

As I have already indicated, the explicit theme of exile in the output of the Group is not especially strong, which suggests that these poets do not fit the typical paradigm of émigré writers. The examples quoted above represent exceptions rather than a rule. Emma Andijewska's poetry completely avoids references to the exilic condition. Vira Vovk hardly ever thematizes exile directly, but occasionally does use childhood memories to re-create the image of the country of her origin. Nonetheless, this imagined Ukraine does not eclipse the exotic beauty of Vovk's adopted homeland, Brazil. It seems that the poet's imagination depends on the harmonious coexistence of these two countries. In this respect, this tendency is deeply rooted in the exilic sensibility. The contrapuntal awareness of simultaneous dimensions (to use Said's words) undoubtedly enriches her vision and widens perspectives, but it also injects a sense of discomfort and indeterminacy:

вони зійшли
несіяні квіти
на передвіконні
чужого дуже
нашого світу
щоб дарувати
смуток бездомних тварин
усмішки білого рижу
в червонім бальоні вечора[23]

---

23 Vira Vovk, *Poezii* (Kyiv: Rodovid, 2000), 255. This is a slightly revised version of the poem originally published in *Meandry* (Rio de Janeiro: Artes Gráficas, 1979).

they sprouted
unsown flowers
on the windowsill
of this foreign
world of ours
to offer
the sadness of homeless creatures
the smiles of white rice
in the red balloon of the evening.

Homelessness is just a hint in this poem, but the dilemma of what is "ours" and what is "foreign" becomes conspicuously centered and underscores the poet's liminal existence.

What unites all six Ukrainian poets of the New York Group (Kylyna, as an American, must be excluded here) is their insistence on producing works in Ukrainian that have a universal appeal. Hence, local and national idiosyncrasies are not particularly revered or cultivated, which is in step with modernism's "international" bias. Yet the latter brings us back to the problematics of the center-periphery dichotomy. The poets' mother tongue excludes them from the cultural mainstream of their adopted countries. Therefore, the propensity to speak through universal forms and content and the embrace of humanism as a philosophical signpost could well stem from their need (conscious or unconscious) to compensate for such marginalization. On the other hand, by resisting émigré parochialism and ghettoization, the poets found themselves on the periphery of a periphery: they were in a linguistically liminal position vis-à-vis the host country, and in a thematically liminal position vis-à-vis their own politicized émigré community. Because the themes the New York Group poets cultivated were by and large universalist, they consciously avoided engaging themselves in issues that would directly correlate to the émigré condition. In other words, patriotic rhetoric (often excessive among exile poets) was eschewed by the group. No wonder that the center—Ukraine— became pivotally important for them. Nevertheless, geographically and politically, they were all "ex-centrics." However, their fateful decision to accept Ukraine as a symbolic and psychological point of reference did launch the New York Group on a life-long creative journey that posited an eventual embrace by the center, defined as a future free and democratic state. Their ambition was to invent their own aesthetics in the realm of Ukrainian poetry as a palliative measure against the ensnaring realities of all the peripheries encroaching on them.

It is often said that exiles never break their psychological links with their points of origin, and that they must keep faith in the possibility of home-coming. The poets of the New York Group indeed nurtured the link with Ukraine as a "spiritual home," but having left their native soil at an early age, they never really entertained the thought of returning to their homeland. The West has become their permanent home. Despite initial insecurities, they found freedom abroad. That in itself was enough to make up for the separation from Ukraine, which, unfortunately, at the time of their creative prime, had little to offer them because of the communist occupation. Zygmunt Bauman put it succinctly: "In exile, uncertainty meets freedom. Creation is the issue of that wedlock."[24] The members of the New York Group found their home in poetry and experienced creativity in freedom.

While a permanent homecoming was never an issue, the poets under discussion did long for a symbolic return, hoping for an eventual literary acceptance by the center.[25] The official contacts they established in the mid-1960s with Ukrainian poets Ivan Drach and Dmytro Pavlychko raised short-lived hopes of being published in Ukraine. That, understandably, did not happen. The majority of the group's members were in fact very realistic about the possibility of cultural exchange. By and large, they were hesitant to cooperate, mindful of political ramifications and careful not to compromise

---

24 Zygmunt Bauman, "Assimilation into Exile: The Jew as a Polish Writer," in *Exile and Creativity: Signposts, Travelers, Outsiders, Backward Glances*, ed. Susan Rubin Suleiman (Durham: Duke University Press, 1998), 321.

25 While official recognition was slow, the group was aware of individual private reactions to their work in Ukraine. Thanks to clandestinely channeled publications by such publishers as Suchasnist', at least some readers in Ukraine were acquainted with overseas writings. Bohdan Boychuk, for example, in a letter to Bohdan Rubchak, mentions one such reaction: "Були деякі відгуки з Києва—позитивно реаґували зокрема на Твої та Емми вірші. Один критик питав, чому нема укр. тематики!" (28 Sept. 1963). ("There were some responses from Kyiv—they reacted positively especially to yours and Emma's poetry. One critic asked why there is no Ukrainian content!") Letter to Bohdan Rubchak, 28 Sept. 1963. Bohdan Rubchak Papers, Rare Book and Manuscript Library, Columbia University, New York. From the tone of the letter, it is clear that such reactions were of great importance to the members of the group.

or undermine their aesthetic integrity. But they welcomed the interaction and knowingly tested its limits. For example, this is how Boychuk saw it:

Але вітри, які тут між нами віяли були свіжі, цікаві—постараємось зробити їх плідними. Обмін думок був гострий, але дружній—колись розкажу, писати не годиться. До 10-го, ювілейного, числа «Нових поезій» ми запросили поетів України (офіційно, через спілку письменників—тобто Дмитра)—якщо поезії не прийдуть, сторінки їхні залишаться порожні, і так підуть в майбутнє. Будемо від тепер ставити їх в доконані ситуації. Чому б ні—там же свобода творчости і людини—це нам вигідно приймати за щире золото.[26]

But the winds that blew between us were fresh and interesting—we'll try to make them fruitful. The exchange of thoughts was sharp but friendly—I'll tell you some time, it's hard to write about it. To our tenth anniversary issue of "New Poetry" we have invited the poets from Ukraine (officially, via the Union of Writers—that is through Dmytro [Pavlychko])—if poetry does not arrive, we shall leave blank pages and this is how the future will read. From now on they will face a fait accompli. Why not? They have "creative and personal freedoms" over there, and it is convenient to us to take these at face value.

Despite the sarcasm about freedom in Soviet Ukraine, this statement pointedly illustrates the confidence with which the group acted vis-à-vis the center. Naturally, none of the invited Ukrainian poets contributed to *Novi poezii*. Nor did the New York Group publish blank pages in the almanac's tenth issue.

Unlike Vira Vovk, who visited Ukraine on a tourist visa three times during the 1960s, others in the group waited for official recognition and invitation. It never arrived—at least not in the sixties. It is interesting to see this development through Kylyna's eyes:

Finally, Drach and his circle dared to invite me and Yuriy [Tarnawsky] to visit Soviet Ukraine. Again, I was to be the door-opener—the "safe" *Amerikanka*. Drach wrote that it would be possible to read our poetry in major cities there.

We were tempted. It was now possible to get U.S. visas to go there. A trickling of American tourists had visited Ukraine. I had debriefed with one American-born college student who told me how he had actually hitchhiked

---

26 Letter to Vira Vovk, 12 Dec. 1966. Vira Vovk Papers, Central State Museum-Archive of Literature and Art, Kyiv.

around the Ukrainian boonies, right into the high mountain country where Pavlychko was from.... But was it safe? The KGB had continued to keep an eye on us. At large Ukrainian social affairs, the KGB was casual about letting one of their guys be visible, with a drink in his hand....

We decided that our trip would be safe only if the Soviet Ukrainian government would issue an official invitation.

Regretably, in the late 1960s, an official invitation was still not possible.[27]

An invitation did arrive some twenty years later, in the late 1980s and the early 1990s, when the Soviet Union was approaching the brink of collapse. All four poets who withstood the temptation to go to Ukraine as tourists—Bohdan Boychuk, Emma Andijewska, Yuriy Tarnawsky, and Bohdan Rubchak— received official invitations from the Writers' Union of Ukraine.

Understandably, the New York Group's dealings with the center in the 1990s changed in proportion to Ukraine's own transformation from a Soviet republic into an independent state. Not only was the group recognized and accepted as a significant contributor to Ukrainian letters, but it also managed to influence the literary process briefly in the first years of Ukraine's independence by publishing the journal *Svito-vyd*. Alliances with the poets in Ukraine shifted as well. For example, Drach and Pavlychko, the leading *shistdesiatnyky*, left literature to become politicians and therefore were no longer viable partners. Consequently, the New York Group aligned itself with the poets of the Kyiv School and the so-called *visimdesiatnyky*, the poets of the 1980s. The latter, however, soon distanced themselves from the New York poets, perhaps because they found them rather passé for their own tastes. Their ties with the Kyiv School, however, remained close.

The poetic affinity between the poets of the Kyiv School—namely, Mykola Vorobiov, Viktor Kordun, Mykhailo Hryhoriv, and Vasyl Holoborodko[28]—

---

27 Patricia Nell Warren, "A Tragedy of Bees: My Years as a Poet in Exile, 1957-1973," *Harvard Gay & Lesbian Review* 2.4 (1995): 20. Kylyna somewhat exaggerates the safety issue. After all, Vira Vovk travelled to Ukraine without incident. Therefore, the reluctance to make a trip to the native land seems to have been a matter more of principle than of safety.

28 These poets are also called *postshistdesiatnyky*, a label which, for example, Volodymyr Morenets' dismisses as misleading. He suggests it would be more appropriate to call the poets of the Kyiv School *neshistdesiatnyky*, for according to him their approach to poetry is very different from that of the *shistdesiatnyky*. See his introduction to Mykhailo Hryhoriv's book *Sady Marii* (Kyiv: Svito-vyd, 1997), 17.

and the New York Group is obvious to anyone acquainted with their works. I want to elaborate on this connection slightly by pointing beyond the sphere of poetry. For example, both groups experienced the condition of exile, but differently. The poets of the Kyiv School demonstrated that it is quite possible to be an exile in one's own country. In this respect, Paul Ilie dismisses the view that geographical displacement constitutes the basic criterion for identifying exile. He proposes the concept of inner exile in order to focus not only on those who left, but also on those who were bound to stay and had to build their own space for cultural communion. According to him: "Inner exile ... is an emptiness that awaits restoration, much the same way that territorial exile is the absence that compensates itself by nostalgia and hopeful anticipation."[29] It took approximately two decades for the Kyiv School to overcome its sense of inner exile and have its contributions acknowledged. On the other hand, the New York Group only made a symbolic, i.e. literary, return to Ukraine after about thirty-five years.

The exilic experience of both groups, unique as it was, left its mark. The aesthetic nonconformism and principled defense of freedom by these poets invariably isolated them from their respective audiences. Alienated writers are free to write as they please, but as a rule they have difficulty in defining their public. Each literary generation has only a limited time to flourish. If for some reason it cannot use this opportunity effectively, then its work may be marginalized.

The New York Group flourished from the mid-1950s to the early 1970s. This period witnessed a flurry of activities—intensive writing, publishing, editing, and translating—but these remained peripheral to and unappreciated by the center. When these poets "returned" to their native land, their achievements were necessarily historicized, no longer perceived as contemporaneous, and therefore had little impact in Ukraine. To some degree, the Kyiv School shared the fate of the New York poets. By the time Vorobiov, Kordun, Holoborodko, and many other "silenced" poets began publishing their work anew, they were competing with a younger and more aggressive literary generation. The time lag of some twenty years turned out to be extremely difficult to

---

29 Paul Ilie, *Literature and Inner Exile: Authoritarian Spain, 1939-1975* (Baltimore: John Hopkins University Press, 1980), 14.

overcome. While no longer exiled, the poets of both groups remained off-center in Ukrainian literature of the 1990s.

There can be no doubt that, geographically speaking, the position of the members of the New York Group has always remained peripheral in relation to Ukraine. After all, their physical displacement stayed intact. However, in aesthetic and historical terms, this peripherality is illusory. During the cultural stagnation of the Stalinist period, the status of Ukrainian émigré literature grew and the exiled community spearheaded the literary process for at least two decades, becoming in some respects the "center." But with the emergence of the *shistdesiatnyky* at the end of the 1950s, this changed dramatically. It is safe to say that since then the literary center coincided with the territorial. Nevertheless, without freedom of expression, the poets in Ukraine could not fully develop their potential; the most talented of them, namely the Kyiv School, were silenced. Therefore, the aesthetic center lost some of its authority. The poets of the New York Group, on the other hand, introduced many innovative features into Ukrainian letters; arguably, they crowned and exhausted the possibilities of Ukrainian modernism. It is therefore my contention that, although these poets were territorially peripheral, they were aesthetically central to the development of Ukrainian literature in the 1960s. However, because their innovations became widely known only some twenty years later, their centrality can only be appreciated historically.

CHAPTER 4

From Surrealism to Postmodernism: The Poetics of Liminality

The way I employ the concept of liminality in this study, it implies both a transitional state and a fixed position, that is, a zone in which liminars (whether individuals or groups) find themselves operating for a certain period of time or permanently. In the previous chapter, I used the term to delineate the New York Group's exilic position and to designate the spatial relationship between a center (Ukraine) and its periphery (émigré milieu); here I want to concentrate on a transitory aspect of liminality by discussing the ambiguities and shifts that occurred in the group's output with regard to the modernism-postmodernism continuum. I argue that the transition from the homogenous, purely modernist mode of the "vocal" period of the 1950s and 1960s to the individually diversified modes of the late 1980s and 1990s would not have been possible had literature not passed through the indeterminate, ambiguous, impure, liminal phase of the silent 1970s, a decade of soul-searching and reevaluation of the group and individual accomplishments.

There is a direct correlation between the changes in the poets' creative approaches and the evolution that the New York Group itself underwent. In other words, the shift in the group's internal structure, that is, a loosening of the cohesiveness of its boundaries, coincides with the shift in the members' aesthetic attitudes and practices. No longer is the modernist premise overbearing the poets' writings. Beginning with the 1970s, one can discern a qualitative transition from the decisively modernist/surrealist posture to the more ambiguous, indeterminate stance vis-à-vis the then-emerging postmodernist trends as well as the still-entrenched and active modernist practices. The poetry of some members of the group in that period reflects and/or incorporates quite a few elements that can be labeled postmodernist, but they are inextricably intertwined with modernist assumptions and come across more as the trimmings than as the main dish. This impure, hybridized modernist/postmodernist quality of the poetry coming from the New York Group belongs to the realm of the liminal. Hence, my use of this term necessarily entails hybridization, indeterminacy, impurity, and the disintegration of the hierarchical distinction between high and popular culture.

In order to elucidate the qualitative shifts that have occurred in the poets' oeuvre since the early seventies, I shall first examine the extensiveness of the surrealist vision in their work of the "vocal" period, then contrast the group's avant-garde posture with that of their American counterparts, namely the poets of the Beat Generation, and finally proceed to discuss the interplay between modernism and postmodernism as reflected in the texts themselves.

Surrealism, as approached and practiced by the members of the New York Group, does not manifest itself solely in the more or less faithful application of surrealist poetics. It is also embedded in the very attitudes toward art and life that the poets assume. First and foremost, the desire for complete freedom, for creative nonconformism, characteristic of all who evolved toward surrealism, remains invariably central to all the endeavors of the New York Group. Overcoming the barrier between reason and the instinctual depths, reflected in the apparent exploitation of eroticism, also figures quite prominently in the poets' output. Finally, the foregrounding of love as the source of unity and release as well as the emphasis on self-exploration and, perhaps, self-revelation, all point to the surrealist mode of perception and individuation. Of course, the degree of involvement in surrealism is not the same among the individual members of the group. Nonetheless, to a lesser or greater degree, each poet reveals at least some aspect of the spirit of surrealism. I contend that the surrealist project was particularly determinative and constitutive of the group's poetic formation, but this is a view that others have questioned.[1]

Bohdan Boychuk, for example, looking back at the group's achievements and giving his assessment of the poetry of each individual member, challenges the tagging of Emma Andijewska as a surrealist.[2] He believes that her "surrealism" is too idiosyncratic to warrant such a label and does not have much in common with its Western counterpart:

> ... можна вже говорити про своєрідний сюрреалізм, бо іншого окреслення не маю, але не в західньому сенсі. Це наскрізь індивідуальний «сюрреалізм» Андієвської, і типово східній чи, якщо хочете, український. Бо в кожній метафорі, в кожному, дослівно, рядку, читач натрапляє на якесь слово, чи образ, чи лише натяк ... , що виводиться десь з глибин українського минулого.[3]

> ... We can talk perhaps about idiosyncratic surrealism, because I don't have any other fitting term, but not in the Western sense. This is through and through Andijewska's individual "surrealism," one that is thoroughly Eastern, or, if you prefer, Ukrainian. For in every metaphor, in literally every line, the reader will stumble on a word, or an image, or an allusion ... that springs from the depths of the Ukrainian past.

Boychuk fails to concede, however, that the choice of lexicon alone cannot engender the surrealist character of a poem. Rather, surreality emerges from the unusual juxtapositions of words, images, and thoughts, all alluding to the "presentness" of reality (which becomes super-reality) and to the inherent instability of experience. Andijewska's poems abound in such juxtapositions,

---

1   See Anna Bila, *Ukrains'kyi literaturnyi avangard: poshuky, styl'ovi napriamky* (Kyiv: Smoloskyp, 2006), 357-82. Bila acknowledges Andijewska's surrealism and sees its influence on Tarnawsky's oeuvre, but denies the same for other members of the group.

2   See his article "Dekil'ka dumok pro N'iu-Iorks'ku hrupu i dekil'ka zadnikh dumok," *Suchasnist'* 1 (1979): 20-33. Boychuk writes there: "Критики (і некритики, як от автор цієї статті) часто намагалися обмежити Емму Андієвську наліпкою 'сюрреаліст', коли ж Емма сама *і ні з чиєї волі*" (23). ("The critics [and non-critics, as the author of this article] frequently strove to limit Emma Andijewska with the tag 'surrealist,' when the case is that Emma is all by herself *and of no one's will*.") No doubt Boychuk opposes here the view advanced especially by Volodymyr Derzhavyn, the critic who was overly harsh in his comments to the poet's first collection *Chas boliu*.

3   Ibid., 25.

and her imputed "Ukrainianness" is simply irrelevant here. She delights in the incongruous, in the unconventional, if not plain bizarre:

З пальців скапують звірі.[4]

Animals drip from the fingers.

Він роздмухує дзвін, як рукав.
На тілі у нього замість руки ріка
І кілька гаків, щоб тримати маркізи над
прилавками.[5]

He blows the bell like a sleeve.
His body has a river instead of a hand
And a few hooks to hold marquises over the
counter.

Гусячу шкірку неба
Шпаки зібрали у миску.[6]

Goose bumps of the sky
Starlings gathered into the bowl.

In fact, her vision, with its stress on the marvelous and the spontaneous, closely correlates to the surrealist principles advocated originally by André Breton. Andijewska's imagery strongly evinces the desire to transcend ordinary life and to undermine logical language. She has an extraordinary ability to impart abstract properties to the concrete or vice versa,[7] or even to provoke

---

4   Emma Andiievs'ka, *Poezii* (Ukraina: N. p., 1951), 24.
5   Emma Andiievs'ka, *Ryba i rozmir* (New York: V-vo N'iu-Iorks'koi hrupy, 1961), 29.
6   Emma Andiievs'ka, *Kuty opostin'* (New York: V-vo N'iu-Iorks'koi hrupy, 1962), 7.
7   This is the quality that Boychuk himself pointed out: "А ота несподівана асоціяція конкретних елементів з абстрактними (звуком, формою, кольором, смаком і ін.)— творить стрижень її образотворення" ("Dekil'ka dumok," 24). ("This unexpected association of concrete elements with the abstract [sound, form, colour, taste and so on]— lies at the core of her imagery.")

laughter.[8] These characteristics, together with contradiction, concealment, negation of physical properties, and hallucinatory aspects, according to Breton, lie at the heart of what constitutes the surrealist image.[9] For Breton, the surrealist image is precisely the surprising juxtaposition of images of disparate realities. Andijewska's surrealist poems draw from sharply different contexts:

> Дорога вогником знялася.
> Жене в повітрі кінь з меляси
> Через тераси і тарелі—
> Жовток всесвітній розпороли.[10]

> The road lifted like a flame.
> In the air the horse of molasses gallops
> Through terraces and plates—
> Cosmic yolk got ripped.

In the above stanza, the road and the horse generate the speed and force which strike at the very source of cosmic existence. On the other hand, the preceding two stanzas also allow the interpretation in which we simply deal with the defamiliarized description of a sunrise (here "yolk" could well stand for the sun).

Andijewska's "de-realizing" aesthetics undoubtedly stems from a belief in the creative powers of the unconscious. Her startling juxtapositions merely attempt to unleash the potential of primitive or elemental impulses. Ultimately, it is all about bringing forth a new consciousness, a consciousness in which, according to Breton, "life and death, the real and the imagined, past and future, the communicable and the incommunicable, high and low cease to be perceived as contradictions."[11]

If one were to create a surrealist continuum for the poets of the New York Group, no doubt Andijewska would have taken up the most "surrealist"

---

8   For example, these lines from Andijewska's poem "Radist'" (Joy) cannot but provoke a smile: "В картоплі ангели цибаті/ Хропуть, на сонце звівши зад" ("In the potato field long-legged angels/ Snore, turning up their bums to the sun"). (See her *Narodzhennia idola*, 8).

9   André Breton, *Manifestoes of Surrealism*, trans. Richard Seaver and Helen R. Lane (Ann Arbor, MI: University of Michigan Press, 1969), 38.

10 Emma Andiievs'ka, *Pervni* (Munich: Suchasnist', 1964), 25.

11 Breton, *Manifestoes of Surrealism*, 123.

position, and Vira Vovk and Bohdan Rubchak would have stood on the opposite end. Vira Vovk's somewhat distant link with surrealism could be partly explained by her strong Christian conviction. Her religious bent clearly clashes with the surrealists' preferred way of life, but it does not prevent her from coming up with an array of surprising images that frequently juxtapose incompatible elements in a way that unmistakably echoes the surrealist approach:

Дерево сипле червоно-чорну квасолю
На довгі низанки дітям.[12]

A tree scatters red-black beans
For children's long strings.

А місяць, як годинник
Без цифер, б'є вічність.
Я чую ... чи то хвиля
Молотить ребра?[13]

And the moon, like a clock
Without hours, strikes eternity.
I hear ... is it a wave
That grinds ribs?

Скрипки кружляють у крові,[14]

Violins circulate in the blood,

Палить сонце з сокир,
Хмара в кущах шелестить.[15]

The sun of axes burns,
A cloud rustles in the bushes.

12 Vira Vovk, *Chorni akatsii* (Munich: Na hori, 1961), 11.
13 Ibid., 35.
14 Ibid., 55.
15 Vira Vovk, *Kappa Khresta* (Munich: Suchasnist', 1969), 10.

Of course, these images are not as startling or as cryptic as Andijewska's, but they also discard logic in the mating of words and point to an unexpected chance encounter of two different realities, bridged only with the help of imagination.

Bohdan Rubchak's connection with surrealism is also weak, but mostly because of the immensely structured and intellectual character of his poetry. His is a vision that leaves very little room for spontaneity and dreamlike associations. Even his haiku (which by nature are supposed to remain beyond the intellect's comprehension and involve only a moment of pure perception) suffer from intellectualization and reflected apprehension of reality:

(Місяць)

Сумна ніч носить
медалик коханого,
    що вчора згинув.[16]

A sad night carries
beloved's holy medal
    who died yesterday.

Зелені мислі
морозом слів убиті:
старість поета[17]

Green thoughts
killed by the ice of words:
poet's old age.

Neither of these miniatures exudes the immediacy of a now-moment, nor are they free of discriminative or reflected thought. Rubchak seems unable to let go of conscious control in constructing his poems, and this is what makes his participation in the surrealist project even more dubious than that

---

16 Bohdan Rubchak, *Kaminnyi sad* (New York: Slovo, 1956), 11.
17 Bohdan Rubchak, *Osobysta Klio* (New York: V-vo N'iu-Iorks'koi hrupy, 1967), 40.

of Vira Vovk. But like Vovk, he also comes up with a number of surrealist images, foregrounding especially contradiction and concealment:

> Вздовж асфальту бульварів
> Між темно-синім листям
> Дозріли цитрини-зорі.[18]

> Along the asphalt boulevards
> Among the dark-blue leaves
> The lemon-stars ripened.

> З піску виростають колючі руки,
> уста, мов ножі, кущі шорсткого волосся—
> тіло з піску м'якогрудої жертви шукає,
> що дощ в зіницях несе, що має зелені руки.[19]

> From beneath the sand thorny hands grow,
> and lips like knives, and bushes of harsh hair—
> the body out of the sand looks for a soft-breasted victim,
> whom rain carries in its eyes, the one that has green hands.

> Дівчина жагуче
> пульсує споминому
> з червоних печер праночі.[20]

> Girl passionately
> pulsates with the memory
> of red caves of primeval night.

The remaining four members of the group, each in his/her own more or less pronounced way, displayed affinity with at least some aspect of the surrealist movement. Amongst these, Bohdan Boychuk's surrealist proclivities

---

18 Rubchak, *Kaminnyi sad*, 14.
19 Bohdan Rubchak, *Promenysta zrada* (New York: V-vo N'iu-Iorks'koi hrupy, 1960), 9.
20 Rubchak, *Osobysta Klio*, 36.

are arguably most tangential. In this respect, he is closer to Vira Vovk and Bohdan Rubchak than to Emma Andijewska. What links his poetic vision with surrealism is, in my view, the glorification of love and the privileged position reserved for women. Like the surrealists, Boychuk sees woman as mediator between the alienated man and the world. Through love man may hope for redemption; through woman he may dream of regeneration:

> Мої стежки просохли спрагою в устах,
> мої шляхи шукають чаші ніжности твоєї, жінко,
> моє життя:
> вертається до піль твоїх рамен,
> де білі джерела
> хвилюють кров: любов'ю, ласкою, барвінком.[21]

> My paths dried up thirst in my mouth,
> my roads seek the goblet of your grace, oh woman,
> my life:
> goes back to the fields of your arms
> where white springs
> arouse blood with love, charity, periwinkle.

His poetic language is by and large free of the illogical juxtapositions revered by the surrealists; moreover, his metaphors are built on analogy rather than contradiction and disjunction. Hence, Boychuk's affinity with surrealism is first and foremost thematic and philosophical. It is not based on the utilization of surrealist poetics, but on the insistence on freedom from limitations and boundaries of any kind (embracing transgressions), including the freedom to convey poetically sexual and sensual experiences.

Zhenia Vasylkivska's poetry lends itself easily to interpretation from the surrealist perspective. She stands quite close to Andijewska in her foregrounding of the word's enchanting potential and in elevating the irrational. Her images, although less incongruous than those of Andijewska, startle nonetheless and implicate the whole nexus of the poetic persona's unconscious

---

21 Bohdan Boichuk, *Spomyny liubovy* (New York: V-vo N'iu-Iorks'koi hrupy, 1963), 65.

desires and impulses, which reify themselves in contrary oxymoronic juxtapositions, taken straight from the impersonal world of nature:

> На порожнечі
> дня безтурботного
> виріж глибоку
> борозну вітру.[22]

In the emptiness
of the careless day
carve a deep
furrow of wind.

> І погасли
> руки вітру—
> і світанок
> хлібом світить.[23]

And the wind's hands
dimmed out—
and the dawn
shines with bread.

> Місяць—як ребро молока,
> місяць, як біла лисиця,
> чорним крилом над веслом
> хлипає зранена хвиля.[24]

The moon—like milk's rib,
the moon like a white fox,
with a black wing over the oar
an injured wave sobs.

---

22 Zhenia Vasyl'kivs'ka, *Korotki viddali* (New York: Slovo, 1959), 9.
23 Ibid., 45.
24 Ibid., 14.

Vasylkivska's reticent lyricism carries unmistakable erotic overtones. In the last stanza, for example, the image of the crescent moon as milk's rib possibly subsumes phallic connotations which might have been entirely contingent or unconscious for the poet herself at the moment of the creative act. The unconscious workings of the inner self no doubt affect Vasylkivska's imagery. By giving in to illogical impulses the poet brings her own desires, of which she may well be unaware, into the world she poetically perceives. Surrealist poems—in the words of Charles Russell—"may bring together states of mind, absurd landscapes, physical sensations, and illogical arguments."[25] Vasylkivska displays a penchant for the aesthetics of free association, and precisely that places her close to the surrealist camp.

It is a well-known fact that the surrealists turned to dreams for inspiration. Dreaming secured for them incongruity and a notable release from logical restraint. Breton, for example, expressed his amazement that so little credence had been given to dream states:

> Freud very rightly brought his critical faculties to bear upon the dream. It is, in fact, inadmissible that this considerable portion of psychic activity ... has still today been so grossly neglected. I have always been amazed at the way an ordinary observer lends so much more credence and attaches so much more importance to waking events than those occurring in dreams.[26]

Patricia Kylyna and Yuriy Tarnawsky are the only two poets of the New York Group who utilized dreamlike associations in their creative processes. They did not aspire to escape reality through dreams but, rather, they used them as a tool in furthering self-exploration and self-knowledge.

Patricia Kylyna's second book, *Legendy i sny* (Legends and Dreams, 1964), consists of a number of surrealist poems that foreground the relationship between the dream and the waking state. Her long poem "Legenda abo son" (Legend or Dream) attests to how masterfully she blends the real with the unexpected and the imaginary:

---

25   Charles Russell, *Poets, Prophets, and Revolutionaries*, 137.
26   Breton, *Manifestoes of Surrealism*, 10-11.

«Тату,» вона сказала, «ти поранений.»
«Я знаю.»
«Тату, в твоїй рані сидить пташка.»
«Я знаю. Тримайся міцно.»
«Я можу сама стояти,» вона сказала
й стала на ноги.[27]

"Daddy," she said, "you are injured."
"I know."
"Daddy, in your wound there is a little bird."
"I know. Hold yourself tight."
"I can stand on my own," she said
and got up.

Kylyna's insistence on the simple and the concrete only enhances the surprising effect of the fantastic, interlaced imperceptibly into the fabric of the poem. On the one hand, "Legenda abo son" describes the homebound journey of an injured father and his daughter in a manner bordering on realism; on the other hand, because of occasional surreal images, the whole poem reads (quite in line with the title itself) like a retelling of a dream. Surreality emerges here in the interstices of the realistic scenery and the oneiric happenings. By mixing different contexts, Kylyna creates thereof a new reality, which is far removed from ordinary life.

Yuriy Tarnawsky's surrealist turn is arguably as pronounced as Andijewska's, although he approaches the movement from an entirely different angle. While both poets believe in the power of language to engender new modes of perception, Tarnawsky, unlike Andijewska, abhors unnecessary intricacy and complications, preferring in every case the simple to the elaborate. Andijewska's inspired, spontaneous exuberance finds a countermeasure in Tarnawsky's austere word efficiency and induced dreamlike streams of associations, especially in his prose poems *Spomyny* (Memories, 1964) and *Bez Espanii* (Without Spain, 1969). This does not mean that his poetry lacks occasional hermetic

---

27 Patrytsiia Kylyna, *Legendy i sny* (New York: V-vo N'iu-Iorks'koi hrupy, 1964), 23.

proclivity, but his hermeticism stems more from ascetic reductiveness than from excessive wordplay.

In *Spomyny*, Tarnawsky introduces alienating disjointed images in order to deal with the remembrances of his mother's illness and death. He uses the contradictory logic of the dream to structure the sequence of events, so that the incongruity itself provides the organization of the disparate parts:

Ріка, нараз стаючи вулицею. На ній пес із собором, замість пащі, із болем твого тіла, як клаптем матерії, в зубах.[28]

The river's becoming the street suddenly. There's the dog with a cathedral instead of mouth, with the pain of your body, as if with the piece of fabric in the jaws.

В будинку, на столі, сяйво хліба, виповненого світлом, видобутим з масла і яєць. Мертва жінка одягнена у жовту шкіру, душа якої перейшла в муху.[29]

In the building, on the table, the radiance of bread, filled with light, extracted from butter and eggs. A dead woman, dressed in yellow skin, whose soul turned to a fly.

Рожеве, спінене вино, як закривавлене мереживо, визирає із твоїх уст. Веселка з помаранчів, що починається в північній Африці, зникає у твоїм роті.[30]

Pink, foamy wine, like a bloody lace, peers out from your lips. The rainbow of oranges that begins in North Africa, disappears in your mouth.

Відчиняється хвіртка. Замість звуку, вона видає місячне світло. Входить у сад твоя баба у чорному одязі, просторому, як ніч. Лягає на ліжко, що, наче тінь, висить у повітрі над яблунею.[31]

The gate opens. Instead of sound, it releases the moon's light. Your grandmother, in black attire spacious as night, enters the orchard. She lies down on the bed, which, like a shadow, hangs in the air over the apple tree.

---

28 Iurii Tarnavs'kyi, *Spomyny* (Munich: Suchasnist', 1964), 11.

29 Ibid., 17.

30 Ibid., 22.

31 Ibid., 32.

It is not the lighthearted "marvelous" that transpires through these excerpts. Rather, it is the dreamlike and the hallucinatory that seem to govern Tarnawsky's poetics. The elaborateness of language and imagery give way to the modern simplicity of ordinary objects. Yet the way the poet externalizes his interior reality has much in common with the surrealist self-exploratory process, the goal of which is to uncover the hidden self's emotional life. This subjective turn, evident especially in Tarnawsky's prose poems, corresponds to the surrealists' attempt to "reunite the conscious self not only with the unconscious self, but with its/their past."[32]

In their glorification of the incongruous, the surrealists often advocated "automatic" writing. This feature has not been utilized in the output of the New York Group. Even the French surrealists were not entirely consistent in this sphere.[33] The Ukrainian poets also did not share the political activism of the surrealists, especially their leftist and communist inclinations. The New York Group identified itself more with surrealism's passive phase of the 1920s than with the politically activist phase of the 1930s. However, the group's gravitation toward assembling could well have its roots in the tradition of the European avant-garde. Arguably, without the initial group interaction, the poets' paths could conceivably have developed differently.

There can be no doubt that the European connection proved to be strong and quite pervasive among the poets of New York Group, even though almost all of them found themselves in an American setting. Lisa Efimov-Schneider, writing comparatively about the poetry of the New York Group, contends that there are "significant parallels between the New York Group and their

---

32 Russell, *Poets, Prophets, and Revolutionaries*, 143.

33 This is how Ihab Hassan summarizes the surrealists' attitude toward automatic writing: "The Surrealist theory of language, of creativity, accords, then with its poetic mysticism. Its applications, however, are equivocal. Aragon, for instance, confesses that Surrealism entails *practiced* inspiration; Eluard gives himself to automatic writing very little. Even Breton ends by admitting that pure automatism is never more than an ideal or hyperbole. Though the Surrealists want to believe that poetry lives in images of direct revelation, neither their verse nor their prose depends entirely on images. They still argue and still exhort. Their immense hope is to create, through objective chance, sleep, automatism, a new kind of language, a new consciousness, something larger than art or literature." See his *The Dismemberment of Orpheus: Toward a Postmodern Literature*, 2nd ed. (Madison: University of Wisconsin, 1982), 76-77.

American contemporaries."[34] She refers here to the American movement of the Beat Generation. Efimov-Schneider sees these parallels not only in the subversive attitudes both groups assumed toward their respective literary traditions, but also in the sphere of thematic and formal innovations. In the end she comes to the following conclusion:

> Both the American underground and the Ukrainian New York group in the 1950s try to deal with change, with their own cultural displacement, and with their desire to prevent the petrification of poetry. The similarities between the two groups suggest that the readiness of the Ukrainian poets for new ideas and methods might not have developed in quite the way it did, had they not found themselves in a cultural milieu that was undergoing similar upheavals.[35]

While it is true that a rebellious spirit and a desire for change was deeply ingrained in both the Ukrainian poets and their American counterparts, Efimov-Schneider fails to perceive the fundamental differences between them. The similarities she refers to are, in fact, somewhat perfunctory. First of all, unlike the Beats, the New York Group embraced the achievements of high modernism, including the poetry of T.S. Eliot and Ezra Pound. The Beat Generation was considerably more radical in its rejection of the social, political, religious, and artistic values of its time. The Beats abhorred the cerebralism of existentialism and instead pursued the extremes of experience: the use of drugs, sexual experimentation, criminality, and mysticism. This mode of life then found its reflection in their writings, which elevated the themes of obscenity, (homo)sexuality, delinquency, and madness. By contrast, all the members of the New York Group from the very beginning considered themselves law-abiding citizens who valued comfortable (if not bourgeois) existences. The Ukrainian poets did not share the Beats' love for jazz or Zen Buddhism; they did not place as much emphasis on spiritual development and sacred vision as their American counterparts did. The conception of a literary career and status (even if eroded by the condition of exile) was still quite important to them.

---

34 Lisa Efimov-Schneider, "Poetry of the New York Group: Ukrainian Poets in an American Setting," *Canadian Slavonic Papers* 23 (1981): 291.

35 Ibid., 301.

Also questionable is Efimov-Schneider's assertion that "the situation of the American poets is similar to that of the New York Group. The image of Walt Whitman is as central to their struggle as the figure of Shevchenko is for the Ukrainians."[36] It is a misstatement (to say the least) to suggest that Shevchenko constituted for the poets of the New York Group an influence with which they had to struggle. It would be more accurate to say that the Ukrainian futurists as well as other poets of the 1920s avant-garde struggled to overcome Shevchenko's domination. Finally, Lisa Efimov-Schneider misses the mark by not appreciating the differences in the sphere of general attitudes of the respective groups. Against the prevailing pessimism of the early poetry of the Ukrainian group (spurred no doubt by the tenets of existentialism), the Beats presented a literature full of optimism and offered an artistic vision exuding energy, activism, and movement, both outward and inward. Such an approach to life and art, together with their anti-formalist and anti-elitist stance, places them, according to some critics, closer to the poetics of postmodernism. Matei Calinescu, for example, is of the opinion that it is possible to speak of American postmodernism as early as the late 1940s:

> ... the term *postmodernism* first came into literary use in the United States, where a number of poets of the later 1940s used it to distance themselves from the symbolist kind of modernism represented by T.S. Eliot. Like the early postmoderns, most of those who subsequently joined the antimodernist reaction were aesthetic radicals and often intellectually close to the spirit of the counterculture. The works of these writers constitute the historical nucleus of literary postmodernism. In poetry, the corpus of American postmodernist writing would include the Black Mountain poets (Charles Olson, Robert Duncan, Robert Creely), the Beats (Allen Ginsberg, Jack Kerouac, Laurence Ferlinghetti, Gregory Corso), and the representatives of the San Francisco Renaissance (Gary Snyder) or those of the New York School (John Ashbery, Kenneth Koch).[37]

The debates on modernism and postmodernism and their interrelation seem themselves to betray many liminal qualities. There is no firm agreement on whether postmodernism constitutes the "exhaustive" or endgame phase of modernism or entails an entirely new aesthetic formation. Thus,

---

36 Ibid., 296.
37 Matei Calinescu, *Five Faces of Modernity: Modernism, Avant-Garde, Decadence, Kitsch, Postmodernism* (Durham, NC: Duke University Press, 1987), 297.

postmodernism can be apprehended as differing from modernism either because it extends modernist principles further than modernists themselves did or because it rejects them. Gerald Graff, for example, sees postmodernism as essentially a continuation of modernism, rather than as a sharp break from it. According to him, it is simply a more rigorous and consistent acceptance of the implications of modern skepticism. If modernists turned to art as a source of consolation in the face of a reality perceived as disordered and lacking enduring values, postmodernists, more consistent in their skepticism, "conclude that art provides no more consolation than any other discredited cultural institution."[38]

Ihab Hassan, on the other hand, while admitting the fluidity and instability of the terms, nevertheless charts a number of bipolar characteristics for modernism and postmodernism alike, seeing the former as foregrounding form, purpose, design, metaphor, depth, metaphysics, determinacy, and transcendence, and the latter underscoring antiform, play, chance, metonymy, surface, irony, indeterminacy, and immanence.[39] Fredric Jameson, conceptualizing the modernism/postmodernism dichotomy and coming from an entirely different ideological angle (Marxism to be precise), appears even more radical:

> The first point to be made about the conception of periodization in dominance, therefore, is that even if all the constitutive features of postmodernism were identical and continuous with those of an older modernism—a position I feel to be demonstrably erroneous but which only an even lengthier analysis of modernism proper could dispel—the two phenomena would still remain utterly distinct in their meaning and social function, owing to the very different positioning of postmodernism in the economic system of late capital, and beyond that, to the transformation of the very sphere of culture in contemporary society.[40]

In other words, Jameson views postmodernism not merely as a period or style, but rather as a cultural dominant in which aesthetic production has been integrated into commodity production. This conception, according to

---

38 Gerald Graff, *Literature against Itself: Literary Ideas in Modern Society* (Chicago: University of Chicago Press, 1979), 55.

39 See his *The Dismemberment of Orpheus*, 267-68.

40 Fredric Jameson, "Postmodernism, or The Cultural Logic of the Late Capitalism," *New Left Review* 146 (1984): 57.

him, "allows for the presence and coexistence of a range of very different, yet subordinate features."[41]

While the break with modernism was unmistakably visible in architecture and the visual arts, the notion of a postmodern rupture in literature has been much more difficult to establish. John Barth, an American writer tagged as a postmodernist, in a 1967 essay referred to the contemporary literary production as "the literature of exhaustion," implying the situation in which "the used-upness of certain forms or exhaustion of certain possibilities"[42] prevails. Some dozen years later, in the essay "The Literature of Replenishment," he clarified his position by saying that his earlier article was really about "the effective 'exhaustion' not of language or of literature but of the aesthetic of high modernism,"[43] that is, the latter's insistence on the autonomy of the art work, its hostility to mass culture (or to the culture of everyday life), and its detachment from political and social concerns.

Some critics, Andreas Huyssen being the most prominent among them, contemplate the existence of a variety of postmodernisms, differentiating the trends predominant in the 1960s from those of the 1970s. Huyssen sums this up as follows:

> Against the codified high modernism of the preceding decades, the post-modernism of the 1960s tried to revitalize the heritage of the European avantgarde [sic] and to give it an American form along what one could call in short-hand the Duchamp-Cage-Warhol axis. By the 1970s, the avantgardist postmodernism of the 1960s had in turn exhausted its potential, even though some of its manifestations continued well into the new decade. What was new in the 1970s was, on the one hand, the emergence of a culture of eclecticism, a largely affirmative postmodernism which had abandoned any claim to critique, transgression or negation; and, on the other hand, an alternative postmodernism in which resistance, critique, and negation of the status quo were redefined in non-modernist and non-avantgardist terms... [44]

He admits, however, that his periodization is somewhat problematic and dependent on the perspective from which one views the phenomena in

---

41   Ibid., 56.
42   John Barth, "The Literature of Exhaustion," *The Atlantic* 220.2 (1969): 29.
43   John Barth, "The Literature of Replenishment: Postmodernist Fiction," *The Atlantic* 245.1 (1980): 71.
44   Andreas Huyssen, *After the Great Divide: Modernism, Mass Culture, Postmodernism* (Bloomington: Indian University Press, 1986), 188.

question. He also concedes that from a European perspective, the 1960s in the U.S. "looked like the endgame of the historical avantgarde rather than like the breakthrough to new frontiers it claimed to be."[45] Later Huyssen revises his stance by saying that the 1960s could well be considered "the prehistory of the postmodern," but only in order to reemphasize the view that "the notion of postmodernism can only be fully grasped if one takes the late 1950s as the starting point of a mapping of the postmodern."[46]

Huyssen's insights into the workings of cultural and artistic trends in the U.S. of the 1960s are particularly useful in understanding the New York Group's link with the European (historical) avant-garde on the one hand, and with the contemporaneous American neo-avant-garde on the other. Undoubtedly from the very beginning the group felt more aligned with the European artistic movements (after all, all but one of them were born in Europe) than with the emerging underground culture of America. It can be argued that the cultural trends of the 1960s in the U.S. continued the premises of the historical avant-garde by expanding its boundaries, engendering new movements, and giving them a uniquely American flavor. Pop art and the Beat Generation, two inherently American movements, often displayed a tendency to disregard high art by incorporating elements of mass culture. The young Ukrainian émigré poets, on the other hand, looked back at the European avant-garde in order to pick up and extend those trends that were already established and which were especially close to their hearts. They found surrealism's turn to interiority, to the irrational and creative powers of the subconscious mind, quite irresistible and unusually attractive. They incorporated many of the developments of the French surrealists into their writings; at the same time, they succeeded in imbuing them with their own unique visions, creating thus a specifically Ukrainian version of the movement.

The liminal character of the New York Group's output is especially noticeable following the closure of *Novi poezii* in 1971. The dissolution of the group opened the door to individual soul-searching among the poets. It is as if they suddenly became over-saturated with the responsibilities of maintaining the group and wanted to free themselves from the bonds of such structured existence. This attitude resulted in diminished publishing activities and less

---

45 Ibid., 195.
46 Ibid.

frequent personal interaction. In the sphere of poetry, there was a lot of hesitancy as to which way to go, which trend to pursue. They must have been somewhat influenced by the changing tide in American letters, because their oeuvre reflects a curious admixture of modernist and postmodernist attributes. The liminality thus displayed pointed to stylistic impurity and hybridization— that is, the coexistence of modernist and postmodernist features side by side without the subversive potential of the latter.

Patricia Kylyna's entrance into the liminal happened through her adoption of the minimal approach to poetry as early as 1968. Minimalism can be seen as a reaction against modernist aesthetics mainly because it rejected the tendency toward complexity and elitism. It promoted simplicity of form and a deliberate lack of expressive content. Minimal poetry did not shy away from repetition, impersonality, and cliché. The following is Kylyna's minimal poem no. 2, printed in *Novi poezii* no. 10:

> Око, моє око, твоє око.
> Його око дивиться на голу жінку,
> або на Бога, або на іржаве залізо.
> Наші очі, без яких ми сліпі, є,
>   мов окуляри, або телескоп.
> Ваші очі без вас, що котяться по світу,
>   бачачи цілі фільми тротуарів.
> Їхні мертві очі, що далі стогнуть у трунах.
> Та очі загублені між плянетами:
>   кожне з них знає свою орбіту і своє сонце.[47]

Eye, my eye, your eye.
His eye looks at a naked woman,
or at God, or at rusty iron.
Our eyes, without which we're blind, are
        like glasses or a telescope.
Your eyes without you, they roll all over the world
        seeing whole movies of side-walks.

---

47 Patrytsiia Kylyna, "Z minimal'nykh poezii," *Novi poezii* 10 (1968): 74.

Their dead eyes which still moan in coffins.
And eyes lost in-between planets:
each of them knows its orbit and its sun.

The juxtaposition of a "naked woman" with "God" is a prime example of Kyly-na's attempt to demolish the modernist boundary between "high" and "low" subject matter. Yet the last line "each of them knows its orbit and its sun" still points to the modernist need for center and point of reference. Thus, such vicis-situdes ensnare the poem in the liminal space. On the one hand, the poet displays an urge to destroy the high/low dichotomy; on the other hand, she still clings to universalist notions.

The turn to simplicity, although not necessarily of the minimalist kind, touched the poetry of the other poets as well. Emma Andijewska's *Nauka pro zemliu* (A Lesson about the Earth, 1975) includes a considerable number of miniatures, which, as in Kylyna's case, delight in mixing highbrow subjects with the most ordinary, everyday objects:

Вічність—дерево з котячим стовбуром.
Чашка чаю, горнятко цикути.
Усі в дорозі—п'ятою, копитом, крильми.
В тіні від розп'яття грають у кості.
І знову червоним малюють брами
Для новоприбульців.[48]

Eternity—a tree with a cat's trunk.
A cup of tea, a mug of cowbane.
All travelling—on heel, on hoof, on wings.
They play with dice in the crucifixion's shadow.
And again they paint in red the gates
For newcomers.

Andijewska relativizes and removes an aura of mystery from such notions as eternity or crucifixion by juxtaposing them with a cup of tea or a mug of

---

48   Emma Andiievs'ka, *Nauka pro zemliu* (Munich: Suchasnist', 1975), 74.

cowbane, or with the gamble of dice. The surrealist images, however, strip Andijewska's poetry of transparency. Even though *Nauka pro zemliu* and the preceding collection *Pisni bez tekstu* (Songs Without a Text, 1968) are less opaque than her other poetic books, they still betray elitist tendencies. Andijewska's postmodern dabbling remains ambiguous and liminal.

Two other poets who experimented with minimalist simplicity to some degree are Yuriy Tarnawsky and Vira Vovk. Tarnawsky's *Os', iak ia vyduzhuiu* (This Is How I Get Well, 1978) introduces poems that read like prose statements chopped into extremely short lines, sometimes no longer than a word:

Тайна

Коли
вони
зрозуміють
що ціле
життя
я тільки й те
робив,
що шукав
тебе,
мамо,
жінко,
дочко?[49]

Secret

When
will they
realize
that all
I ever
did

---

49   Iurii Tarnavs'kyi, *Os' iak ia vyduzhuiu* (Munich: Suchasnist', 1978), 55.

was look
for you,
mother,
wife,
daughter?[50]

However, the extreme formal simplicity of the poems included in this collection is not backed up by the emotional detachment typical of minimalism. *Os', iak ia vyduzhuiu* is quite expressive and lyrical in conveying the feelings of the poet's alter ego:

Дощ

Дощ,
як тихий
голос,
будить
рослини,
коли
він збудить
моє щастя?[51]

Rain

The rain,
like a soft
voice,
wakes up
the plants,
when
will it
wake up
my happiness?

---

50 This poem as well as the next one were translated by the author himself.
51 Ibid., 79.

The clichéd banality of the question posed in this poem undermines the seriousness with which one would expect the reader might have approached it. One could argue that such a subversive (if indeed so) move entails something inherently typical to postmodernism. Again, here we have a case where modernist and postmodernist attributes clash with each other and form an entity with uncertain belonging.

Vira Vovk's *Meandry* (Meanders, 1979) and *Mandalia* (Mandala, 1980), two collections that are composed exclusively of miniature poems, visibly attempt to introduce postmodern chance, playfulness, and inconsequence. Both collections, for example, lack pagination, as if deliberately inviting the reader to come up with his/her own sequence. In *Meandry*, the fragmentary, disjointed, almost enumerative manner of poetic expression allows a considerable interpretative freedom. One is somehow prompted to re-sequence or play with lines or stanzas within a single poem, as if looking for nuances of comprehension:

> вібрації світла
> тераси сходи голуби
>
> Дафна офірує
> коси на вівтарі
>
> ніщо не мре
> і дещо з голубизни
> твоїх очей
> лявандою
> в щілинах мурів[52]

> vibrations of light
> terraces steps pigeons
>
> Daphne
> offers plaits of hair on the altar

---

52 Vira Vovk, *Meandry* (Rio de Janeiro: Artes Gráficas, 1979).

nothing dies
and something from the dove-blue
of your eyes
lavender
in the cracks of walls.[53]

The poem, in a fragmentary fashion, evokes the memories of unrequited love, linked to some kind of self-sacrifice, and ultimately to acceptance, because "nothing dies" and the remembrance of "the dove-blue of your eyes" will live on.[54]

Vovk's other collection, *Mandalia*, is considerably less emotive, and stylistically more minimal. It is a cycle of concise, detached, impersonal observations, describing various aspects of ordinary life from a deeply spiritual perspective, not without the influence of Eastern philosophies. In the poem "Molytvy" (Prayers), for instance, the poet contemplates the various manifestations of spirituality:

Буддистський монах
меле молитви на млинці,
чернець нанизує їх на чотки,
сіяч їх сипле в землю.

Різниця вся—в обряді.[55]

---

53 Translated by Maria Lukianowicz.

54 Bohdan Rubchak interprets the lines "Daphne offers/ plaits of hair on the altar" in the following way: "У своєму відчитуванні цього місця, я подумав про схрещення старогрецького жертвоприношення й українського весілля: синхронічне поєднання цих двох ритуалів насвітлило б ролю Аполлона в відповідному міті з досить несподіваної точки. Сама поетка, одначе, зауважила в прилюдній розмові, що вона в цьому образі хотіла натякнути на пострижения дівчини в черниці. В світлі такої автоінтерпретації, одержуємо ще цікавішу багатогранність—схрещення постаті української дівчини, старогрецького міту з обертонами насильної еротики та церковного обряду самозречення ..." See his "Meandramy Viry Vovk," *Suchasnist'* 1 (1980): 41. ("In my own reading of these lines, I thought of crossing between the Old Greek offering and the Ukrainian wedding: a synchronic combination of these two rituals would elucidate Apollo's role in the respective myth from an unexpected angle. The poet herself, however, made a remark in an open conversation that she wanted to allude in this image to the ritual linked with ordaining the nuns. In the light of such self-interpretation, we receive even more intriguing multifariousness—a crossing between the figure of the Ukrainian girl and the Old Greek mythology and the church ritual of renunciation....").

55 Vira Vovk, *Mandalia* (Rio de Janeiro: Artes Gráficas, 1980).

The Buddist [sic] monk
grinds his prayers in the mill,
the Christian threads them on a rosary,
the ploughman sows them on the soil.

The difference is in the ritual.[56]

The simplicity rests not only in form but also in diction and tone. The metaphor is rare, and the prosaic mode dominates the manner of expression.

Bohdan Boychuk published just one collection in the 1970s, *Podorozh z uchytelem* (Journey with a Teacher, 1976), but this long modernist poem was originally conceived and written in the 1960s, and does not reflect the qualitative shift that occurred in his late oeuvre. There is no evidence that Boychuk entertained minimalism with the same conviction as, for example, Kylyna. But what can be found in his poems of the 1970s and the early 1980s, collected in *Virshi, vybrani i peredostanni* (Poems, Selected and Next to the Last, 1983), is a turn toward the simplification of poetic language. His mature poetry admits mixing of genres and prosaic motifs, and expands on themes of love and sensuality. This tendency is especially conspicuous in Boychuk's poem "Liubov u tr'okh chasakh" (Three-Dimensional Love, 1974-76). It can be argued that the juxtapositions of the lyrical song-like beginning stanzas with the rough vers libre sections of this long poem resemble and invoke the liminal collapse between high and mass culture:

Одинадцять
1.
Напне на грудях перкаль ночі,
обпарить губи кропом сосок;
знепритомнівши, неспокоєм
закропиш очі.

---

56 Translated by Aïla de Oliveira Gomes.

Зануриш голову у білу
гущавину грудей кипучих,
бажаючи ще раз вернутись
в жіноче тіло.

2.
роздерши на грудях перкаль
вона переходить times square
і віддається кожному
хто прагне кохання
за гроші

і ти
самотній
також злягаєшся з нею
бо не маєш нікого
ближчого[57]

Eleven
1.
She'll shed the night's percale,
burn your lips with her breasts,
infect your moistened eyes
with unrest,

you'll dip your anxious brow
in the white foam of her flesh,
turning to return
into her.

2.
tearing apart her cotton dress
she crosses Times Square
and gives herself to everyone
who hungers for flesh
and pays

---

57 Bohdan Boichuk, *Virshi, vybrani i peredostanni* (New York: Suchasnist', 1983), 160.

you
also make love to her
having no one
closer.[58]

Boychuk leaves behind complex baroque metaphors and replaces them with language that foregrounds an emotional immediacy, focuses on the personal, and prefers an individual experience and directness of communication.[59] There is a marked departure from formal to more flexible verse forms, resulting in verbal clarity and simplicity of idiom. To label the above change as postmodern would be far-fetched, but it does signal a slight move to the surface and away from overly metaphoric language. His poetry escapes liminal impurity, although brushes with it slightly. A remarkable philosophical continuity and consistency in his worldview grounds his late work firmly in the modernist camp.[60]

In addition to the simplicity and "prosaic" turn of the 1970s, one can discern another tendency in the group's output of that period: the universal concerns and transnational attitudes gradually give way to the local and the national. While it was unthinkable to be politically *engagé* in the 1950s, in the eighties it almost became fashionable. For instance, Vira Vovk and Yuriy Tarnawsky turned to explicitly national and political themes.[61] Tarnawsky's cycle "Dorosli virshi" (Adult Poems) and *U ra na* (1993) are especially emblematic in this regard.[62]

U ra na, a ten-part poem having as its subject the well-being of Ukraine and her past, present, and future, incorporates many features of postmodern technique: numerous allusions (literary, historical, political, cultural) shuffled and reshuffled, direct quotations, and play with clichés and various

---

58 Bohdan Boychuk, *Memories of Love: The Selected Poems of Bohdan Boychuk* (Riverdale-on-Hudson, NY: The Sheep Meadow Press, 1989), 36. Translated by Mark Rudman.

59 In the 1970s, Boychuk began a fruitful cooperation with young American poets in order to translate works by Ivan Drach and other contemporary Ukrainian poets. It is quite conceivable that this project had a considerable impact on Boychuk's own poetic style.

60 His two volumes of collected poems published in Kyiv in 2007 only attest to this remarkable continuity. See his *Zibrani tvory*, 2 vols. (Kyiv: Fakt, 2007).

61 This tendency is less true for Vovk's poetic output, but is very strong in her dramatic works.

62 At a private reading of *U ra na* in 1991, Tarnawsky commented that this particular work of his is written not without the rampant influence of postmodernism.

intertexts bordering on collage, but the subject matter is conveyed in such a passionate, subjective manner that the tone underlying the narration does not leave any doubt as to what kind of message the author wants to convey. These unambiguous underpinnings of *U ra na* virtually eliminate postmodern double-coding and preclude readings on more than one level. Again, this poem ventures out into new territories, but seems incapable of dropping its bag of old habits before entering them. One could argue that such liminality is precisely Tarnawsky's attempt at double-coding, but there is no evidence in the poem itself that the poet consciously employs indeterminacy as a way of showing his postmodernist proclivity for playing with various modes of expression.

The period of the 1990s, which coincided with the publication of *Svito-vyd* and witnessed the emergence of independent Ukraine, manifested a number of choices the poets of the New York Group assumed. The poetry of Rubchak and Andijewska continues to display liminal ambiguity. After independence, Boychuk and Vovk reemerged as hard-core modernists, returning to the themes that preoccupied them during the "vocal" period. In Boychuk's case we see a deepening and simultaneous intertwining of his two main fixations: metaphysics and eroticism; in Vovk's case, it is the return to mythic and nostalgic motifs. Arguably, Tarnawsky is the only poet of the New York Group who managed to transcend his liminal hesitancy and decisively embrace postmodern poetics. This embrace is evident only in one work thus far, namely the long poem "Misto kyiv ta iam" (The City of Sticks and Holes), included as the last work in the book *Ikh nemaie* (They Are Not There, 1999), but it is not inconceivable that it perhaps signals the beginning of the poet's adoption of a new mode.[63]

Boychuk's first book published in Ukraine, *Tretia osin'* (The Third Autumn, 1991), in addition to selected poems from the previous collections, also introduces two new cycles: "Pro zhinku i poru zhovtinnia" (About a Woman and the Time of Yellowing) and "Molytvy" (Prayers). The former presents a story about a mature love and a subsequent break-up, and foregrounds a typically modernist preference for design and totalization rather than chance and

---

63 Iurii Tarnavs'kyi, *Ikh nemaie* (Kyiv: Rodovid, 1999), 335-408. One should note that Tarnawsky's collection of plays titled 6 x 0, published in Kyiv by Rodovid in 1998, definitely signals a postmodern turn in his oeuvre.

deconstruction (using Hassan's classification), evident especially in the poet's choice of an idiosyncratic form (all seventy five-poems in this cycle are built the same way: two short stanzas—a tercet and a couplet—the last lines of which rhyme):

> Наші життя розминалися мимо,
>> коли ти пристала, щоб
>> гілку нагнути,
>
>> коли нахилився світанок,
>> щоб я тебе міг досягнути.[64]

Our lives were passing by,
>> when you stopped to
>> bend the branch,

> when the dawn bowed,
> so I could reach you.

The "Molytvy" cycle elevates the religious introspection by dwelling on the significance of Logos and transcendence. This dialogue with God, however, is less skeptical and rebellious than the one presented in Boychuk's early work. It very much underscores the poet's thirst for the center and a meaningful point of reference.[65]

Vira Vovk's *Poezii* (2000), published in Kyiv, includes four new collections, almost all written in the 1990s and one in 2000. They expand on themes familiar to her oeuvre—the mythic and the feminine: *Zhinochi masky* (Women's Masks); the religious: *Moleben' do Bohorodytsi* (A Supplication to the Mother of God); the native Ukrainian: *Pysani kakhli* (Painted Stove Tiles); and the personal: *Violia pid vechir* (Viola in the Evening). The pensive tone of the last collection harmonizes well with philosophical reflections on the passing of time, aging, and the meaning of life:

---

64 Bohdan Boichuk, *Tretia osin'* (Kyiv: Dnipro, 1991), 212.

65 This cycle was reprinted in a new collection titled *Virshi kokhannia i molytvy*, published in Kyiv by Fakt in 2002.

приходять дні і відлітають
пориви на високих закаблуках
яскраві надії бажання
все відцвітає
і лише свічка на вустах
пелюстка в зіниці
і жайворон у серці після жнив[66]

days come and fly off
impulses on high heels
bright hopes desires
everything withers away
and only the candle on the lips
a petal in the eye
and a lark in the heart after the harvest are left

The preoccupation with temporal rather than spatial aspects of existence points to the pervasiveness of modernist tenets: the insistence on metaphysics, purpose, and the signified. The poems in the last collection of *Poezii* also invoke the symbols of sharing:

тут мій робочий стіл
моя книгозбірня
мій клявікорд
кілька картин на стінах
килим з дитинства

все це дочасне
моє і ваше[67]

---

66 Vira Vovk, *Poezii* (Kyiv: Rodovid, 2000), 392.
67 Ibid., 393.

here's my desk
my library
my clavichord
a few paintings on the walls
a rug from my childhood

all that is transient
mine and yours

This reaching out to the readers in Ukraine is clouded by the realization of the temporary nature of all things. Nevertheless, Vovk's poetic return to Ukraine undoubtedly constitutes a crowning moment of her entire life.

Tarnawsky's turn to postmodernism is best exemplified in the previously mentioned poem "Misto kyiv i iam." The title displays a considerable dose of intertextual double-coding—it could easily read "The City of Sticks and Holes" or "The City of Kyiv and Holes." The interplay between "sticks" and "Kyiv" could have its origin in the events of the early 1990s, before Ukraine's declaration of independence, when people demonstrating in the capital were literally beaten up by special units of the militia armed with sticks. On the other hand, there are other beatings in the poem which appear to have nothing to do with the political reality.[68]

"Misto kyiv ta iam" is on one level a story of a romantic relationship going nowhere. The male protagonist moves disjointedly from one situation to another as in a dream, seemingly more and more abused and tortured by a cruel woman. But on another level, the poem reads like a parody of the poet's own obsession with love and search for an ideal woman (cf. his other cycle, "For an Ideal Woman"). In the process, he deconstructs many emblems associated with such famous lovers as, for example, Orpheus:

---

68 Tarnawsky's commentary in the endnotes actually allows both interpretations:
    "... поема може бути інтерпретована по-різному, згідно з асоціяціями й здібностями читача. Та автор хотів би підказати, що одною з таких можливостей є розглядання її як опису морального розкладу української людини, а тим самим і розкладу України, в умовах Сов'єтського Союзу, і смерти кохання в такім контексті" (420) ("... The poem can be interpreted in many different ways, according to the reader's associations and abilities. But the author would like to suggest that one way to approach it is to see it as a description of the moral degradation of Ukrainian people, and thereby the degradation of Ukraine in the Soviet Union, and as a depiction of love's death in the context of the above.")

дивиться не себе—
він увесь голий,
тіло біле,
немов з мармуру,
думає про себе,
як про античну статую,
задоволений
з цього,
в руці в нього
сопілка,
він прикладає її
до уст,
грає,
виходять звуки,
прекрасні,
він здивований,
що може грати так
гарно,[69]

he looks at himself—
he's all naked,
the body's white
as if made of marble,
he thinks of himself
like of an antique statue,
feels satisfied
thinking like that,
in his hand
a flute,
he brings it
to his lips,
plays,
the sound comes out,
beautiful,
he's surprised
that he can play so
well

---

69   Tarnavs'kyi, *Ikh nemaie*, 340.

He also laughs at the banality of love scenes, not without a reference to the hackneyed "nightingale" and "cherry tree":

> вона співає,
> наслідує тьохкання
> соловейка,
> прекрасно,
> неймовірно подібно
> до соловейка,
> він у захопленні,
> вона під деревом,
> воно в цвіту,
> вишня, очевидно[70]

> she sings,
> imitates warbling
> of a nightingale,
> beautiful,
> incredibly alike
> to a nightingale,
> he's ecstatic,
> she's under the tree,
> it blossoms,
> it's a cherry tree, of course

and delights in the repulsive:

---

70 Ibid., 359.

чоловік щось белькоче,
нараз блює
на груди жінці,
він саме минає їх
в ту мить,

бачить напівголі,
важкі,
стиснені
жінчині перса,
щось зелене на них,
ворушиться,
це жаба,
чоловік її виблював,
мусів її ковтнути,
йому стає недобре
на думку,[71]

a man mumbles something,
then suddenly vomits
on the woman's breasts,
he was just passing them
that very moment,
he sees half-naked,
heavy,
squeezed
woman's breasts,
something green moves
on them,
it's a frog,
the man threw it up,
must've swallowed it,
he feels nauseous
at the mere thought of it.

---

71   Ibid., 366-67.

The disintegration of myths, beliefs, morals, and love projected by Tarnawsky in this poem recalls Hassan's variation on the theme of deformation, which, according to him, pervades postmodernism:

> The latter alone [i.e. deformation] subsumes a dozen current terms of unmaking: decreation, disintegration, deconstruction, decenterment, displacement, difference, discontinuity, disjunction, disappearance, decomposition, de-definition, demystification, detotalization, deligitimation—let alone more technical terms referring to the rhetoric of irony, rupture, silence. Through all these signs moves a vast will to unmaking, affecting the body politic, the body cognitive, the erotic body, the individual psyche—the entire realm of discourse in the West.[72]

Tarnawsky's multilayered unmaking in "Misto kyiv ta iam" amounts to the strongest postmodernist statement that he has ever presented.

The four poets who remain poetically active up to the present moment, Emma Andijewska, Bohdan Boychuk, Yuriy Tarnawsky, and Vira Vovk,[73] have all demonstrated that writing can achieve life and substance. Their prolonged creativity has on the one hand paved the road for new poetic discoveries, and on the other hand petrified past achievements. On the whole, the majority of the poets of the New York Group confined themselves for the most part to the realm of personal experience, within which they showed impressive skill. Others (especially Andijewska and Rubchak) sought creative comfort behind facades of various masks. However, regardless of personal preferences, the period of their poetic activity, by now spanning more than half a century, shows their gradual opening up to new demands and fashions and reveals their willingness and overall receptivity to aesthetic pluralism. And pluralism has become, according to Ihab Hassan, the condition of postmodern discourses.[74]

---

72 Hassan, *The Dismemberment of Orpheus*, 269.

73 It is not without significance that in 2008 she was awarded the Shevchenko Prize, Ukraine's most prestigious literary honor.

74 Ihab Hassan, *The Postmodern Turn: Essays in Postmodern Theory and Culture* (Columbus: Ohio State University Press, 1987), 167.

CHAPTER 5

(Post)Modernist Masks: The Aesthetics of the Play-Element

In his 1968 portrait of the New York Group of Ukrainian poets, Jurij Solovij depicted Emma Andijewska as wearing a mask. According to him, she alone among the poets in the group evoked the image of a person who likes disguises. This image, however, is not a product of Solovij's fancy, but rather a reflection of the attitude Andijewska herself cultivated and assumed in her poetry. Her third collection, *Ryba i rozmir* (Fish and Dimension, 1961), is a case in point. It includes a chapter of her own poetry, presented as translations of the works of two imaginary poets—Aristidimos Likhnos and Barubu Bdrumbhu. (To obscure the project even further, the latter happens to be a pseudonym of the fictional John Williams). The playfulness of such a literary mystification is so pronounced that it cannot escape notice. No wonder Solovij made Andijewska wear a mask in his portrait.

Johan Huizinga, a leading theorist of play, underscores the secrecy with which play loves to surround itself. He states:

> The "differentness" and secrecy of play are most vividly expressed in "dressing up." Here the "extra-ordinary" nature of play reaches perfection. The disguised or masked individual "plays" another part, another being. He *is* another being. The terrors of childhood, open-hearted gaiety, mystic

fantasy and sacred awe are all inextricably entangled in this strange business of masks and disguises.[1]

But, as I claim in this chapter, Andijewska is not the only poet of the New York Group to have toyed with the ludic and all its tacit implications. Bohdan Rubchak, for example, perhaps more subtly and less noticeably, has matched Andijewska's playful poetic exuberance with his own treatment of poetry as a creative, intellectual, and interactive histrionic game.

The purpose of this chapter is twofold. On the one hand, I shall trace the internal evolution that these two poets underwent in their treatment of the play-element; on the other, I shall attempt to pinpoint the shifts in their poetic texts from modernism to postmodernism. The latter question presupposes that it is possible to localize the borderline between these two literary and artistic trends in the poetry of Andijewska and Rubchak and to show how it is aesthetically reified in the texts.

Modern discussions of play always involve a polarity of play and serious-ness. This radical opposition, although questioned by a number of younger theorists of play,[2] is rather pervasive in the classic studies of Johan Huizinga and Roger Caillois.[3] Huizinga, for example, defines play as "a voluntary activity or occupation executed within certain fixed limits of time and place, according to rules freely accepted but absolutely binding, having its aim in itself and accompanied by a feeling of tension, joy, and the consciousness that it is 'different' from 'ordinary life.'"[4] He essentially identifies "ordinary

---

1   Johan Huizinga, *Homo Ludens: A Study of the Play-Element in Culture* (Boston: Beacon, 1955), 13.

2   Most notable among them is Jacques Ehrmann, the author of "*Homo Ludens* Revisited," trans. Cathy and Phil Lewis, in *Game, Play, Literature*, ed. Jacques Ehrmann. Special issue of *Yale French* Studies 41 (1968) (Boston: Beacon, 1971), 31-57. See also James H. Hans, *The Play of the World* (Amherst, MA: University of Massachusetts Press, 1981); Warren Motte, *Playtexts: Ludics in Contemporary Literature* (Lincoln: University of Nebraska Press, 1995); and Ruth E. Burke, *The Games of Poetics: Ludic Criticism and Postmodern Fiction* (New York: Peter Lang, 1994).

3   I am referring to his *Man, Play, and Games*, trans. Meyer Barash (New York: The Free Press of Glencoe, 1961).

4   *Homo Ludens*, 28. This definition seems to underplay the opposition of play/seriousness. On page 13, however, Huizinga provides another definition which brings this opposition more to the forefront: "Summing up the formal characteristics of play we might call it a free activity standing quite consciously outside 'ordinary' life as being 'not serious,' but at the same time

life" with seriousness. In other words, one plays in a ludic spirit, but one faces ordinary life in a spirit of seriousness. Bohdan Rubchak expressed this beautifully in the poem "V kimnati sta liuster" (In the Room of a Hundred Mirrors) from his first collection, *Kaminnyi sad* (1956):

> Часто я зодягаю пишні шати. Вони
> щедробарвно блищать на мені
> на мініятюрній сцені мого інтимного театру.
> Але у голім
>
> білім світлі, між кущами камінного саду,
> убрання зовсім сіріє, блідне казкова маска, стікає
> ґрим ґротеску, і я
> знову стаю собою.[5]

> I often put on ornate garments. They
> colorfully glitter on me
> on the miniature stage of my intimate theatre.
> But in the naked
>
> white light, among the bushes of the stone orchard,
> the clothes fade completely, the fairy-tale mask pales,
> the mascara of the grotesque runs, and I
> become myself again.

Although the play vs. seriousness opposition poses some problems,[6] I find it a useful classificatory device that enables me to differentiate the poets of the

---

absorbing the player intensely and utterly. It is an activity connected with no material interest, and no profit can be gained by it. It proceeds within its own proper boundaries of time and space according to fixed rules and in an orderly manner. It promotes the formation of social groupings which tend to surround themselves with secrecy and to stress their difference from the common world by disguise or other means."

5   Bohdan Rubchak, *Kaminnyi sad* (New York: Slovo, 1956), 5.

6   Even Huizinga recognized this. At the beginning of *Homo Ludens* he states: "Examined more closely, however, the contrast between play and seriousness proves to be neither conclusive nor fixed. We can say: play is non-seriousness. But apart from the fact that this proposition tells us nothing about the positive qualities of play, it is extraordinarily easy to refute. As soon

New York Group according to the presence or absence of the play-element in their works. My understanding of this opposition is rather commonsensical. It is difficult not to read the poetry of Andijewska and Rubchak as somehow inherently diverting, especially in comparison to that of the other members of the group.[7] A certain distancing and literariness, if not plain artificiality, permeate these two poets' texts. By and large such qualities are absent from the poetry of Bohdan Boychuk, Yuriy Tarnawsky, or Vira Vovk. For them, poetry is existential and mingled with real life to such an extent that the boundary between life and art is blurred. That is not to suggest that their poetry is, for the most part, confessional or autobiographical, but it is fair to say that they feel and express in their texts the "heaviness" or absurdity of life. In that sense their poetry is serious rather than playful.

Yet I am aware that such a differentiation poses another problem if one adheres to the conception of play Huizinga proposed. According to him, poetry (*poiesis*) is a play-function, and, moreover, it will never rise to the level of seriousness.[8] In other words, it is inherently "extra-ordinary" and immutably removed from "ordinary" life. I believe this apparent contradiction stems from the double nature of play. It is both an activity rooted in intention and an outcome of such activity. If one accepts the broad view that all creative activity is animated by a strong ludic spirit, then all poetry can indeed be treated as a play-function. But even within such an assumption, one should be able to recognize that a playful activity does not necessarily lead to a playful outcome, or, to put it differently, play does not always result in a plaything.

Going back to Andijewska and Rubchak, I would like to point out that in addition to their shared interest in the play-element, they both seem to display

---

as we proceed from 'play is non-seriousness' to 'play is not serious,' the contrast leaves us in the lurch—for some play can be very serious indeed" (5).

7   Rubchak's proclivity for playfulness was noticed by Boychuk very early on. In his letter to Rubchak, Boychuk tried to dissuade the young poet from nurturing this side of his talent: "Одно я запримітив: Ваші поезії (написані навіть в той самий період) дуже відмінні характером. Не знаю, чим це пояснити. Ви або в стадії шукань, або бавитесь з читачем. Це останнє я б волів зовсім відкинути, бо поезія за поважна річ, щоб нею бавитись." Letter to Bohdan Rubchak, 28 Jan. 1956. Bohdan Rubchak Papers, Rare Book and Manuscript Library, Columbia University, New York. ("One thing I noticed: your poems [even those written in the same period] vary in character. You are either in the phase of search or simply play with the reader. The latter I would prefer to dispense with, because poetry is too serious a matter to play with.")

8   *Homo Ludens*, 119.

a preference for traditional poetical forms such as stanza, meter, and rhyme (though imperfect—assonance, dissonance, consonance—rather than perfect); both also seem to exhibit a propensity to experiment with such classical genres as the sonnet. This return to tradition in both formal (poetics) and cultural (context/convention) aspects has some affinity, in my view, to what Linda Hutcheon describes as one of the defining principles of postmodernism, namely "the presence of the past."[9] She emphasizes, however, that to be considered postmodern such a turn has to be first and foremost critical and problematized, rather than merely nostalgic. It has been firmly established that play, parody, and pastiche lie at the core of the postmodern project. What concerns me here is not only the extent to which these attributes are present in the works of the two poets analyzed here, but also the character of the playfulness they employ. Can it be called postmodern? Perhaps, notwithstanding all postmodernist coloring, it is still deeply rooted ideologically in modernism.

I have focused on the similarities between Andijewska's and Rubchak's *ars poetica* because I wanted to set them apart from the other members of the New York Group. It would be a mistake, however, to think that their approaches to the play-element are the same, although on the level of language, i.e., on the level of experimenting with its materiality, especially sound, there is indeed a strong resemblance. Both poets espouse an alliterative technique in building a line and play with words for sound effects, thus often bracketing the meaning. This often occurs in Andijewska's work. For example:

> Габою губиться сузір'я
> Губою голубник порушили[10]

> A constellation lost in a shroud
> The lip has disturbed the pigeon coop.

The same is seen in the poems of Rubchak:

---

9   *A Poetics of Postmodernism: History, Theory, Fiction* (New York: Routledge, 1988), 4.

10   Emma Andiievs'ka, *Kuty opostin'* (New York: V-vo Niu-Iorks'koi hrupy, 1962), 12.

Віршам і снам не вір:
травур, та рев, та вир.
З варив розрив-трави
Скроплений кожен вірш.[11]

Don't believe in poems and dreams:
mourning, and roar, and swirl.
With brews of magic herbs
each verse is sprayed.

I should point out, however, that on the whole that kind of wordplay is more characteristic of Andijewska's poetry than Rubchak's.

As to the differences, they mostly stem from the different attitudes our poets exhibit toward the creative process itself. To some extent, their attitudes coincide with what Nietzsche called the Dionysian and the Apollonian spirit; the first is instinctual, irrational, ecstatic, and unbounded, while the second is rational, restrained, mediated, and balanced. Measured with this yardstick, Andijewska's poetry belongs to the Dionysian camp, while Rubchak's is in the Apollonian one.

Roger Caillois follows Huizinga's model of play quite closely, except that he rejects the latter's insistence on agon (competition) as the essence of every play activity. Caillois turns his attention also to games, which Huizinga by and large ignores, and classifies them in four broad categories: agon (competitive games), alea (games of chance), mimicry (make-believe games), and ilinx (vertigo, or games dominated by confusion and disarray). What is useful in Caillois's work for my purposes is that he also introduces two attitudinal poles, or "ways of playing,"[12] that further qualify these four categories. They are *paidia*, characterized by turbulence, free improvisation, and fantasy, and *ludus*, identified with constraint, arbitrary rules, effort, and ingenuity.[13] These two attitudinal modes are somewhat similar to Nietzsche's famous opposition between the Dionysian and Apollonian ways of viewing the world. In my view, Andijewska's use of the play-element is more in the *paidia* mode,

---

11 Bohdan Rubchak, *Divchyni bez krainy* (New York: V-vo N'iu-Iorks'koi hrupy, 1963), 30.
12 *Man, Play and Games*, 53.
13 Ibid., 13.

whereas Rubchak's is more in the *ludus* mode. Her spontaneous, immediate, child-like associations contrast vividly with his more structured, intellectualized, allusive poetic constructs.

Although these are the general tendencies, one can discern shifts in Andijewska's poetry from the more structured ludic to the more improvised "paidic" treatment of the play-element. Her "as if" translations in *Ryba i rozmir* are quite illustrative. In a letter to Bohdan Boychuk, dated 21 December 1964, Andijewska calls her "Dionysia" (the cycle of poems by Aristidimos Likhnos) a "jest" (насмішка). Notwithstanding her comment about "Dionysia" ("це не еротика, а насмішка"),[14] the cycle does invoke homoerotic themes. Moreover, her imaginary poets Aristidimos Likhnos and John Williams (Andijewska describes the latter as an African-American born in Harlem) either depict minorities (be it according to sexual orientation or race) or actually belong to them. In the early 1960s, when these texts were published, both homosexuals and African-Americans were considered marginal groups. Playing with the notion of alterity on Andijewska's part is not coincidental. It very much reflects the feelings she and her colleagues experienced as young émigré poets realizing themselves in America. This kind of structured, ideological playing is an exception rather than a rule in Andijewska's poetry. Her subsequent collections represent an incessant flow of metaphors, metonymies, and wordplay, all of them grounded in "still-life" descriptiveness, discontinuity, and chance. Here are a few examples:

> Мов сіті, бабку витягнувши з дельт
> Повітря й—замість булочки—на тацю,—
> Хай поруч море мокрим носом тиця
> У литку, щоб—ні лиха, ні недоль.[15]

> Like nets, having pulled a cake out of the deltas
> Of air and put it on a tray instead of a roll—
> Let the sea close by nuzzle my calf
> With a wet nose to spare me affliction and misfortune.

---

14   "This is not eroticism, but a jest" (Bohdan Boichuk Papers, Rare Book and Manuscript Library, Columbia University, New York).

15   "Mors'ka terasa," in Andijewska, *Kavarnia: Poezii* (Munich: Suchasnist, 1983), 40.

Рожева губка, ніж, кілька рибин—
Не стіл—корова—інтер'єр сумирний,
Де око—дійсність—в довгий накомарник
Й поля—під себе—силові гребе.[16]

A pink sponge, knife, and a few small fish,—
Not a table—a cow—a serene interior,
Where an eye pulls reality and fields of force
Into a long mosquito net.

Bohdan Rubchak's toying with the ludic is not as conspicuous in his first collection, *Kaminnyi sad*, as it is in his more mature poetry. Nonetheless, the seeds of playfulness had been planted at an early stage. Hence the opening poem "V kimnati sta liuster," quoted earlier, points to his awareness of a certain theatricality in all creative endeavors. Despite the fact that, on the whole, modernist, existential, and purely imagist qualities prevail here, the allusiveness, intertextuality, and playing with the cultural emblems of the past typical of Rubchak's subsequent poetry have their origins in this first collection. Here we find a reference to Shakespeare's Hamlet and to Mann's main character of the *Buddenbrooks* saga; we encounter hints of the traditions of both Athens (Orpheus) and Jerusalem (The Song of Songs). But this "presence of the past" or intertextual play is not parodic in nature. Rubchak's dialogue with key figures of both the west European (Balzac, Baudelaire, Goethe) and the native Ukrainian (Vyshensky, Kotliarevsky, Franko, Antonych) literary traditions, as well as his invocation of famous literary characters (Cassandra, Dante's Francesca of Canto V, *Inferno*, Faust, and Don Juan, to name just a few) all spring from veneration rather than the desire to subvert this grand humanist tradition. I discern in Rubchak's poetry a certain longing for continuity, an aspiration to preserve the link with the mentioned cultural riches. Consider, for example, the poem "S'ohodni vzhe ne kvity" (Today No Longer Flowers):

---

16 "Stupeni kolyvan," in Andijewska, *Znaky. Tarok* (Kyiv: Dnipro, 1995), 142.

Сьогодні вже не квіти
(*Читаючи Бодлера*)

Хризантемами зло вже не світиться
в вечорах, що мов яд, мов полин.
В нім немає вже місця для місяця,
оксамитних пороків і вин.

В нім немає дощу злотолезого,
навіть плюшу дешевих неслав:
Сатана божевілля тверезого
дим отруйний в квартали послав.

Не шукай, добрий, зла в літніх зорях.
Його чистий, безкровний мороз
продукують у лябораторіях
без поем, без розбещених поз.

В кам'яній, в остаточній самотності,
що забула розпуку і біль,
бачу я твої сльози розкотисті,
і безмірно я заздрю тобі.[17]

Today No Longer Flowers
(*Reading Baudelaire*)

Evil no longer shines through chrysanthemum
in the evenings which are like a venom, like a wormwood.
There is no more room in it for the moon,
velvety vices and wine.

There is no gold-bladed rain in it,
even none of the velvet's cheap infamies:
Satan of sober madness
sent off a poisonous smoke into the dwellings.

---

17   *Divchyni bez krainy*, 26.

Do not seek, dear, evil in the summer stars.
Its pure, bloodless frost
is produced in the laboratories
without poems, without spoiled poses.

In stony finite solitude
which has forgotten despair and pain,
I see your rolling tears
and immensely envy you.

The poet often employs irony and, less often, the grotesque, but diffuses their subversive potential: the ironic tone that permeates his more mature poetry is used as a device for the playful probing of communicative possibilities between the text and the reader. For example, in the opening stanza of the poem "Poetychnyi khlib" (Poetic Bread) the premise about what poetry should be is immediately debunked with irony:

Такого хліба треба б замісити,
щоб в нім було і злетів, і покор,
щоб був їдою хворим, їддю ситим, –
та я ні пекар, ані прокурор.

One should knead such bread
so that it would contain both pride and humility,
so that would feed the sick and poison the sated,
but I am neither a baker nor a prosecutor.

Now we will look at the final stanza of this poem:

А волю світу—бидлову, обидну—
по віядуках мрії обійду
та й тополину виявлю біду
в неділю, після доброго обіду.[18]

---

18   Bohdan Rubchak, *Krylo Ikarove* (Kyiv: Dnipro, 1991), 33.

And the world's will—bovine, offensive—
I'll pass by on the viaducts of daydreams
and reveal the poplar's sorrow
on Sunday, after a good dinner.

This stanza is a far cry from the metaphysical qualities ascribed to poetic activity in his early poem "Ars Poetica":

Шукати лиш суть, лиш голе буття шукати—
       суть буття.
Відчувати простір: літ чорних птахів далеко,
відчувати час: чіткі рисунки в чорних печерах,
і абсолютним вітром розуміти свій день, поете.[19]

To seek only the essence, to seek only bare existence is the
       essence of being.
To feel space: the flight of black birds far away,
to feel time: the distinct drawings in the black caves,
and to understand your own day as the absolute wind, O, poet.

The seriousness of tone in this poem contrasts vividly with the somewhat cynical and even mildly subversive underpinnings of "Poetychnyi khlib." In the latter poem, Rubchak alludes to the century-old modernist formula of "art-for-art's sake" with a considerable dose of skepticism and sarcasm. Yet, I would argue, the poet's mistrust of metaphysical substance both in life and in poetry, which is evident especially in his late oeuvre, does not have nihilistic or subversive undertones. On the contrary, Rubchak does not question the validity of the accepted order of things, whether on the moral or the aesthetic plane, but he does like to reveal its shortcomings. Moreover, his belief in the power of poetry, its transformative and almost transcendent quality, clearly betrays the poet's modernist posture. It is also clear that the poet often uses cultural emblems as vehicles for expressing his own personal dilemmas. For example, in the poem "Luk Filokteta" (Philoctetes's Bow), he contemplates his

---

19 *Kaminnyi sad*, 52.

own poetic return after many years of silence, using the Greek mythological figure of Philoctetes:

> ... і, мабуть, повернусь. Із смерти струнким
>   нарцизом,
> непомильним, блакитним. За біль і за шмаття хмар
> дам відповідь гостру на сонця сердечний визов.
> Плоскорізьбою на фризі застигну. Льодистим
>   бризом
> війну змінити кошмар на кришталький кошмар.
>
> А тепер я з собою. Мій кострубатий острів
> шкірить щоранку порепані ребра скель.
> Наді мною чайки танцюють, прозорі гості,
> піді мною в старечій злості безчасний простір
> корить гирла, джерела, оселі, корені, брості, –
>
> а в мені моя гордість і сором, мій зліт і мій скем.[20]

… and, maybe, I shall return. Out of death as a slender narcissus,
faultless, blue. For all the pain and the clouds' rags
I will give a sharp response to the sun's cordial challenge.
I will congeal like a bas-relief on the frieze. With an icy breeze
I will breathe to change a nightmare into a crystal nightmare.

But now I am with myself. My jagged island
grins the chapped ribs of rocks every morning.
Above me the seagulls, transparent guests, dance,
below me the timeless space in its toothless anger
chides outfalls, springs, dwellings, roots, buds,—

and within me there is my pride and shame, my rise and my pain.

---

20 Bohdan Rubchak, *Krylo Ikarove* (Munchen: Suchasnist', 1983), 13.

As the legend has it, the great archer Philoctetes was bitten by a snake on his way to Troy. Abandoned and forgotten by his friends, he spent nine miserable years on the island Lemnos. It turned out, however, that the destruction of Troy required Philoctetes's bow and his skills as a warrior. In the end, healed of his wound, he killed Paris with the arrows of Heracles, and the city of Troy eventually fell. Undoubtedly, Rubchak also has confidence in his weapon—poetry—and is hopeful that his art can make a difference and, in the end, will bring him deserved recognition, which implies a relationship with the reader.

Rubchak's foregrounding of the dynamic, interactive, or communicative aspects of playful activity invokes yet another model of play: the one presented by Jacques Ehrmann. For Ehrmann, play is economy, communication, and articulation, i.e., "opening and closing of and through language."[21] He further rejects the opposition of play and reality (or seriousness) as false and unproductive. "Each text contains in itself its own reality, which in essence (or by nature!) is put into play by the words which make it up.... In other words, the distinguishing characteristic of reality is that it is played."[22] In this model, culture, play, and games are all forms of communication. Players are at the same time subjects and objects of the play. What I find useful and valuable in Ehrmann's theory is his insistence on the articulative relation of player to player, player to game, and game to world. Using this scheme as another classificatory tool, I would categorize Emma Andijewska's poetry as one that privileges the dynamics between player (writer) and game (text), and Bohdan Rubchak's poetry as one that foregrounds the relation of player to player, i.e., the relation that is manifest in communication between the writer and the reader in the act of reading. By juxtaposing various types of discourse, by creating poetic puns that highlight the ambiguity of words, and by constantly forcing the reader to waver between poetry as communication of an idea or feeling separate from the text and the reader's awareness of how the text is generated by quirks of language rather than by real-life situations, the poet requires the reader to reconsider the reading process, forces her or him to participate in the creative process, and problematizes the conventional approach to the poet's texts. From this standpoint, Rubchak's ludic poetry may well be

---

21 Ehrmann, "*Homo Ludens* Revisited," 56.
22 Ibid.

part of a postmodernist project, although he never calls into question the universalist humanist conceptions of meaning and center. Previous styles, works, and traditions are played with, but never doubted; they are paraphrased, but at the same time cherished and accepted.

Unlike Rubchak, Andijewska seems to be oblivious to the issues of reception. Hers is a world of self-contained poetic constructs, a world in which the word reigns supreme, even though dislocation, surprise, and ambiguity, which are so conspicuous in her oeuvre, frequently undercut the logical foundations of that word. However, this very faithfulness to the authority of the word, the acceptance of its centrality and autonomy, situates Andijewska's poetic output firmly in modernism. The playfulness of her poetry is the byproduct of the game she seems to play with language itself. The intertextuality which is so central to Rubchak takes a back seat in Andijewska's *ars poetica*.[23] There can be no doubt that she is quite mindful of the postmodernist underpinnings of the contemporary cultural scene. For example, the poem "Prymruzhenymy ochyma" (With Squinting Eyes), which opens her collection *Mezhyrichchia* (The Place between the Rivers, 1998), demonstrates Andijewska's view (no doubt ironic, judging by the title) of what postmodernism is all about:

> Буття нема. Є січка-монолог
> Речей. Скрізь замість цілого—частини.
> Єдиний відступ—барва-неврастенік.
> Що—сірниками—селезінку й слух.[24]

> There is no being. There's chopped monologue
> Of things. Everywhere there are parts instead of the whole.
> The only retreat is a neurasthenic color
> That burns the spleen and hearing with matches.

---

23 However, it is by no means absent. Like Rubchak, she displays a penchant for ancient Greek décor and Greek mythological figures (see "Dionisii" in her *Ryba i rozmir* and "Antychni reministsentsii" (Antique Reminiscences) in her *Arkhitekturni ansambli: Sonety* (New York: Suchasnist, 1989). One can also discern in her poetry intertextual play with various kinds of folk literatures. But these tendencies are not as dominant as they are in Rubchak.

24 Emma Andiievs'ka, *Mezhyrichchia: Sonety* (Kyiv: Vsesvit, 1998), 5.

This stanza ironically foregrounds the postmodern contesting of metaphysical premises. It also points to the postmodern preference for fragmentation and discontinuity rather than totality and continuity.

Yet another aspect that moves Andijewska closer to the modernist end on a continuum between modernism and postmodernism is her privileging of ethics. Throughout her poetic output she evinces a strongly defined sense of what is right and wrong, perhaps echoing Kant's categorical imperative. The typical postmodernist relativism in the sphere of ethics (which incidentally goes back to Nietzsche's perspectivism, i.e., his famous statement that there is no truth, only interpretations) is foreign to Andijewska. Herbert Grabes, for instance, asserts that "one of postmodernism's most prominent features is the striving towards a pan-aestheticism which reverses the subordination of aesthetics to ethics."[25] Explicit in her prose, implicit in her poetry, the ever-present undercurrent of clearly defined moral values does not do justice to such a reversal, at least not in Andijewska's case.[26] Ethical issues are as important to her as aesthetics itself. Yet, notwithstanding the strong display of a moral center, one can also easily argue that Andijewska's other tendency, the tendency toward open, associative, and indeterminate poetic texts with a plethora of incongruous juxtapositions of images, toward poetry as a playful process of exploring verbal fields rather than a presentation of a coherent viewpoint or an emotional reaction to some aspect of social or personal reality, place her squarely in the postmodernist camp.[27] She oscillates between the poem as an

---

25 Herbert Grabes, "Ethics, Aesthetics, and Alterity," in *Ethics and Aesthetics: The Moral Turn of Postmodernism*, ed. Gerhard Hoffman and Alfred Hornung (Heidelberg: Universitätsverlag C. Winter, 1996), 13.

26 For example, her 1961 collection *Ryba i rozmir* includes a chapter entitled "Z tsyklu pro dobro i zlo" ("From the Cycle about Goodness and Evil"). Ethical concerns permeate many of her poems, but they are often inconspicuous because of her uncontrolled verbosity.

27 Ihab Hassan, for example, posits indeterminacy, derived from Nietzsche's thought, as a basic feature of postmodernism. He describes this indeterminacy as embracing many features: the rejection of the human being as the measure of all value; the portrayal of the subject as a fiction; and the recognition of "facts" as perspectives or interpretations. See his books *The Postmodern Turn: Essays in Postmodern Theory and Culture* (Columbus: Ohio State University Press, 1987), 47-54, and *The Dismemberment of Orpheus: Toward a Postmodern Literature*, 2d. ed. (Madison, WI: University of Wisconsin Press, 1982), 268-9. As I have shown in my essay "Elementy dehumanizatsii v poezii Emmy Andiievs'koi," *Svito-vyd*, no. 3 (1992): 13, 17, there is no doubt that Andijewska displays a tendency to expose the reality of the poem as pure fiction and makes her poems very impersonal and devoid of the human agent.

exercise in verbal play in which there is a clear disregard for meaning and the poem as semantically "loaded"; paradoxically, this makes her poetry stylistically uniform and yet simultaneously diverse and complex. This double-edged, equivocal quality of her poems greatly contributes to the difficulty of convincingly classifying her work, especially her late poetry, as either modernist or postmodernist.

In spite of employing some typically postmodernist techniques, such as play, intertextuality, and irony, ideologically (or philosophically) both Rubchak and Andijewska are unable or, more likely, unwilling to subvert the metanarratives (to use Lyotard's terminology) of the humanist tradition. Their position may best be defined as liminal with respect to the modernism-postmodernism continuum. The masks they wear may look postmodernist, but the faces behind these masks are modernist.

CHAPTER 6

From Spain with Love, or, Is There a 'Spanish School' in Ukrainian Literature?

With regard to the thematic innovations introduced by the New York Group, the voice of Spain and Latin America assumes a role that cannot be lightly dismissed.[1] The development of a poetic idiom for some poets in the group was predicated to a large extent on their intimate knowledge of poetic works by such literary giants as Pablo Neruda, Federico García Lorca, Juan Ramón Jiménez, and Antonio Machado, to name just a few. While the degree and intensity of Spanish/Latin American influences vary from poet to poet, in the cases of Emma Andijewska and Bohdan Rubchak amounting to nil,[2] nevertheless, if one approaches the poetry of the New York Group in its

---

1   George G. Grabowicz, for example, considers as innovative the following themes: the city, the erotic, death, and alienation. However, he fails to mention the presence of Spanish motifs and themes in the group's output. See his "New Directions in Ukrainian Poetry in the United States," in *The Ukrainian Experience in the United States: A Symposium*, ed. Paul R. Magosci (Cambridge, MA: Harvard Ukrainian Research Institute, 1979), 166-67.

2   Neither Andijewska nor Rubchak has ever ventured to translate Spanish-language poetry. Spanish themes are also conspicuously absent in their respective poetic outputs, although the second issue of the group's journal *Novi poezii* (1960) contains Andijewska's poem "Hommage á Federico García Lorca." To my knowledge, this poem is her one and only attempt at incorporating Spanish themes. Rubchak's first collection *Kaminnyi sad*, on the other hand, contains a poem titled "Kavalero proshchaiet'sia z hitaroiu" (A Cavalier Bids Farewell to his Guitar) which not only alludes to the Spanish setting, but actually uses a

totality, this "Spanish turn" is one of those factors that clearly define the group's uniqueness and cohesiveness. To my knowledge, no other Ukrainian poet or group of poets has incorporated the Spanish themes in such a systematic manner and with so much enthusiasm.[3]

The concept of a "national school" in literature, judging by its application in the historical accounts of specifically Polish and Russian Romantic literatures,[4] entails a considerable degree of fascination with a region or a country, its people, landscapes, lore, and customs, as reflected in the works of a poet or a writer whose national origin and/or language differs from that of the people described. In other words, one can easily infer from such practice that it is literary content alone that justifies the usage of this concept. Here, however, I shall argue that such an approach is too narrow for the description of the New York Group's love for things Spanish because it does not allow the inclu-

---

couple of Spanish words: *adios* and *chiquita*. Interestingly, in the poem "Proiekt dlia baletu v tr'okh aktakh" (A Project for the Three-Act Ballet) of the same book, Boychuk discerns Lorca's influence: "Також дуже вдалий вислів "фіолетно усміхаючись"—коротка і повна характеристика монахині (хоч ці галузки, що носять чорні помаранчі нагадують мені Льорку—його "чорні мелони"—хоч у нього це вжите у зовсім іншому сенсі)" (Letter to Bohdan Rubchak, 1 Apr. 1957. Bohdan Rubchak Papers, Rare Book and Manuscript Library, Columbia University, New York.) ("Also, your expression 'smiling like a violet' is very felicitous—it gives a brief but full characterization of a nun [although, these branches that carry black oranges remind me of Lorca—his 'black melons,' but he uses it in an entirely different sense].") (Cf. Rubchak's "За вікном ходять монахині, фіолетно усміхаючись/ під галузками, що носять чорні помаранчі," *Kaminnyi sad* [16]). ("Outside the window the nuns walk, smiling like a violet,/ under the branches that carry black oranges.") Notwithstanding Boychuk's comments, Rubchak's overall interest in Spanish thematic material is marginal indeed, and does not merit inclusion in the "Spanish School" phenomenon of the New York Group.

3   Singular examples can be found in Bohdan Ihor Antonych (cf. his "Slovo pro Al'kazar" [A Word on Alkazar]), Iurii Klen (cf. "Kortes" [Cortez]), and Vadym Lesych (cf. "Do El' Greko" [To El Greco]). There are also two "Spanish" poems in Iurii Kosach's poetry collection *Kubok Khanimeda* (cf. "El Centauro de la Conquista" and "Frantsisko Goia").

4   I am referring here to the so-called "Ukrainian schools" in Polish and Russian literatures of the Romantic period. In Polish literature this term applies to the works of three Romantic poets, namely Antoni Malczewski, Józef Bohdan Zalewski, and Seweryn Goszczyński, who were born in Ukraine and found Ukrainian folklore and history inspiring. In Russian literature this name designates those Romantics who were attracted to Ukrainian thematic material (e.g. K. Ryleev, N. Gogol, A. Pushkin with his *Poltava*, to name a few). It is often insinuated that this fascination with Ukrainian themes stems from the general Romantic attraction to the exotic. This exoticism, however, for almost all authors just mentioned, was very close to home. To the poets of the New York Group, the Spanish influences meant the reverse of what happened to the Romantics, i.e. going away from home rather than back to the place of origin.

sion of aspects other than thematic. Thematics, while the most conspicuous, are not the only factors that need to be brought to the surface. My coinage "Spanish turn" also entails two other facets, namely the production of numerous Ukrainian translations of Spanish-language poetry and the presence of influences that actually transcend the Spanish content. I am referring here not so much to the influences perceivable on a thematic level, but those present on a formative level, i.e., those having to do with shaping each individual poetic personality. This latter category is no doubt the subtlest and, perhaps, the most controversial one, because hardly any poet readily admits to such influences in her or his oeuvre.

Let me first catalogue the group's achievements in the sphere of translation, specifically from the Spanish. Andijewska and Rubchak aside, the remaining five poets of the New York Group have all been active in bringing Spanish-language poetry to the Ukrainian reader. In 1958, Ihor Kostetsky edited and published the book *Vybranyi Garsiia L'orka*, for which he invited Yuriy Tarnawsky, Zhenia Vasylkivska, and Bohdan Boychuk, among others, to contribute their translations—and they did indeed. Overall, only a handful of books pertaining to Spanish-language literatures in Ukrainian translation have appeared in the West, which is understandable, considering the limited resources of the émigré community. The other works of translation worth mentioning are Juan Ramón Jiménez's *Pliatero i ia* (Platero and I), translated by Boychuk, published in 1968, García Lorca's *Iak kokhavsia don Perlimplin z Belisoiu v sadu* (The Love of Don Perlimplin for Belisa in Their Orchard), translated by Tarnawsky and published in 1967, and two books in Vira Vovk's translation, the first being Pablo Neruda's long poem *Verkhiv'ia Machu Pichu* (The Heights of Macchu Picchu, 1970) and the second Lorca's *Chotyry dramy* (Four Plays, 1974). The bulk of the translations were produced as direct contributions to the group's almanac, the annual *Novi poezii*. This journal introduced to the Ukrainian reader the poetry of the following Spanish-language authors: Pablo Neruda, Cesar Vallejo, Jorge Carrera Andrade, Vicente Aleixandre, Juan Ramón Jiménez, Rafael Alberti, Miguel Hernandez, Federico García Lorca, and Antonio Machado. Collectively, their poems amount to approximately two thirds of all translations included in *Novi poezii*.

By far, however, the most engaging aspect of the "Spanish School" phenomenon is the group's utilization of Spanish thematic material. Octavio

Paz, writing about poetry in the Spanish language, calls it "revelry and funereal dance, erotic dancing and mystical flight."[5] Perhaps it is this unique combination of Eros, death, and mysticism that attracted the young Ukrainian poets to Spanish poetic treasures. Of course, each poet of the group has incorporated the Spanish heritage in his/her own peculiar way: as a background for expressing personal drama or as a pretext for experimentation (Tarnawsky), as a vehicle for contemplation on love, beauty, life, and death (Boychuk), as a means to infuse Ukrainian literature with a certain exotic flavor (Vovk, Vasylkivska), and, finally, as a channel for giving readers a very personalized picture of Spain, imbued with individual impressions, experience, and reflection (Kylyna).

The presence of Spanish themes in the poetry of Vasylkivska is somewhat scant and its significance rather marginal. This marginality stems mostly from the fact that Vasylkivska left the group and literature quite early, having written just one collection of poetry, *Korotki viddali*. And yet this book includes the poem entitled "Flamenco," which deftly captures the spirit of the famed Spanish gypsy-style dance and music. It describes the mournful sound of guitars, the hoarse voices of male singers, and the tense movements of dancers' bodies with the intensity usually associated with flamenco:

> Хриплим відламком
> старечий голос—
> рвучким стаккато
> струни гітари.
>
> Брязнули вістря
> скреготом сталі,
> зойкнули стрілами,
> болем зламались.
>
> Гортанним відгуком
> Згадка—печери,
> босі циганки,
> вежі Севільї.[6]

---

5 Paz, *The Bow and the Lyre*, 75.
6 Vasyl'kivs'ka, *Korotki viddali* (New York: Slovo, 1959), 27.

An elderly voice is
like hoarse splints,
the guitar's sound—
an ardent staccato.

Blades clashed with
a clang of steel,
shrieked with arrows,
broke in pain.

A throaty voice is
a reminder of caves,
barefooted Gypsy girls,
the towers of Seville.

What deserves attention in this poem is Vasylkivska's masterful matching of the poem's rhythm with the actual content. The staccato of the guitar she refers to in the first stanza also characterizes the rhythm of the whole poem. But the three poems that constitute the cycle "Flamenco" are her only contribution to Spanish thematics. Overall, her interest in Spain was by and large confined to translations.

Vira Vovk's poetic output in comparison to Vasylkivska's is more appreciable, and the number of poems dealing with Spain and Latin America is proportionally more substantial. Still, the number of poems directly incorporating Spanish content is rather limited. One should emphasize, however, that a Latin American flavor prevails, most likely because Vovk emigrated to Brazil and settled in Rio de Janeiro.[7] Her poems, especially in *Chorni akatsii* (Black Acacias, 1961) often carry as titles the names of the countries visited (e.g. Chile, Mexico) and can almost be perceived as concise poetic travelogues expressing the poet's impressions and observations. Yet they seem to lack the spirit and immediacy of experience; they seem to be distant and devoid of personal perspective:

---

7   Her work bears a considerable mark of the influences of Brazilian culture, but since Brazil is outside of the Spanish language domain, they are not examined in this chapter.

Мехіко

Хоч добре, що ластівка-стежка
Летіла собі між вульканами
І що стелилися вітру
Злотні, незаймані трави.
І добре, що синє кладовище
Було західною колискою,
Що розцвітало каміння
В оселі, церкви й піраміди.
І кактусів бурі органи
Сурмили зненацька про сонце,
Про місяць крутих візерунків.
Ще в візії Таско засяє.
Й ростуть кривобокі святині
З хиткої землі в Ґвадалюпе.[8]

Mexico

It's good that a trail like a swallow
Flew between the volcanoes
And that gold-tinged innocent grass
Unfurled itself for the wind.
It's also good that a blue cemetery
Was the sunset's cradle
And that stones blossomed
In the dwellings, churches, and pyramids.
The brown organs of cactuses
Suddenly trumpeted about the sun,
And about the moon of sharp patterns.
Taxco will shine in vision.
The tilted sides of sanctuaries
Grow out of the unsteady ground in Guadalupe.

---

8   Vira Vovk, *Chorni akatsii* (Munchen: Na hori, 1961), 32.

In two other poetic books, *Elehii* (Elegies, 1956) and *Kappa khresta* (The Kappa of a Cross, 1969), unlike in *Chorni akatsii*, Spanish/Latin American themes do not occur for their own sake, but rather are inextricably interwoven in the fabric of the poet's personal reflections on God, human justice, and fate. The first elegy, entitled "Toreadory i heroi" (Toreadors and Heroes), for example, brings forth the Spanish people's treasured tradition of bullfighting only in order to undermine the assumed heroism of matadors and spur subsequent ethical reflections, not without a strong mystical underpinning. It is this first "Spanish" poem that exudes genuine passion and compassion, and makes the whole elegy poetically satisfying:

> Тореадори!
> Камелії зарясніли над стрункістю смаглих тіл,
> І Мадрід, отяжілий минулим, і Севілья
> Зідхають за ними шелестячими кедрами.
> … А в рудий пісок арени всякає кров,
> І тур міцногрудий завернув голубіючі очі:
> «Навіщо, людино?»
> Тореадори!
> Горять мандоліни, перляться оплески з рук
>   рожевих:
> … Несуть для тореадорів
> Відрізані вуха і слинявий тура язик …
> Тореадори! Ви посіли землю!
> (Давніше інквізитори палили відьом;
> Їм теж віддавали прилюдну шану,
> І всі подивляли їх міць).[9]

> Toreadors!
> Camellia covered the slenderness of brown bodies,
> And Madrid, heavy with the past, and Seville
> Sigh for them with rustling cedars.
> … And the blood sinks into the rufous sand of arena,
> And a bull with a mighty trunk turned his bluish eyes:

---

9   Vira Vovk, *Elehii* (Munich: Ukrains'ke V-vo, 1956), 7.

"What for, man?"

Toreadors!

Mandolins burn, the applause spills from pink hands like pearls:

... They carry for the toreadors

the bull's cutoff ears and slobbery tongue ...

Toreadors! You inherit the earth!

(Once inquisitors burned witches;

Those men also earned public respect

And everyone admired their might.)

But to talk about the consistent presence of Spanish and/or Latin American themes is to really talk about Tarnawsky, Kylyna, and Boychuk. It is these three poets who truly deserve attention in this area, not only because each of them has brought forth a book of poetry wholly devoted to some aspect of Spanish-language culture, but also because they seem to extol in their poems the spirit of the Spanish people. Ernest Hemingway in his famous book on bullfighting, *Death in the Afternoon*, characterizes this spirit as follows:

> If the people of Spain have one common trait it is pride and if they have another it is common sense and if they have a third it is impracticality. Because they have pride they do not mind killing; feeling that they are worthy to give this gift. As they have common sense they are interested in death and do not spend their lives avoiding the thought of it and hoping it does not exist only to discover it when they come to die.[10]

The theme of death permeates the poetry of all the poets in the New York Group. But Tarnawsky, Boychuk, and Kylyna display that interest in death in a particularly pronounced way. Moreover, Boychuk's poetry is characterized by pride and intense emotionality; Tarnawsky's texts, on the other hand, evince a strong aura of masculinity (which is very much in tune with the perceived macho attitude of the majority of Spanish/Latin American males);[11]

---

10 Ernest Hemingway, *Death in the Afternoon* (New York: Scribner, 1932), 264.

11 By the poet's own admission, Spain with its masculinity has always constituted a point of attraction to him: "What attracts me about Spain and its culture is its masculinity and simplicity, the hoarse, 'afilao' flamenco voice, the tight clothes, the preoccupation with death, and facing it head on. No sentimentality. My critics don't understand that in my writings I strive for the greatest simplicity, and find beauty in roughness, coarseness, not the candy-box cover prettiness. That's why I love Spain" (E-mail to the author, 26 Dec. 1999.)

and finally, Kylyna's "Spanish" poems underscore a certain fatalism and the tragic aspects of life.

In 1964, Bohdan Boychuk published his fourth collection of poetry, *Virshi dlia Mekhiko* (Poems for Mexico). This tiny book of fifteen poems, in which for the first time the poet dispensed with his usual technique of vers libre, has its origin in a trip made to Mexico in 1962. However, Boychuk avoids the passive role of an observer who, like an ordinary tourist, jots down impressions of things encountered. He personifies Mexico, makes it a woman, and then falls in love with her. The eroticism thus introduced emerges as a paramount characteristic of the book. It welds into a coherent whole the feelings, the impressions, the landscapes, and the people:

> А ти торкнулася чомусь мене тремтячою рукою,
> і чудотворними здавалися твої уста
> від хлипання свічок, де гнулись аналої
>
> під воском молитов, розтоплених на теплих і
>   вогких губах
> жінок, що простелялись по землі хрестами:
> і я схотів тебе.[12]

> You touched me with the trembling hand
> and your lips seemed miraculous
> through flickering sobs of candles bending
>
> over women lying cross-like on the ground
> whose prayers melted on their moist lips:
> then I desired you.

This personalized vision of Mexico, combined with the typical Boychuk metaphysical bent, yields poetry that foregrounds the emotive and existential aspects of human experience. It also points to the fragility and temporality of life:

---

12   Bohdan Boichuk, *Virshi dlia Mekhiko* (Munich: V-vo N'iu-Iorks'koi hrupy, 1964), 8.

Час затримався тут пів дороги,
задихнувся і впав на горі,
і проїде з обличчям серйозним і вбогим
темношкірий Христос на ослі.

А понурі, глухі барабани
б'ють у глиняні мозки домів,
що влипають до скель кам'яними хребтами,
і стікає череп'я з дахів

на вузькі вулиці. І свобідно
час не ступить сюди ні звідсіль,—
а простягнені в нутрощі руки по срібло
остигають на серці землі.[13]

Time pauses halfway up—
gasps and collapses on the hill.
A dark-skinned Christ rides a donkey
with a poor man's face.

Hollow drums beat over
the clay skulls of the houses
whose spines grow into the rocks;
rooftiles melt and flow

down narrow streets. Time
finds it hard to come or go,
and the hands grasping for silver
stiffen in the deep earth.[14]

Critics were not particularly generous to Boychuk following his debut in 1957. With the appearance of *Virshi dlia Mekhiko*, this trend was reversed. The book was warmly received and the reviews were positive. Iurii Dyvnych

13 Ibid., 16.
14 Translated by Mark Rudman in *Memories of Love: The Selected Poems of Bohdan Boychuk* (Riverdale-on-Hudson: Sheep Meadow Press, 1989), 93.

(a pseudonym of Lavrinenko), for example, praised this book for stylistic continuity:

> ... суцільність цього твору «Вірші для Мехіко» твориться всім: сюжетом, внутрішньою напругою єдности антитез і контрастів; важкуватим, мов кроки долі, ритмом; густим мов застигла кров колоритом, нарешті фаталістичним відтинком настрою, і диханням на всі велетенські легені цієї країни.[15]

> ... The continuity of this work, "Virshi dlia Mekhiko," unfolds on every level: on the level of subject matter; on the level of inner tension engendered by the unity between antitheses and contrasts; on the level of rhythm, heavy like the steps of fate; on the level of color, thick like a hardened blood; finally, on the level of atmosphere, tinged with fatality and breathed through the grand lungs of this country.

Boychuk reintroduced Spanish thematic material almost a decade later in the poem entitled "Dovha podorozh II" (A Long Journey II), which was included in his selected poems, published in 1983 (cf. his *Virshi, vybrani i peredostanni*, 120-22). "Dovha podorozh" represents a series of interwoven narrative and lyrical reminiscences following the trip to Spain Boychuk made in 1969. Yet these prose poems and song-like interludes transcend a mere descriptiveness and, in fact, contain very few references to the actual places visited. The poet does mention Toledo, Granada, and Valencia, but in the main he is interested not so much in conveying the picturesque details of Spanish cities as in poetically re-creating the atmosphere and spirit of the Spanish people, interlaced with his own meditations on love, death, and God. Boychuk's "Dovha podorozh" truly matches Paz's characterization of Spanish poetry mentioned earlier: it is itself "a funereal dance," "erotic dancing" as well as "a mystical flight."

Undoubtedly, at the core of the New York Group's Spanish phenomenon lies the poetry of Yuriy Tarnawsky and Patricia Kylyna. Both have become fluent in the language, both actually went to Spain and lived there for more than a year, and finally, both published books directly related to that sojourn. Here is how Kylyna describes this experience:

---

15 Iurii Dyvnych, "Mekhikans'ko-ukrains'ke vydyvo v poezii Bohdana Boichuka," *Lysty do pryiateliv* 13.8-10 (1965): 25.

Yuriy and I were in and out of Spain frequently between 1964 and 1971. We went there because we wanted to take a sabbatical from our jobs and Spain was then the cheapest place in Europe to live (the peseta was then very devalued against the dollar), but also because we wanted to immerse ourselves in Spanish culture. We lived there full time for a year and a half, from 1964 into mid-1965, and spent a month of every year there after that, till 1972. During those years we traveled all over Spain … there was hardly a remote corner that we didn't poke into, enjoying the diversity of Spain's cultural and ethnic heritage.[16]

Patricia Kylyna's third book, *Rozhevi mista* (The Pink Cities, 1969), reflects this diversity aptly and refreshingly. These poems could also be labeled "poetic travelogues," since they mainly describe the visited places, yet the treatment of the subject, unlike in the case of Vira Vovk's poetry, is exhaustive and very personal. The moods, attitudes, and everyday details of city life observed during the numerous trips, are almost always used for subjective effects. Kylyna not only captures the beauty of Spanish cities but also presents her own reflections. Stylistically diverse, often written in long but flexible lines, *Rozhevi mista* foregrounds the narrative approach to poetry and thereby points to Kylyna's natural tendency toward storytelling. The contemporary scene is frequently blended with historic, literary, and art references as, for instance, in the poem "Toledo:"

> Ель Ґреко каже правду: Толедо підноситься
> у небо так, як він його намалював.
> Я входжу в картину, немов крізь дзеркало:
> на вулиці люди стають обнаженими святими,
> і там, на червоних горбах за Толедо,
> під оливами, непритомніють тисячі Христів.
> У вітрі, бешкет оксамитних шат. Скляні очі.
> Тіла видовжуються, відлітають. Відрубують
> голову
> римському воїнові. Золоті ґотицькі вівтарі
> верхом у низ.
> Собор відходить під вітрилами. З'єднуються
> полумені

16 E-mail to the author, 10 Jan. 2000.

двох свічок. Світло! Екстаза! Шизофренія!
Наркомани! Астигматизм! І раптом
таксі пролітає крізь шати, трублячи страшно,
і лишаються вузькі вулиці, що тхнуть сечею і
       ладаном,
і базар, де продають арабський посуд, капусту і
       дзеркала.

Недаром Ель Ґреко, коли хотів
малювати портрети апостолів,
шукав натурників у божевільні Толедо.[17]

El Greco was right. Toledo lifts up toward
the sky exactly the way he painted it.
I enter the painting as if through a mirror:
people on the streets become bare saints,
and on the red hills outside Toledo,
thousands of Christs faint under olive trees.
In the wind's a turmoil of velvet garments. Glassy eyes.
The bodies elongate and fly off. A Roman warrior
is beheaded. The golden Gothic altars hang upside down.
A cathedral sails away. The flames of two candles
unite. Light! Ecstasy! Schizophrenia!
Drug addicts! Astigmatism! Suddenly
a taxi cab flies through honking viciously,
then only narrow streets remain, smelling of urine and incense,
and the marketplace where Arabic pottery, cabbage and
       mirrors are sold.

No wonder that El Greco
when painting apostles,
looked for models in a madhouse.

---

17   Patrytsiia Kylyna, *Rozhevi mista* (Munich: Suchasnist', 1969), 27.

Rozhevi mista also includes two long poems, often considered Kylyna's best poetic works in Ukrainian, entitled "Polum'ianyi byk" (Fiery Bull) and "Plach na smert' Antoniia Risa Pastora" (Lament for Antonio Riso Pastor).[18] Both deal with the famous Spanish tradition of bullfighting. The intensity of tragedy and level of empathy expressed in these two poems are in harmony with the mastery of language and freshness of images. But underlying all this is the pervasively existentialist theme of death with its absurdity and randomness, related poetically in a manner that mixes compassion, anger, and awe.

Yuriy Tarnawsky's passion for things Spanish has found many outlets. Thematically, there are many allusions to Spain even in his early collections, most notably in *Popoludni v Pokipsi* (Afternoons in Poughkeepsie, 1960), but the culmination arrived in 1969 with the publication of his prose poem collection *Bez Espanii* (Without Spain). In this book (highly experimental in its conception), the vision of Spain is internalized to the point that it dissolves into various parts of the lyrical hero's body. This "anatomical" approach underscores the obsessiveness of reminiscences over a farewell with a lover, i.e. Spain, and at the same time elevates body rather than mind as a source of memories.

Bez Espanii has a well-defined structure. Part One is composed as a series of poems depicting various phases of departure and arrival, thereby contrasting the beauty of the lost lover (Spain) with a mundane existence in the United States, but both come about not so much as descriptions of external realities of either country but rather as verbalizations of internal states of the lyrical hero, rooted in the unconscious and the irrational. Part Two consists of a series of addresses directed to specific places in Santander (a city in which Tarnawsky and Kylyna resided while in Spain) as well as to other Spanish cities, interspersed with a number of interludes titled "Tysha" (Silence), in which the lyrical hero is transported back to the present time. However, whether we are dealing with the hero's reminiscences or his "here and now," both are conveyed in a manner relying on a freely associative stream of consciousness. Frequent surrealist juxtapositions occasionally undermine the poems' logic and comprehensibility as, for example, in the excerpt below:

---

18 Kylyna's "Lament for Antonio Riso Pastor" was originally published in *Novi Poezii*, no. 8 (1966).

Звернення V

(Валенсія)

Чи в килимі, чи в моїх костях, чи в цій фарбі, близькій до паперу і недалекій від крови, міститься твій вогонь і простір, що відбулися без моїх уст, і моє обличчя? Я переступаю слова, і думки, і свою шкіру, і напрямлюю руки до твоєї води, що витекла крізь дельти площ до шкаралущ паристих чисел і океанів, та знаходжу лише поверхні в моїх пальцях, і папір у моїх устах, і квадрат килима, який намарне намагається вмістити моє тіло. О, поверни до мене обличчя твоєї речовини, і збери полки моїх кроків і усмішок, помножених твоїми вітами, які я зоставив на твоїх тінях і цеглі, і згуртуй свої рухомі білі мости, і пальми, з вершниками в вітах і в корінні, і безстрашні музеї з моторизованими картинами, і пошли їх мені на поміч, до піль бою під моїми нігтями і на моїх вилицях![19]

Address V

(Valencia)

Is it in the rug or in my bones, or, perhaps, in this ink close to the sheet of paper and my blood that your fire and space are held without my lips and face? I pass beyond words, thoughts, and my skin, directing my hand to your water which ran out through the delta of squares to the shells of even numbers and oceans, but I find only the surfaces of my fingers and a paper in my mouth, and a contour of the rug which in vain strives to hold my body. Oh, turn to me the face of your substance, and gather the regiments of my steps and smiles, multiplied by your branches which I left in the shadows and in the bricks, unite your white drawbridges and palm trees with riders in the branches and in the roots, and fearless museums with motorized paintings and send them all to help me in the battlefields under my nails and on my cheek-bones!

When *Bez Espanii* was first published in *Suchasnist'*, it triggered a flow of angry letters from the readers, forcing the editor–in–chief, Wolfram Burghardt, to conduct an interview with Yuriy Tarnawsky in order to dispel at least some of the concerns brought forth. This interview, provocatively titled "Bez Espanii chy bez znachennia?" (Without Spain or Without Meaning?), dealt with issues concerning the communicative role of poetry and, to some extent, forced Tarnawsky to explain his approach to poetry in general and in *Bez Espanii* in particular. The poet emphasized the significance of perception on an emotional rather than rational level, and reiterated the fact that this long

---

19 Iurii Tarnavs'kyi, *Bez Espanii* (Munich: Suchasnist', 1969), 41.

poem reflects his emotional state following the departure from Spain. It becomes clear from the context that the "emotional level" Tarnawsky refers to is essentially equal to what is generally called the unconscious. Disregarding his quite idiosyncratic views on reception (whereby the reader ought to be able to re-create the author's emotions and, as it stands, has very little autonomy), the fact remains that the real subject of the poet's texts is he himself:

... я хотів вглибитися в свою свідомість, віднайти те, що я шукав, закодувати це в найпростішій мові, і це все. Тоді я припускав і далі припускаю, що коли хтось читатиме ці картини, вони відтворять у нього, на емоційному рівні, емоції приблизно того роду, що й мої.[20]

... I wanted to penetrate deep into my own consciousness, to find there something I was looking for, to encode it in the simplest language, and that is it. I assumed then, and still assume, that when someone reads these pieces, s/he will re-create on the emotional level emotions approximately of the same kind as my own.

When in the mid-1970s, inspired by the trip he made to Mexico in 1975, Tarnawsky re-introduced Spanish American motifs in his poetry, he did so as a background for unfolding his own personal drama (with all its emotions and concerns), rather than for sharing his own impressions. As in *Bez Espanii*, Mexico becomes for him a mere pretext for dealing with his own subjectivity. The text I am referring to is titled "Operene sertse" (Fledged Heart).[21] This long poem, comprised of seventeen short-line parts, gives very few details about the places visited. In fact, if not for the author's footnotes,[22] one could hardly (if at all) guess what region or city the poet alludes to (cf. parts 1-4; 6-10; 12). But even the poems that include references to specific places (like those, for example, about Mexico City) lack the reality of a concrete geographical entity. The poet does not reflect the city, or its people, or its

20 Iurii Tarnavs'kyi, "Bez Espanii chy bez znachennia?," *Suchasnist'* 12 (1969): 14.

21 The poem has had three printings so far. Originally, it was published in *Suchasnist'* 1-2, 4 (1986). It was then reprinted in the book of selected poems *Bez nichoho*, published in Kyiv by the "Dnipro" Publishing House in 1991. Finally, the third edition (which I am using here) was included in *Ikh nemaie*, published also in Kyiv in 1999.

22 The only edition of "Operene sertse" that includes the explanatory footnotes is the one included in *Ikh nemaie*.

atmosphere, but rather it is the city that reflects him and his inner emotional states. In this poem the only clue we have that the action takes place in Mexico City is the title, for it includes a reference to the "Pink Zone," a fashionable district in the Mexican capital. Otherwise, what we encounter here are not the details and dynamics of the Pink Zone, but personal, inexorably existential, struggles to make life livable and meaningful.

It is evident from the poems analyzed above that each poet of the New York Group who has incorporated Spanish and/or Spanish American content in his/her poetry, approached it differently and utilized it for various effects. I argue, however, that underlying this "Spanish turn" among them (no matter how heterogeneous on the surface) was their being very much in tune with the prevailing trends and tastes within the literary establishment in the United States or in the West in general. In 1954, the Nobel Prize in literature was awarded to Ernest Hemingway, a writer who happened to be a champion for things Spanish in American literature.[23] Two years later, the same prize went to the Spanish poet Juan Ramón Jiménez. The poetry of Pablo Neruda and Cesar Vallejo was widely admired and extensively translated by such young (at the time) American poets as Robert Bly and James Wright. These are but a few instances indicating a rather pervasive fascination with Spanish culture at the time of the New York Group's formation. Patricia Kylyna conveys this climate quite succinctly:

> Typically, liberal and leftie young American writers of the 1950s and 1960s admired whatever they could learn of leftie and liberal European and Latin American poetry. It was part of a new internationalism in young U.S. vision, and an effort to end our Yankee parochialism. The New York Group members had similar tastes and vision, though their internationalism came from being dragged through various countries as war refugee children, and speaking various languages to survive. So García Lorca and Neruda were big favorites with the New York Group.[24]

Therefore, the variety of translation projects that the members of the group were involved in reflected as much their own personal tastes as those that were generally in literary vogue at the time. Reading extensively Spanish-

---

23 Tarnawsky admitted, for instance, that he liked *Death in the Afternoon* very much and that it was one of the reasons he went to Spain.

24 E-mail to the author, 10 Jan. 2000.

language poetry, rendering it into Ukrainian, and keeping step with the prevailing literary trends had a tremendous impact on the emergence and poetic growth of each poet thus discussed. Again, this impact varies from poet to poet. Nevertheless, the influences on the formative level are discernible and worthy of closer scrutiny.

Thematically and stylistically, Tarnawsky's early poetry, and especially his first collection, *Zhyttia v misti* (Life in the City, 1956), can be traced back to Pablo Neruda. Tarnawsky himself draws a parallel here, noting that the title of his first book was suggested by Neruda's *Residencia en la tierra* (Life on Earth, 1933), but he is unwilling to go further than that: "I was haunted by the topic of death and Neruda's poetry seemed to release me from it because it dealt with it. When I put together 'Life in the City' I think the title was partly suggested by his 'Residencia en la tierra.' But it also alluded to the subject of a large industrialized city, which stifled me after the peaceful Ulm in Germany, and to existentialism ('life')."[25] However, when in 1958 Patricia Kylyna submitted her own and Tarnawsky's poems for publication in the journal *The Fifties*, this is the response she received from the editor, Robert Bly:

> In the case of Mr. Tarnawsky's book, I think the translations are good, and the poetry shows great ability, but when I read many of them together, they seem to me too much like Neruda. A group of poems not only creates images and music, but also a personality which stands behind the poems. I think when we say poetry is new, we mean that behind it, we can sense a new personality created by it. But behind these poems the personality I see, as in the third part of "Thoughts About My Death," is not new to me, but one I have seen before in Neruda. This is not surprising or terrible; you both are very young, but I think I would try to get rid of these echoes; and I think gradually, as you write more, the poetry will become more and more like yourself, with much more of your own accent, and I would definitely like to see more later.[26]

What connects Neruda's *Residencia en la tierra* and Tarnawsky's *Zhyttia v misti* is the same existential anguish expressed as the individual's doomed struggle to overcome alienation, because he is destined to be an outsider, facing in the end nothing but his own death. The enchantment with

---

25 E-mail to the author, 26 Dec.1999.
26 Letter to Patricia Kylyna, 5 May 1959. Iurii Tarnavs'kyi Papers, Rare Book and Manuscript Library, Columbia University, New York.

existentialism and profound pessimism found in *Zhyttia v misti* is as pronounced as it is in Neruda's poetry. Yet this thematic affinity is complemented also by the closeness in poetic style, including versification techniques and syntax. According to Marjorie Agosin, "the techniques characteristic of *Residence on Earth* are the syncopated use of words, the absence of adverbs and adjectives, and the constant use of similes that invoke incongruous images."[27] Tarnawsky's love for the use of similes, anaphoras, and prosaic rhetoric (labeled by Rubchak as "anti-poetry"[28]) might have found in Neruda's poetry a source of inspiration, for these poetic devices are the hallmarks of the latter's poetry as well. One can definitely say that by the time *Bez Espanii* appeared, Tarnawsky had managed to cast away Nerudian echoes. Yet this Chilean poet was no doubt his hero in the beginning of his poetic career, and someone who, in some ways, haunted him throughout much of his adult life, despite the poet's declarations to the contrary.[29] But, like *Residencia en la tierra* to Spanish-language poetry, *Zhyttia v misti* undeniably introduced a new modern diction to poetry in Ukrainian.

As for the other two poets I have mainly focused on in this section, Bohdan Boychuk and Patricia Kylyna, one can say that they too have had their own favorite Spanish poets. Kylyna was undoubtedly at first influenced by the poetry of Federico García Lorca. There is enough "green" imagery in her poems to remind us of Lorca's famous: "Green, oh how I love you green." Unmistakably, his "green" transcends mere color. It refers to a state of mind, which is indefinable and irrational. Kylyna's images "zelenyi bil'" (green pain), "zelena krov" (green blood), "zelena literatura" (green literature), "zabuty zelenity" (to forget how to turn green), not unlike similar expressions in Lorca, foreground a certain ineffability associated with this word.

---

27 Marjorie Agosin, *Pablo Neruda*, trans. Lorraine Roses (Boston: Twayne, 1986), 40.

28 Cf. Bohdan Rubchak, "Poeziia antypoezii: Zahal'ni obrysy Iurii Tarnavs'koho," *Suchasnist'* 4 (1968): 44-55.

29 On many occasions Tarnawsky made statements that it is Rimbaud, not Neruda, who is his favorite poet (Cf. "Bez Espanii chy bez znachennia?," 25). Yet the quality that is particularly striking in both Neruda and Tarnawsky is their constant need to search for a new method of expression. Like Neruda, Tarnawsky has had many turns in his poetic development: the anguished existentialist of *Zhyttia v misti*, the experimenter of *Bez Espanii*, and the politically committed intellectual of *U ra na*, to name just a few. However, unlike the mature Neruda, who in his late poetry refused to take himself seriously, Tarnawsky has never really been able to dispense with existential heaviness.

Her long poem "Lament for Antonio Riso Pastor" is more likely modeled on Lorca's "Lament for Ignacio Sanchez Mejias," but here she has brought so much of her own background and personality that it is impossible to accuse her of any kind of imitation. Lorca's "Lament" is elegiac, somewhat stylized (especially the first part, with an obsessively repeated line "at five o'clock in the afternoon"), and stylistically diverse (the poet switches from free-flowing lines in the first two parts to more formal stanzaic arrangement in part three and four). Kylyna's poem, by contrast, written in long versatile lines, is stylistically homogenous; moreover, it exudes unity and continuity in terms of both tone (direct and personal) and approach (narrative).

The influences of Spanish and/or Spanish-American poets on Bohdan Boychuk's formative beginnings are less obvious. Arguably, Juan Ramón Jiménez, with his almost religious reverence for poetry, left a mark on Boychuk's philosophical and artistic premises. The poets share a preoccupation with such eternally poetic themes as love, woman, and death. Yet stylistically, this thematic affinity becomes less manifest, especially when one juxtaposes Jiménez's lyricism and serenity with Boychuk's propensity for dramatic effects. Here is how the poet himself describes his involvement in things Spanish:

> Я завжди відчував, що існує глибока емоційна співзвучність між українцями й еспанцями. Тому й захоплювався еспанською й особливо еспаномовною, тобто південно-американською, літературами. Можливо, це відчуття було витвором моєї уяви, але цього вистачало, щоб, їдучи на початках шістдесятих років до Мехіко, я був навстіж відкритий для чуда. І чудо сталося. Мехіканські історичні краєвиди, їхня мітологія, їхні перекази й побут натхнули образи, музику і зміст мого циклу *Вірші для Мехіко*. Точно те саме відноситься до другої частини циклу «Довга подорож», який постав під час моєї подорожі по Еспанії наприкінці шістдесятих років.[30]

I've always felt that there is a deep emotional affinity between Ukrainians and Spaniards. That is why I've been fascinated with Spanish and especially Spanish-language, i.e. Latin American, literatures. Perhaps, that feeling was the product of my own imagination, but that was enough for me to open myself up for a miracle when I went to Mexico in the early 1960s. And the miracle did happen. Mexican historical sites, their mythology, legends, a people's way of life gave a spur to the images, music and subject matter of my

---

30   E-mail to the author, 25 Dec. 1999.

cycle *Poems for Mexico*. The same can be said about my second part of the cycle "A Long Journey," which came forth during my trip to Spain at the end of the 1960s.

It is interesting to note that Dyvnych (Lavrinenko), in his review of Boychuk's *Virshi dlia Mekhiko*, also tried to find parallels between Ukrainian and Mexican mentalities, as if justifying before the émigré reading public the poet's thematic choice:

> Що ж може бути спільне між Мехіко і Україною? Про якусь подібність між ними говорить чимало українців, які відвідали Мехіко. Може, це поєднання багатої природи з бідною колоніяльною долею? Може, незмірна глибина історії—через конквістадорів і ацтеків аж до майї, як у нас—через вікінгів до трипільців? Може, насиченість цієї історії і землі кров'ю, стражданнями, видержливістю? Може, та вільність, що в найстрашніших іспитах зберігає силу любити і виявити ту любов у ліричному мистецтві, поруч із монументалізмом?[31]

> What could Ukraine and Mexico possibly have in common? Many Ukrainians who traveled to Mexico talk about some kind of affinity. Is it perhaps a combination of luxuriant nature with the poverty of colonial fate? Or, is it an immeasurable depth of history—stretching from the conquistadors through Aztecs to Maya, or like in our case—from the Vikings to Trypilians? Or, is it perhaps this saturation of history and soil with the blood, suffering, and endurance? Or, is it a vitality, which under most trying circumstances preserves the strength to love and manifests this love in the lyrical arts side by side with the monumentalism?

Notwithstanding Lavrinenko's rather unconvincing argument (ascribing to *Virshi dlia Mekhiko* a "monumentalism"), his insistence on finding correspondences between Ukrainian and Mexican cultures is quite emblematic; he is simply displaying the symptoms of an émigré condition.

As the poetic excerpts above illustrate, the poets' embrace of Hispanic cultures was intense and tangible. Their love for Spanish language literatures found its expression in poetic explorations of Spanish content as well as in numerous translations they undertook. That work was not a call of duty. Rather, it stemmed from their deeply-felt need for expansive experiences. Spain (or Spanish America), with its proud people and bullfighting tradition of defying

---

31   Dyvnych, "Mekhikans'ko-ukrains'ke vydyvo," 27.

death, offered them an unusual escape from the narrow confines of exile. They have always considered themselves citizens of the Western world who simply happened to come from Ukraine. In fact, it should be pointed out that the poets' gravitation toward Spanish motifs had a definite rebellious ring to it. The "Spanish turn" was yet another challenge to the expectations of the émigré community.

Freedom of expression, including an unrestricted selection of themes, has always been at the heart of the New York Group's activity. The emergence of the "Spanish School" phenomenon, unique in Ukrainian literature, has been a byproduct of that artistic freedom, longed for and practiced by all the poets of the group. Clearly, underlying this "Spanish turn" among the members of the New York Group was, on the one hand, a reluctance on their part to allow themselves to be ensnared in the typically émigré nostalgia, and, on the other hand, an identification with the cosmopolitan mode and mood of the modernist and avant-garde movements, particularly of Spanish and Latin American provenance. No one can accuse these poets of not loving their own country, but they have always felt at home in America, in Mexico, or, for that matter, in Spain. The "Spanish School" phenomenon of the New York Group, as I have attempted to delineate it here, happens to be but a guise of the poets' deeply-felt and espoused internationalism.

CHAPTER 7

Transforming Desire: The Many Faces of Eroticism

In the poem "Kinets' dnia" (The Day's End), Bohdan Boychuk celebrates life through erotic activity and underscores its undeniable worthiness in the face of unavoidable death:

> віддай
> мені в долоні теплоту
> м'якого голосу,
> і синій трепет крови,
> і галузку тіла:
> все віддай,
> ....
> аж поки темними устами ніч
> не вип'є пісню твого тіла,
> поки не оставить лиш
> холодну пам'ять костей[1]

---

1   Bohdan Boichuk, *Spomyny liubovy* (New York: V-vo N'iu-Iorks'koi hrupy, 1963), 11.

give back
into my hands the warmth
of your soft voice,
and blue trembling of your blood,
and a branch of body:
give back to me everything,

....

until the night with dark lips
does not drink out the song of your body,
until it does not leave just
the cold memory of bones

This poem inadvertently elaborates and complements Georges Bataille's understanding of eroticism. Eroticism, he says, "is assenting to life even in death." Bataille was aware that such a formulation might appear too general, so he qualified it further:

> Strictly speaking, this is not a definition, but I think the formula gives the meaning of eroticism better than any other. If a precise definition were called for, the starting-point would certainly have to be sexual reproductive activity, of which eroticism is a special form. Sexual reproductive activity is common to sexual animals and men, but only men appear to have turned their sexual activity into erotic activity. Eroticism, unlike simple sexual activity, is a psychological quest independent of the natural goal: reproduction and the desire for children.[2]

Interestingly, his broad formula found its devotees.

Eroticism, understood as something that is "more than sex, more than life, more than death,"[3] to use Octavio Paz's formulation, is one of those thematic forces that figures quite prominently in the poetry of the New York Group and brings a substantial degree of unity into the group's otherwise stylistically diverse poetic production. Erotic motifs permeate the works of all the members of the group. The eroticism of their poetic texts from the "vocal"

---

2   Georges Bataille, *Erotism: Death and Sensuality*, trans. Mary Dalwood (San Francisco: City Lights, 1986), 11.

3   Octavio Paz, *An Erotic Beyond: Sade*, trans. Eliot Weinberger (New York: Harcourt, 1998), 20.

period (1950s and 1960s) is saturated with a similar, if not identical, body of signifying information. Understandably, the extent, intensity, and measure of explicitness in utilizing sexual content vary considerably from one poet to another. In fact, it is even possible to divide the group into two camps: those poets who openly and consciously experimented with the various aspects of erotica (Andijewska, Boychuk, and Tarnawsky), and those for whom eroticism emerges as a kind of "behind-the-scenes" compulsion, inferred from the tension between the symbolically libidinal images and their contextual position, rather than expressed by sexually explicit poetic language (Rubchak, Vovk, Kylyna, and Vasylkivska).

This chapter argues that despite a seeming unevenness in emphasis, the erotic imagery brought forth by the poets of the New York Group became for them a vehicle for conveying existentialist views, especially the need for freedom and responsibility for each individual choice. The weight and discursiveness of such a posture, that is, an open advocacy of an existentialist platform, points to yet another important component in the way the erotic metaphor was employed by the poets under scrutiny, namely their almost combative willingness to probe the boundaries of the transgressive, the taboo, and the Other.[4] It is within the framework of these two aspects, existentialism on the one hand and transgression on the other, that the eroticism evinced in the poetry of each individual member of the group will be analyzed.

The broad formulations regarding eroticism quoted above perhaps do not give justice to Bataille's and Paz's understanding of the term. However, these formulations do signal their general orientation, which sees eroticism as the point of tension or instability in the nature/culture opposition. For Paz,

---

4   These terms play a significant role in Georges Bataille's conceptualization of erotism. For him transgression was an "inner experience" inseparable from the consciousness of the constraint or prohibition it violates, because "there exists no prohibition that cannot be transgressed" (*Erotism*, 63). In other words, it is only through the transgression that the force of a prohibition becomes fully realized. By valorizing the aesthetics of transgression, the members of the New York Group unveiled a host of constraints and restrictions imposed on them by the émigré milieu in the realm of subject matter or forms of language. Whereas the erotic necessarily entails some violation of sexual taboos, one should emphasize that in the case of the New York Group and its particular set of social and historical circumstances, the existentialist turn on their part was already viewed in and of itself as "transgressive," regardless of whether or not it was coiled with any aspect of eroticism.

eroticism is "socialized sexuality"[5] because it unfolds in society and in history. He further states: "What distinguishes a sexual act from an erotic one is that, in the former, nature serves the species, while in the latter, human society is served by nature."[6] Bataille also elaborates his initial formula: "Human eroticism differs from animal sexuality precisely in this, that it calls inner life to play. In human consciousness, eroticism is that within man which calls his being into question."[7]

There is an unmistakable parallel between the erotic experience and the awareness of death: both belong exclusively to the domain of the human. Thus eroticism inexorably reveals the nature of the human predicament. On the one hand, it points to man's simultaneous desire for continuity and discontinuity; on the other, it entails "a fusion with the animal world and a rupture, a separation from that world, an irremediable solitude"[8]—that is, a desire to follow an instinct and, at the same time, to obey a set of prohibitions imposed by society. The existential character of that dialectic cannot be overlooked. Bataille's conception of the erotic as "assenting to life even in death" found a fascinating realization in the New York Group's poetic output. Like the surrealists, many members of the group placed eroticism (love) at the center of their attention and used it subversively as a tool in their rebellion against the aesthetic entrenched within the émigré community in which they were active.

It is impossible to understand the New York Group's eroticism without looking closely at its love poetry. In fact, the group's erotica and love poetry are inextricably intertwined simply because of the latter's unmistakable sensuality. Not only are the carnal and the instinctual at the core of many love poems offered by the group, but, more importantly, they also insinuate novel significations. The fact that the poets of the New York Group incorporated erotica in their creative work fails to constitute any particular innovation on their part. The unique in their work can be found exclusively within the sphere of signification.

Regardless of its explicitness in depicting sexuality, erotica very often transcends this sexuality, and by doing so transports the reader/viewer into a

---

5   Octavio Paz, *The Double Flame: Love and Eroticism*, trans. Helen Lane (New York: Harcourt, 1993), 8.
6   Paz, *An Erotic Beyond*, 12.
7   Bataille, *Erotism: Death and Sensuality*, 29.
8   Paz, *An Erotic Beyond*, 17.

different plane of meaning. The passage or leap from the level of representation (or mimesis, to use Michael Riffaterre's terminology[9]) to the level of significance is not always straightforward. In order to facilitate the leap from the mimetic level to that of significance, Riffaterre introduces the concept of the hypogram. Serving as the generator of the poetic text, the hypogram is the original semantic matrix, indispensable to the process of interpretation. It can consist of a word, a phrase, a cliché, a quote, an intricate thematic complex, or a string of associations, which on the mimetic level discernibly break off and fragment. The peculiar dissonance by which they are differentiated within the text draws the reader's attention toward the symbolic key, which reveals the structure of the meaning.

It would be erroneous to claim that erotica dominates the poetry of Emma Andijewska. But in her 1961 collection, *Ryba i rozmir* (Fish and Dimension), she delivered a cycle of homoerotic poems entitled "Dionisii" (Dionysia). The debut of this cycle was actually realized through the imaginary persona of Aristidimos Likhnos, invented by the author herself, who even endowed her created character with a short biography. The very fact of such literary mystification conceals within itself an unusual, if not extraordinary, message for the critic. I argue that both the title "Dionisii" and this very mystification constitute the key to decoding the meaning of the entire cycle, or comprise its hypogram.

Andijewska's cycle "Dionisii" invokes the rituals connected to the Dionysian festivals in honor of the Hellenic god of fertility and wine.[10] Moreover, there is a reference to the ancient Greek rites and traditions, wherein homosexuality, and especially pederasty, was tolerated. Finally, it is impossible to overlook the association with Nietzsche's *The Birth of Tragedy* and the allusion to the Apollonian and the Dionysian aspects of the creative process. These intertexts provide a necessary context for interpretation. Thematically, "Dionisii" recounts the romantic obstacles and reversals of fortune experienced by the lyrical hero and his young lover. Following is one of the poems from the series, entitled "Napys na muri" (Sign on the Wall):

---

9   See his *Semiotics of Poetry* (Bloomington, IN: Indiana University Press, 1978).

10   As I indicated in Chapter 5, Andijewska calls this cycle "a jest." However, I intend to show here that there is more substance in these poems than the author's offhand remark would otherwise indicate.

Він, з гронами винограду в голосі,
Нехай залишить свою флейту
І підійде до мене.
Сьогодні я його любитиму,
Я, ім'я якого бояться вимовляти.
Нехай він скине одяг,
Що поганить його тіло,
І перестане червоніти, як дівчина,
Затуляючи руками
Свій божественний фаллос.
Сьогодні я його любитиму,
Я, ім'я якого соромляться вимовляти.[11]

He, with the clusters of grapes in his voice,
Let him abandon his flute
And come toward me.
Today I shall love him,
I, whose name they fear to speak.
Let him take off the clothing,
That defiles his body,
And cease blushing, like a girl,
With his hands
Covering his divine phallus.
Today I shall love him,
I, whose name they are ashamed to pronounce.[12]

With the exception of the first line, which clearly does not conform to the mimetic framework and which can be understood only in the context of the Dionysian cult of wine and its attendant emphasis on the cultivation of the grapevine, this poem strikes the reader with its prosaic directness, generally atypical to Andijewska's poetic style. The poem becomes delineated and acquires imagery in the dynamics of the choice faced by the lyrical hero's

---

11   Emma Andiievs'ka, *Ryba i rozmir* (New York: V-vo N'iu-Iorks'koi hrupy), 80.
12   Translated by Luba Gawur. Hereafter in this chapter all the excerpts translated by Gawur will be followed by her initials (LG).

object of desire: to either continue playing the flute, or to surrender to the act of lovemaking. Paradoxically, and herein lies the beauty of it, this choice is illusory, for both music and the delights of carnal knowledge, according to Nietzsche, spring from the selfsame Dionysian origin. There is truly only one choice: to be oneself, to be authentic and not ashamed of one's own personal power, as symbolized by the "divine phallus"—the source of creative energy and ecstasy. Freedom and choice lie at the core of existentialist thought, and there is no doubt that the erotica inherent in the "Dionisii" cycle projects these very principles. The following poem conveys the angst that is so characteristic of existentialists:

> Ти прийшов на моє ложе.
> Ти, якого я чекав від інших.
> Ти прийшов і лежиш,
> Сховавши фаллос між ногами,
> І виглядаючи зовсім, як жінка.
> Але ти помилився.
> Я сам, і твоя присутність
> Проходить крізь мене, як простирало.
> Я сам, і ти з жахом дивишся,
> Як від тиші
> Твоє тіло розпадається на помаранчеві голуби,
> Що зникають за вікном.[13]

You came to my bed.
You, for whom I waited from among others.
You came and reclined,
Having hidden your phallus between your legs,
And looking altogether like a woman.
But you are mistaken.
I am alone, and your presence
Passes through me like a bed sheet.
I am alone, and with awe you watch,

---

13   *Ryba i rozmir*, 88.

As from the silence
Your body disintegrates into orange doves,
Which disappear behind the window. (LG)

Neither love, nor the presence of another, is capable of surmounting the feeling of solitude. And this very much echoes what Bataille says in his seminal book on eroticism, namely that "when all is said and done that which in eroticism bears us to pinnacles of intensity also lays the curse of solitude upon us at the same time."[14] Ultimately, the self-realization of the incomprehensibility, even absurdity, of existence produces a numbing and encumbering effect. As always, it is death looming large on the horizon that speaks through and to the bodies embraced by Eros:

Епітафія

Ти не знав, що моїми вустами ходить смерть
І бахвалився серед товаришів своєю відвагою.
Тепер твоє тіло вивіває вітер крихту за
                                   крихтою,
Твоє рожеве тіло, що годувало голубів.
Твоє тіло ранніх заморозків, настурцій і
                              шафрану.
Ти мене бачив тільки два рази.
Тоді, коли я зупинив на тобі погляд,
Ти знав мою славу, і ти бахвалився своєю
                              відвагою.
Ти не знав, що моїми вустами ходить смерть.[15]

Epitaph

You did not know that death dwells in my mouth
And bragged about your courage among friends.
Now your body is dispersed by the wind bit
                              by bit.

---

14   *Erotism: Death and Sensuality*, 262.
15   *Ryba i rozmir*, 79.

Your pink body that fed the pigeons.
Your body of early frosts, nasturtium and
saffron.
You saw me only twice.
Then, when I rested my eyes on you,
You knew my fame, and you boasted of your
courage.
You did not know that death dwells in my mouth.

The stratification of existentialist constructs in Andijewska's erotica is masked, and for the most part concealed. Therefore the criticism that followed the publication of *Ryba i rozmir* focused on the outrageousness of the sexually explicit images rather than on the pessimism inherent in existentialist philosophy. Here is how Bohdan Boychuk describes the commotion in New York's circles in a letter to Andijewska:

> Your collection "Fish and Dimension" made a revolution in New York.... But let me get back to the "revolution"—it all began at the "Slovo" meeting—Halyna Zhurba and Humenna were almost jumping out of anger, excommunicating you from literature, and Kostiuk, the archpriest, said: "Well, how is it possible that a man apparently tosses his rotten phallus from hand to hand, etc." Well, I sat there with satisfaction and only from time to time poured oil on troubled waters highly praising the collection. But Halyna and Humenna were jumping even higher. They decided to print a rebuttal in the [newspaper] "Svoboda," denying that it is the "Slovo's" publication. (By the way, why did you use their logo? This is our publication and we have our own logo.) Afterwards, when Lasovsky's son read your collection and lost his innocence, Lasovsky with great outrage wrote an apostolic epistle to "Svoboda," questioning your morality. I responded to him (it will be published in "Lysty do pryiateliv"). Moreover, Lesych read to me his review of the collection (good), which should soon be published (I still don't know where). In other words, your book became a legend.[16]

---

16 Letter to Andiievs'ka, 5 Nov. 1961, Emma Andiievs'ka Papers, Columbia University, New York. The original text reads: "Твоя збірка "Риба і розмір" зробила цілу революцію в Нью-Йорку. ... Але вернуся до "революції"—почалось на сходинах "Слова"—Галина Журба і Гуменна аж підскакували з люті, виклинаючи Тебе з літератури, а архиєрей Костюк каже: 'ну як можна, це немовби чоловік перекидав з долоні в долоню гнилого фалоса ... іт. д.' Ну я собі з задоволенням сидів і тільки час-від-часу доливав вогню, високо

Lesych's review[17] referred to in Boychuk's letter represents an apology of sorts or justification for Andijewska's explicit homoeroticism. The author of the review runs the gamut of well-known works in world literature and art that incorporate erotic motifs in order to defend Andijewska's artistic position. While Lesych admits that Andijewska's "spirit of rebelliousness" makes her poetry inaccessible to an average reader and, de facto, necessarily feeds the perceptions of her elitist inclinations, he fails to notice the existentialist premises of such a rebellious stance on her part.[18]

Unlike in the case of Andijewska's oeuvre, the existentialism intrinsic to the poetry of Yuriy Tarnawsky is obvious and consistent. In his collection of poems *Idealizovana biohrafiia* (Idealized Biography, 1964), which fuses the amorous and erotic into an indissoluble whole, the optimism of the lyrical hero and his faith in love are progressively superseded by the angst so typical of existentialists:

вихваляючи збірку, а Галина і Гуменна тоді вище підскакували. Рішили вони подати спростування в *Свободі*, що це не видання Слова. (До речі пощо Ти ставила їхній значок? Це наше видання, і в нас є свій значок). Опісля, як син Ласовського прочитав Твою збірку і втратив невинність, Ласовський з великим обуренням написав у *Свободі* апостольське посланіє, викидаючи Тебе з моральних людей. Я відповів йому (буде надруковане в *Листах до приятелів*). Крім того Лесич читав мені рецензію (добру) на збірку, яка скоро появиться (не знаю ще де). Одним словом, Твоя книжка стала леґендою."
Boychuk's response to Lasovsky's letter in "Svoboda" was never published, as the poet himself clarified in a subsequent letter to Andijewska: "Моєї статті в обороні "Риби" ніхто не схотів містити, але Лесич дав дуже вдалу оцінку книжки в "Листах до приятелів", і Барка ніби збирається відповідати. Якщо будеш щаслива—то попадеш на католицький індекс!..." (10 Feb. 1962, Emma Andiievs'ka Papers, Rare Book and Manuscript Library, Columbia University, New York). ("No one wanted to publish my article in defense of your 'Fish,' but Lesych contributed a very apt evaluation of the book in 'Lysty do pryiateliv,' and Barka, apparently, is thinking to respond. If you are lucky—you might be included in Index Librorum Prohibitorum!...") Boychuk's offhand tone and the use of the ecclesiastical terminology (e.g., calling the critic, Kostiuk, an archpriest) in his letters to Andijewska only underscores his overall satisfaction with and, not so oddly, sarcastic enjoyment of the controversy surrounding one of the New York Group's publications.
17 See his "Andiievs'ka, Kylyna, Iurii Tarnavs'kyi," *Lysty do pryiateliv* 9.11-12 (1961): 26-29.
18 Existentialism as a source of poetic inspiration notably recedes in Andijewska's late poetry. For example, her 1985 collection *Spokusy Sviatoho Antoniia* (The Temptations of St. Anthony), whose eroticism is implied rather than expressed, lacks any existentialist subtext. It is written in a manner more typical to Andijewska's poetic style; the poetry in this book (exclusively in the sonnet form) is playful, associative, occasionally grotesque, and opaque.

XLII

Не вірю,
що тебе кохаю,
що хочу засвітити
свічі
моїх очей
ясним полум'ям
твоїх
що хочу розплескати
свої уста
і пам'ять
об м'який ґраніт
твойого рота!

Лежу,
й завжди
остануся лежати
у чорній ямі
мого серця.[19]

I don't believe,
that I love you,
that I want to light
the candles
of my eyes
with the bright flames
of yours
that I want to smash
my lips
and consciousness
against the soft granite
of your mouth!

---

19 Iurii Tarnavs'kyi, *Idealizovana biohrafiia* (Munich: Suchasnist', 1964), 46.

I lay,
and shall always
remain lying
in the black hole
of my heart. (LG)

The mimesis in this poem is destroyed by the phrase "candles/ of my eyes" and this refutation of representation culminates with the oxymoron "the soft granite/ of your mouth!" The parallelisms "I don't believe,/ that I love you,/ that I want to light [...]/ that I want to smash" should, it seems, underscore a certain level of determination and steadfastness, yet they actually signal nothing but the lyrical hero's profound doubt, which is, as it were, kindled by the possibility of a choice. For the luminosity of love's flame truly entices, and despite his words the lyrical hero craves this luminosity. Nevertheless, "the granite/ ... mouth," i.e., the a priori conviction of the unattainability of genuine interaction or intercommunication with the beloved (very much in line with the Sartrean notion of relationship as perpetual conflict), thrusts him inevitably toward loneliness. There, the heart transmutes into a black hole, thus contorting and corrupting its conventional symbolism. Again, ultimately, in the face of death, each person always stands alone. Yet the illusion that the act of love-making (no matter how poisonous—in fact, the more poisonous the better, for the resulting death is viewed as a supreme liberator) mutes an unfathomable absence is nevertheless strongly upheld by the poet:

XLIII

Де ти?
У лябіринті
твого тіла
тебе шукаю.
Немов луна,
літають
мої руки
по білих коридорах
твоїх членів.

Знайти,
як келех
холодної отрути,
твої уста,
і притиснути
до своїх ...

До самого кінця,
до смерти![20]

Where are you?
I'm looking for you
in the labyrinths
of your body.
Like an echo
my hands
fly over
the white corridors
of your limbs.

To find
like a chalice
of cold poison
your lips
and press them
to mine ...
To the very end,
to death!

Lovemaking, like death, is absurd because of its leveling inevitability and insipid commonality:

---

20 Ibid., 47.

моя любов
банальна,
як смак банана
в роті,
та я мушу
цілувати
холодні уста
моєї дівчини,
доторкатись пальцями
її шкіри,
як цитрина, твердої,
і казати:
я кохаю тебе!
бо я людина[21]

my love
is banal
like the taste of banana
in the mouth,
but I must
kiss
the cold lips
of my girlfriend,
touching with fingertips
her skin,
hard like lemon,
and say:
I love you!
because I am a human being

The above poem from Tarnawsky's debut collection foregrounds his obsession with yet another existentialist (Sartrean) premise, that of the Other as an

---

21 Iurii Tarnavs'kyi, *Zhyttia v misti* (New York: Slovo, 1956), 7.

indispensable mirror for one's own identity. However, as the poems quoted above attest, that "Other" is often inaccessible and opaque.

Following his *Idealizovana biohrafiia*, Tarnawsky rather infrequently resorted to either love or erotic poetry. But when he did make use of erotic motifs, his method in conveying them became radicalized. Two prose poems, found in the 1978 collection *Os', iak ia vyduzhuiu* (This Is How I Am Getting Well) and sharing the French title "Les dessert (sic!) de l'amour," can serve as illustrations. What comes to the forefront in these two prose poems is Tarnawsky's rare toying with the obscene (if not pornographic) as an experimental device for stretching the limits of the forms of language that can be judged as aesthetically valid:

> … В готелі на краю міста й неба, при навстіж відчинених вікнах, ми кохалися безперестанку одинадцять годин. Холодні іскри, як бенгальські вогні, сипалися з отворів між м'язами позаду моїх стегон, і я боявся за своє життя. Та я дожив до світанку. Обнявшись, голими, ми підійшли до приязного вікна й погодилися, що світ наш брат. …
>
> Під цей час, її лице вже було, як багнет, що пролежав роками в землі, поїджений іржею, так, що я ледве міг її розпізнати. Та все ж вона була красива. Вона була гола. Вона стояла на тлі вікна, обернена правим боком до мене. Її груди були конічні й бузкового кольору. Вони виглядали, як два мурашники білих мурашок молока. Від зарисів її грудей і, на диво, теж від їхнього кольору, боліли мої очі. Тоді, дослівно із повітря, вона дістала жменю калу в праву руку, замазала ним свої груди, вилізла на підвіконня, й ступила в простір. Він був без низу й верху, і мав запах та барву матіолі.[22]

> … In a hotel on the edge of a city and the sky, with the window wide open, we made love without stopping for eleven hours. Cold sparks, like those of sparklers, flowed continually out of the openings between the muscles in the back of my thighs and I was afraid for my life. But I lived to see the dawn. Naked and embracing, we went up then to the friendly window and agreed with the world [sic] it was our brother. …
>
> By then her face had gotten like a bayonet that'd been buried in the ground for a long time, eaten away by rust, so that I could hardly recognize it. But still she was beautiful. She was naked. She stood on the background of the window, her right side turned toward me. Her breasts were painfully sharp and so, strangely enough, was their color. Then, literally out of thin air, she took a handful of excrement in her right hand, smeared her breasts with

---

22 Iurii Tarnavs'kyi, *Os' iak ia vyduzhuiu* (Munich: Suchasnist', 1978), 109.

it, got up onto the window sill, and stepped out into space. It had no top nor bottom and was the smell and color of mountain pinks.[23]

This excerpt not only points to the lingering presence of existentialist residue (motifs of alienation and death), but also betrays the poet's sexist (or, arguably, misogynist) tendencies. Clearly, unlike Andijewska, Tarnawsky adheres to existentialist tenets even in his more mature poetry.

Erotica in the poetry of Bohdan Boychuk has gradually evolved into a position of significant force. His is a poetic world in search of the meaning of life, from the painful moments of birth up to the inscrutable silence of death. His eroticism, compared to that of his colleagues, has the most elemental quality. As his first book of poems, *Chas boliu* (1957), attests, life and death come from the same dimension, that of pain. A tripartite poem opening this collection, entitled "Pisni boliu" (The Songs of Pain), contemplates love, faithfulness, and birth as functions of time, the linear flow of which engenders nothing but pain:

> Я бачу все:
> час нігтями обличчя зриє
> (твоє обличчя, свіже
> і прекрасне),
> а злото кучерів
> покриє іней
> незчисленних
> зим.
>
> Я бачу … і люблю.
>
> А висохлі уста,
> як листя,
> шелестітимуть незрозуміло.
> В очах—не ласка,
> тільки біль.[24]

---

23 *Os', iak ia vyduzhuiu* is a bilingual collection. Therefore this translation is the author's own rendering.

24 Bohdan Boichuk, *Chas boliu* (New York: Slovo, 1957), 3.

I see everything:
time will rake the face with fingernails
(your face, fresh
and beautiful),
and cover
your golden locks
with the frost
of countless winters.

I see ... and love.

And shriveled lips
like leaves,
will rustle incomprehensibly.
In your eyes—not grace
but pain.

For Boychuk, love and the erotic experience must not bracket off reproduction. The poet eroticizes the act of birth and elevates its elemental significance to the point that the experience usually associated with it (pain) symbolically replaces the authority of Logos:

присіла,
розклавши коліна,
й
взяла у долоні
вагітність.

спроквола лягла.

у лоні:
життя затремтіло,
як крапля надії;
по ній—
розливалася
млость.

і взнала:
спочатку був біль,
а не слово
. . . .
й кінець буде біль.[25]

she reclined,
spreading her knees,
and
embraced
the pregnancy.

she lay down unhurriedly.

in the womb:
life trembled
like a drop of hope;
faint overcame
her.

and she understood:
in the beginning was the pain
not the word
… … … … … … … … … … …
and in the end there will be pain.

The poet's concentration on one of the most elemental aspects of human reality, the reality of being painfully "thrown" into existence (after Heidegger), betrays his affinity with some basic existentialist concerns, especially an anxiety in the presence of death. Every act of birth entails the imminence of death, and thus is a reminder of human discontinuity (using Bataille's terminology). Yet, paradoxically, this discontinuity appears to be alleviated, at least momentarily, through the sexual/erotic experience. Love, sexuality,

---

25 Ibid., 5.

reproduction, and death are all inextricably intertwined in Boychuk's poetry, and thereby create a space in which the uniqueness of each individual human mysteriously unfolds.

These existentialist tenets are particularly pronounced in Boychuk's subsequent collections, specifically in *Spomyny liubovy* (Memories of Love, 1963) and *Mandrivka til* (The Journey of Bodies, 1967). In these poems, the anguish of death is almost always offset by the vitality inherent in the reproductive urge of a human being:

Вітер гне до обрію безликі[26]
постаті жінок, в полях забуті,
що вросли утробами великими
в майбутнє.[27]

From over the horizon the wind
inclines the tall women,
left behind in the fields.
They push their pregnant bellies
into the coming years.[28]

Interestingly, Boychuk's images of women, always fertile, full of life, and life-giving, represent (unlike those in Tarnawsky's oeuvre) the positive, earthy, regenerative force, seemingly the only force that is capable of counterbalancing the despair of a man faced with the burden of his own perplexing existence:

Вечір

Гарячка дня спалила спекотою землю,
яка лежить, натягнувши на очі сумерк,
і тяжко дихає.

26 The poet changed the word "безликі" (faceless) to "високі" (tall) in his book of selected poems *Virshi, vybrani i peredostanni* (1983). The translation below, rendered by David Ignatow, reflects this change.

27 Bohdan Boichuk, *Mandrivka til* (New York: V-vo N'iu-Iorks'koi hrupy, 1967), 36.

28 Bohdan Boychuk, *Memories of Love: The Selected Poems of Bohdan Boychuk* (Riverdale-on Hudson: The Sheep Meadow Press, 1989), 55.

Під простертим веретищем неба
повніє місяць,
і яснішає на землі.

До жінок, що широкими клубами
вросли у призьби, поволі ідуть мужчини, –
і яснішає на душі.[29]

The Evening

Fever scorches the earth
which lies breathing heavily
with dusk pulled over its eyes

Under the burlap sky
the full moon rounds,
and the earth grows light.

Men drift toward women
whose hips grow into clay huts.
And their hearts grow light.[30]

Thus the feminine, approached by the poet with an awe usually reserved for the sacred and the unknowable, becomes a point of departure for metaphysical contemplation:

Спочатку відколовся час,
і світло потекло—як сік глевкий, від ночі,
з колосся рук його—упав тяжкий врожай
у глеки глиняні утроб жіночих:

яким, як пляму, виплюнув життя,—
на образ і подобу.
І сам застиг в обличчя кам'яне
без виразу жадоби.[31]

---

29 *Mandrivka til*, 26.
30 *Memories of Love*, 56. Translated by Mark Rudman.
31 *Mandrivka til*, 40.

At first time split off,
and the light flowed like a gluey juice out of darkness,
the heavy harvest fell from his hands
into the clay jars of women's wombs:

He spat life for them like a stain
in his own image and likeness.
But he congealed himself into a stony face
without a trace of desire.

The aforementioned feminine perspective dominates the cycle "Zaklynannia" (Incantations), which was written in 1968 and first published in the 1983 collection *Virshi, vybrani i peredostanni* (Poems, Selected and Next to the Last). The lyrical heroine of this cycle transcends loneliness through her dream-like states, choosing her own clairvoyant imagination as a wellspring of ultimate freedom, an imagination that offers infinite configurations of various contingencies, including the possibility of conjuring up the ideal lover:

3

бо я
перебреду водою снів
шукати
за його можливістю
водою снів
шукати
за його присутністю
бо я
росту бажанням плоті[32]

for I
will wade through the waters of dreams
to search

32　Bohdan Boichuk, *Virshi, vybrani i peredostanni* (New York: Suchasnist, 1983), 107.

for his contingency
through waters of dreams
to search
for his presence
for I
grow through the desire of the flesh (LG)

Here, like in Andijewska's case above, the cycle's title is pivotal, for the connotative possibilities of the word "zaklynannia" are rather wide-ranging. The word signifies not only the ensnaring or enchanting of someone or something with the aid of magic, but also exorcising, liberating from evil spirits. In the given text, such an evil spirit appears to the heroine in the form of life's temporality, which, paradoxically, can be vanquished by the act of love:

14

бо
тіла в любові
протискаються
щілинами крізь
стіни
небуття
і задихаючись
вдихають час
який спиняється на мить
і рухається
по утробах
в напрямі
майбутнього[33]

for
in love-making, bodies
squeeze through

---

33 Ibid., 110-11.

the crevices
of the walls
of non-being
and panting for air
inhale time
which stops for an instant
and moves
in the direction
of the future (LG)

Thus, through sexual love, carnality, whose essence is characterized by imper-manence and inconstancy, acquires certain transcendental qualities.

Boychuk's preoccupation with the erotic and its temporal, transient dimension reaches a pinnacle in the long poem "Liubov u tr'okh chasakh" (Three-Dimensional Love),[34] written in the mid-1970s and published in 1983. This sixteen-part cycle juxtaposes the innocence of adolescent sexuality, both imagined and recollected, with the cruelty of the war (the Holocaust in partic-ular) on the one hand, and with the alienation and carnal depravity that face modern man on the other.

The story unfolds through a cascade of discontinuous episodes, each representing a different dimension of the lyrical hero's incessant quest for love. A tripartite structure of each individual part underscores the reality of time-bound existence, in which the present tense (represented by a tale of a Manhattan man making love to a prostitute) is not accepted as it is, but used as a kind of launching pad into the world of imagination (dreamlike states of idealized explorations of pure sensuality) and memories, no matter how painful (e.g., the narrative recounting a young boy's infatuation with a Jewish girl killed by the Gestapo). These mental projections (the future) and recollections (the past) constitute the lyrical hero's erotic and, simultaneously, purifying forms of escape from the unbearable urban reality in which "you stand alone/ in this apocalyptic city/ inhaling the fumes/ of bodies worn out/ from making love."[35]

---

34   This is not a literal translation, but it was rendered this way by Mark Rudman in his translation of this poem. Cf. *Memories of Love*, 16.

35   *Memories of Love*, 24. All excerpts from this poem were translated by Mark Rudman. The original reads:

They also symbolically represent life's journey from the innocence lost to the innocence regained.

The poem evinces a strong sense of redemptive call, a need for shedding the guilt of the one who survived. "Liubov u tr'okh chasakh" blends erotic, existential, and historical motifs into a whole of unprecedented expressive power:

Обличчя дівчини горіло піді мною, а збуджені рожеві соски проникали в серцевину крови. Її живіт, мов сполоханий птах, бився об мої клуби, а ноги обтискали стан. Зворушений вечір розпливав на наші спини ретину свого одного ока в синьому моноклі.

Подірявлена кулями ніч хиталася зі скелі, а чорні ями в мурах нерухоміли, коли ґестапо з перебитими хрестами, замість лиць, гупало підошвами по бруку й полювало між блідими стінами на тих, які осталися живими. Коли їх витягали на поверхню, місяць застрявав їм в горлі, і не могли кричати у нелюдний світ.[36]

Her face shone under me and her stiff nipples pressed into my flesh. Her belly, like a frightened bird, fluttered against my hips, her legs squeezed my waist. The evening spilled the white of its solitary eye over our bodies.

The night, torn apart by bullets, hung over the precipice. The Gestapo stunned the black holes in the walls with swastikas instead of faces, heavy boots thumping over the cobblestones, hunting for those still alive. When they pulled them out, the moon caught in the victim's throats and they could not shout into the vanquished world.[37]

Rarely, the explicitness and raw quality of sexual scenes destroy the overall sense of beauty inherent in human sexuality:

Помариш ще білолистям,
щоб виросло білими персами,
дівочі бедра облистило,
щоби обпестило;

"і так стоїш
у місті одкровення
захлинаєшся чадом
відлюблених тіл" (*Virshi, vybrani i peredostanni*, 148).

36 *Virshi, vybrani i peredostanni*, 157.
37 *Memories of Love*, 33.

помариш лопушим листям,
щоб стегна зеленим розплавило,
а потім плоскими долонями
щоб обласкавило.[38]

You will dream that birch-white leaves
will cup her whitening breasts,
wrap around her hips and caress
her legs;

you'll dream of burdock leaves,
their sap pressing against her thighs,
lifting her toward you
on flat green hands.[39]

Despite a number of unmistakably existentialist themes such as alienation, despair, and loneliness, the subtle and implicit celebration of the act of love-making in the poem above marks a turning point in Boychuk's poetry. Hereafter, existentialism as a source of poetic inspiration incontrovertibly recedes.

Love poetry does not emerge as a dominant force in Bohdan Rubchak's oeuvre, yet the handful of love poems that he does offer (especially those included in his second collection, *Promenysta zrada* [Bright Betrayal, 1960]) unquestionably hover around the connection between an erotic impulse and death. His reflections on love invariably betray existential underpinnings: according to him, loneliness and alienation are so rooted in human existence that even a union between a man and a woman (no matter how passionate) cannot alleviate them. Rubchak selects the famous story of Abelard and Heloïse in order to underscore the transience and inherent frailty of any physical relationship:

І навіть нам
прийшлось розстатися. Нашу прекрасну Цілість
розбито на Північ і Південь. Ніжне

---

38 *Virshi, vybrani i peredostanni*, 144.
39 *Memories of Love*, 20.

майже-щастя (майже-вітер, майже-цвіт)
немов ніколи не було. Нічого не було. Пустка.[40]
. . . .
Всю нашу вічність, Абелярде,
ми не зазнаємо найвищого щастя—
щастя закінчености.[41]

Even we
had to part. Our beautiful Wholeness
was split into the North and the South. Gentle
almost-happiness (almost-wind, almost-flower)
appears as if it never was. Nothing was. Only emptiness.
. . . .
All our eternity, oh Abelard,
we shall not know the highest happiness—
the happiness of finality.

Sexually explicit images are largely absent in Rubchak's poetic output. His eroticism is very much insinuated, never straightforwardly revealed. As in the poem "Spomyn pro misiats'" (Recollections of Moon), it is an intricate play of images in which traditional symbolism intertwines with the imaginary to spur the unexpected. In this poem, the poet follows the symbolism of Ukrainian folk tradition and imbues the moon with masculine attributes, despite the fact that in other traditions it is usually thought of as female. Images of the moon's light penetrating deeper and deeper or of the moon as an ultimate authority necessarily intimate a phallic bias. The seductive powers of the moon are also underscored:

Самотні дівчата
носять на грудях стигми місяця—
два відображення його обличчя,
що сповнюються жадібним стражданням, коли ніч—
що сповнюються нестримною спрагою
і п'ють його повню.

---

40 Bohdan Rubchak, *Promenysta zrada* (New York: V-vo N'iu-Iorks'koi hrupy, 1960), 27.
41 Ibid., 29.

І тоді
в золотих плесах їхнього волосся
палає повня місяця,
а їхні білі тіла
є палати для нього.[42]

Lonely girls
carry the stigmas of the moon on their breasts—
two reflections of his face
that are filled with the desirous suffering at night
that are filled with the irrepressible thirst
so they drink his fullness.

And then
on the golden surfaces of their hair
the moon burns in full blaze
and their white bodies
become his chambers.

The mimetic aspects of the poem are undermined by the grammatical uncertainty surrounding the verb "are filled with." For it very well may refer to the "stigmas of the moon" or to the "lonely girls." In Riffaterre's view, a poem will always violate the very grammar it evokes on the mimetic level. This apparent ungrammaticality undoubtedly functions as a hypogram: it helps to overshadow the illusion of reciprocity or, more likely, the illusion that it is the moon (the male) rather than the girls being seduced. But the line "so they drink his fullness" as well as the stanza which follows it abruptly reverse such an interpretation and make it clear that the male is really in charge. The moon's ultimate goal is to possess the female, so that she can be enveloped by the power of his "full blaze." Quite in line with the lunar symbolism, the erotic act insinuated here entails both destructive and regenerative aspects simultaneously. As Bataille points out in his book on eroticism, the climax of any sexual act is very often referred to as a "little death." This, in turn, might shed

---

42 Ibid., 25-26.

some light on the poet's penchant for converging on the darker side of the human nature. His preoccupation with nothingness, emptiness, and impermanence unmistakably has an existentialist origin.

Rubchak's eroticism evinces a strong aura of authority and power, and these qualities are challenged by Vira Vovk's love poetry. Her collection *Liubovni lysty kniazhny Veroniky do kardynala Dzhovannibattisty* (Love Letters of Princess Veronica to Cardinal Giovannibattista, 1967) quite explicitly addresses the issue of gender inequality:

> Світ наш, Друже, вживає
> Чоловічу мораль:
> Що мужчині вигідне—
> Пристойне.[43]

> Our world, my friend, employs
> The male morality:
> What's convenient for a man
> Is also decent.

The poem conveys the story of an unconsummated love affair between Princess Veronica, a woman of superb intelligence, proud and worldly, and Cardinal Giovannibattista, a man of questionable integrity, fickle and untrustworthy. Unlike Andijewska and Tarnawsky, Vovk avoids the transgressive forms of language and explores instead the nature of a transgressive relationship. After all, a sexual love between a layperson and a Catholic church official is strictly forbidden. This element of prohibition is essential to the poem's gradual buildup of erotic tension. The lyrical heroine goes through a series of love stages, from the first half-conscious romantic longings: "Схопити в долоню блискавку/ Й заховати енергію!"[44] ("To seize lightning in the palm/ And preserve its energy!"),[45] through the hopes of deliverance:

---

43 Vira Vovk, *Liubovni lysty kniazhny Veroniky do kardynala Dzhovannibattisty* (Munich: Na hori, 1967), 32.

44 Ibid., 10.

45 In analytical psychology, lightning is seen as a symbol of masculine vitality and power. One can certainly speak of this image as one with phallocentric connotations.

Друже мій, як Вам бажається
Мене не тільки листовно,
Прохайте дозволення в Папи,
Щоб висвятив мене швидко
Кардиналихою.
Зрештою, Вам скажу тайну:
Зовсім не надаюся
На пляшку, що гріє ліжко.
Моя любов і в подружжі
Була б полохливою ланню.[46]

My friend, if you desire me
Not only through letters,
Ask the Pope for permission
To swiftly consecrate me
A cardinal's wife.
Besides, I'll tell you a secret:
I'm no good
As a bottle that warms the bed.
My love even in marriage
Would be like a fearful hind.

to the realization of nil prospects for a reciprocal union:

Тоді любов зазирає у вічі
Страшна, як давніше
Мистці малювали смерть.[47]

Then love looks into the eyes,
Horrible like death
Painted by artists long ago.

---

46   Ibid., 20.
47   Ibid., 22.

Such evoking of death is not coincidental. Both love and death entail the same existential dilemma: the human yearning for continuity. Bataille sums it up succinctly: "The urge towards love, pushed to its limit, is an urge toward death."[48]

It would be a mistake, however, to assume that the theme of death figures as prominently in Vovk's poetry as in that of Tarnawsky and Boychuk. It is true that a handful of love poems in her most existentialist book, *Chorni akatsii* (1961), indeed underscore the inextricable connection between Eros and Thanatos, but her *Liubovni lysty* seems to go beyond that. What is particularly interesting about this collection is that it makes the case for femininity without the appearance of giving in to masculine dominance. In fact, the most fascinating phase of Princess Veronica's love affair is the last phase, the phase of healing. The lyrical heroine is not apologetic, regains her pride, and calmly contemplates unfulfilled pleasures:

> Друже, Ви не відчуєте
> Свіжости цього тіла
> Й поцілунків, диких фіялок,
> Що я їх сховала для Вас.[49]

> My friend, you will never know
> The freshness of this body
> And the kisses, wild violets
> That I reserved for you.

The voice of reason suppresses carnal desires and paves the way for regaining personal freedom:

> Друже мій, я зробила
> Велику похибку, що розповіла
> Вам про свій біль.
> Немає на світі
> Ворога більшого жінці, ніж чоловік.

---

48 *Erotism: Death and Sensibility*, 42.
49 *Liubovni lysty*, 44.

Ви відчували міць надо мною
Й погордили слабою.
Спасибі Вам. Я позбиралася:
Знов я спокійна й горда,
Зайві мені вже Ваші втішання.[50]

My friend, I made
A big mistake telling you
About my pain.
There is no bigger enemy for a woman
In this world than a man.
You felt power over me
And despised my weakness.
Thank you. I've collected myself:
I'm calm and proud again
And your sympathy is redundant.

Taking responsibility for one's own actions, toying with the notions of freedom and choice, as intimated by the passage above, invariably betray Vira Vovk's indebtedness to the existentialist project.

Patricia Kylyna's interest in the erotic is slight, though, not unlike in Vira Vovk's oeuvre, gender-sensitive. Looking at the entirety of her poetic evolution, one notices that this interest arrived rather late. Curiously, her first two collections are notably free of any erotic, or even romantic, motifs. Only in the third collection, *Rozhevi mista*, does the poet reveal a more lyrical side of her poetic persona. This collection includes the cycle of sonnets entitled "Aliuminii i rozha" (Aluminum and Rose), in which the themes of love, freedom, temporality, fate, and death constitute indispensable links in the chain of life. Death is not viewed as an inevitable evil, but as a measure against which things are weighed. It adds value to ordinary events and makes love doubly precious:

---

50   Ibid., 34.

Бо, без кінця, життю бракує буйність—
Кохання вдвічі світле перед смертю.
У розриві тримаємось, далекі,
Щоб нас з'єднала візаʼ[51] смерти в леті.[52]

For without the end, life lacks exuberance—
Love's twice as luminous facing death.
We hold in rupture, distant,
To be united by the death's vision in flight.

The temporality of life is serenely accepted, not argued with. Moreover, while existentialist concerns are still evident (in the motifs of alienation, strife, and responsibility without illusions), Kylyna seems to reject "nothingness" as an answer to a world without God. Her last poem in the cycle "Nevira" (Unbelief) moves her close to the mystical realm in which God is all and faith alone has power to enlighten: "Бо навіть скло є Бог; із горна—світ./ О, віри, з серця та з уму, світіть!"[53] ("Because even glass is God; the world out of furnace./ Oh, let the faiths of hearts and minds shine!").

The love presented in "Aliuminii i rozha" lacks carnal dimension. It exudes certain ethereal qualities and lends itself easily to philosophical considerations. However, the erotic element is present (though in an insinuated rather than explicit manner) in Kylyna's other cycle, entitled "Minimal'ni poezii" (Minimal Poems):

Твоє кохання—промінь лейзера,
такий блискучий, що просвічує
мою речовину, непрозору, немов сталь.
Навіть через мене вони побачать тебе:
зелений промінь, такий невидимий,
що в мені, неначе в воді, мутній від молока,
вони побачать твоє таємниче просвітлення:

---

51 This is more likely a typo. It should read: "візія" (vision).
52 Patrytsiia Kylyna, *Rozhevi mista* (Munich: Suchasnist', 1969), 10.
53 Ibid., 12.

такий страшний, що від мене, необхідного
    дзеркала,
відсвітить цілий твій смертельний спектр.
Та від надмірности світла я сама
стаю променем, а ти—моєю прозорою сталлю.[54]

Your lovemaking is a laser's ray
so bright that it shines through
my substance, opaque, like steel.
Even through me they will see you:
the green ray, so invisible,
that's inside me like in water, muddy from milk,
they will see your mysterious transformation:
the ray so frightening that it will reflect
your mortal spectrum from me, the necessary mirror.
But from the light's plethora I myself
become a ray, and you—my transparent steel.

The image of a ray shining through (penetrating) no doubt carries phallic connotations. The beauty of this poem lies in the capturing of the essence of an erotic act: the moment in which the roles of agent and patient become meaningless. The perpetrator is simultaneously the one being perpetrated ("I myself/ become a ray, and you—my transparent steel"). The confluence of subject and object in the act of lovemaking underscores the instability of socially constructed gender roles. The "Other" becomes an indispensable mirror for an agent, and conversely, because of this indispensability, the "Other" itself becomes an agent. The lyrical heroine in the above poem herself becomes "a ray" (here: a symbol of phallic power) because without her presence (real or imaginary) the whole act of lovemaking loses its purport.

Zhenia Vasylkivska's poetic hermeticism defies hasty attempts at categorization.[55] Existentialism as a source of inspiration, it seems, dwells on the margins. Human concerns, conflicts, and emotions hide well behind a facade of

---

54 *Novi poezii* no. 10 (1968): 82.
55 The difficulty also stems from the fact that she contributed just one book of poems, *Korotki viddali*. That is why it is an almost impossible task to trace a poetic evolution in her case. In

dense metaphors, which, at least on the surface, implicate nothing other than the world of nature. The erotic, so inherently human, does not lie bare for easy recognition. Arguably, hers is a poetry of repressed desires, which resurface in the images intimating libidinous subtext. Throughout Vasylkivska's *Korotki viddali*, nature is eroticized: "солоні груди моря" (36) ("salty breasts of sea"), or: "Золотий пил сонця/ медово-пряного,/ що між ребрами залізними/ млісно зідхає ..." (4) ("The golden dust of the sun,/ honeylike, spicy,/ that sighs lustfully/ in between the iron ribs ..."). It is a poetry rich in images suggesting the attributes of the male reproductive organ: "stovpy" (poles), "stovbury" (tree trunks), "rebra" (ribs), crescent moons ("Місяць—як ребро молока") (14) (The moon like a rib of milk), hard stones, swords, thunders, and piercing rays; a poetry which endows nature with human eroticism as if it too, like a man, should feel and face death. Here is a fragment of a monologue by the stone that contemplates its imminent end in the poem "Kamin' hovoryt'" (The Stone Speaks):

> я лежатиму
> тут довго. Поки на всохлий поклад
> не скинеться, як цвіль, ґрунтова крига,
> і я поверну чоло, розірву
> безсилий трепіт стежки, і в темряві
> спливу останнім, безпідставним гнівом.[56]

I will lie
here long. Till the ground's ice-field,
like mould, piles onto the withered bed,
I'll turn my forehead and tear
the impotent tremble of a trail, then in darkness
I'll emerge with the last unjustified rage.

To a varying extent and with varying success, Eros inspired all the poets in the group. Following the devastation of World War II, which they

---

terms of her relation to the rest of the group, it is quite clear that her affinity with her colleagues lies more in the sphere of poetic forms than in the sphere of thematics.

56 Zhenia Vasyl'kivs'ka, *Korotki viddali* (New York: Slovo, 1959), 61.

witnessed either as youths or as children, the poets turned to existentialism (which was fashionable at the time) for answers. Death became an obsessive subject for them, because only by facing it could the issues of freedom, personal responsibility, and choice of actions have an authentic ring to them. Erotic urges and death, as Bataille so aptly demonstrated, go hand in hand. It is impossible to discuss death without a glimpse into the dawn of existence, and by the same token, the sexual act, no matter how much it is extricated from issues of reproduction, always foregrounds it as a possibility and an inherent potential.

The strong undercurrent of eroticism in the poetic texts of the New York Group was not only an expression of their aesthetic inclinations, it was also very much an active undermining and challenging of the petite-bourgeois mentality of the contemporary Ukrainian émigré reader. Their rebelliousness becomes especially transparent when juxtaposed with Bataille's assertion that "eroticism always entails a breaking down of established patterns, the patterns ... of the regulated social order basic to our discontinuous mode of existence as defined and separate individuals."[57] This unwavering individualism and freedom of expression lie at the core of the New York Group's erotica, and define the essence of the poets' creative activity.

---

57 *Erotism: Death and Sensibility,* 18

CHAPTER 8

Eros and Exile

The connection between Eros and exile when it comes to creativity is not as startling as it might initially seem. The most quoted classic example is Ovid, whose erotic work *Art of Love*, which praised adultery among other things, was not well received by the Roman emperor Augustus, and this poor reception resulted in the poet's exile in 8 CE to Tomis, a frontier town on the west coast of the Black Sea, until his death a decade later.[1] Exile as punishment conveys its most narrow sense. It was as true for Dante as it was, more recently, for Joseph Brodsky. As I have already elaborated in Chapter 3, taken metaphorically, exile designates every kind of estrangement and displacement, from the geographical and linguistic to the spiritual. Some scholars like to further qualify exile as voluntary or involuntary, extraverted or introverted, internal/spiritual or political. Bettina Knapp, for example, speaks of two kinds of exile: exoteric, which stands for "permanent

---

1 Irina Grigorescu Pana, *The Tomis Complex: Exile and Eros in Australian Literature* (Berne: Peter Lang, 1996), 9; Bettina L. Knapp, *Exile and the Writer: Exoteric and Esoteric Experiences: A Jungian Approach* (University Park, PA: Pennsylvania State University Press, 1991), 4; Thomas Pavel, "Exile as Romance and as Tragedy," in *Exile and Creativity: Signposts, Travelers, Outsiders, Backward Glances*, ed. Susan Rubin Suleiman (Durham and London: Duke University Press, 1998), 25.

physical departure from the land and banishment to areas outside of the boundaries of the country"[2] and esoteric, which "suggests a withdrawal on the part of individuals from the empirical realm and a desire or need to live predominantly in their inner world."[3] However, regardless of how we choose to define exile, broadly or narrowly, the question I want to consider here is whether the link between Eros and exile is more than circumstantial or coincidental, as in Ovid's case, and how it can be applied to the poetic output of the New York Group of Ukrainian émigré poets.

Eros, traditionally the god of love, points well beyond a mere personification. It is a force of irresistible attraction, which, if not controlled, can lead to destruction. According to Anne Carson, "the Greek word *eros* denotes 'want,' 'lack,' 'desire for that which is missing.'"[4] Eros, in other words, is essentially lack and desire to possess what is perceived as valuable, yet absent. Or, as in Plato, Eros is the soul's striving for the Good and the Beautiful. Exile, not surprisingly, implies lack as well. It uncovers the nostalgia for a lost home and entails an irresistible desire to recover that precious and loved space. (Whether or not this space or home lost necessarily refers to the place of origin is an entirely different question, and I will return to it later.) Eros and exile, therefore, represent strife and hence are dynamic, yet provisional; both involve a movement, a shift, either physical or psychological; and both deal with an issue of boundaries, whether political or emotional. Carson puts it beautifully: "In the interval between reach and grasp, between glance and counterglance, between 'I love you' and 'I love you too,' the absent presence of desire comes alive. [...] And it is only, suddenly, at the moment when I could dissolve that boundary, I realize I never can."[5] What should become clear by now is that Eros and exile do not serve as technical terms for me. Rather, they constitute images or signposts for my exploration of the New York Group's poetic visions.

The original contingent of seven founding poets, namely Boychuk, Tarnawsky, Rubchak, Andijewska, Vasylkivska, Kylyna, and Vovk, lends itself exceptionally well to analysis from the erotic and exilic angles. Eros and exile,

---

2   Knapp, *Exile and the Writer*, 1.
3   Ibid., 2.
4   Anne Carson, *Eros the Bittersweet: An Essay* (Princeton: Princeton University Press, 1986), 10.
5   Ibid., 30.

to various degrees, are explored in their poems. But more importantly, I argue, Eros and exile act as powerful drives behind the poets' creative endeavors. That is, I would like to make a distinction between the thematic and the ontological. In other words, Eros and exile figure both as a theme and as a particular state of being, a condition which all the poets mentioned above, consciously or subconsciously, found themselves thrown into.

In many ways, one could perhaps question the appropriateness of imposing the exilic condition upon the members of the New York Group. After all, they settled in their adopted homeland as children or young adults and established themselves professionally; the memories of their native land were by and large imagined and constructed rather than based on actual recollections. Yet, as I argued regarding the New York Group's poetics of exile,[6] despite this seeming adjustment, they did not escape the grips of exilic sensibility. The postwar physical displacement the poets experienced was involuntary, and thus punitive. Whether they found themselves in the West on their own or together with their parents, going back to Ukraine under Soviet rule would entail at best a lack of freedom, and at worst imprisonment and persecution. Moreover, the linguistic choice they made—selecting the Ukrainian language as a medium for artistic expression—forced them early on to deal with issues of identity, "otherness," and cultural loyalties. Contrary to the prevailing paradigm of an exile, in which the Other, the foreign land, is unloved and only reminds the subject of unbearable loss and separation, the New York Group embraced its exilic condition as something positive and enriching. However, the linguistic factor and the tyranny of difference or existential "in-betweenness" brought about by displacement (i.e., dealing with more than one culture, more than one home, or with what Edward Said calls a "contrapuntal awareness") have situated the poets in the unenviable space of "non-belonging."

Thomas Pavel once remarked that exile as punishment is reserved for those who count.[7] The political expulsion of such personae stirs attention and compels the Other to learn more about them. If these figures happen to be artists or writers, there is a thirst on the part of an educated foreigner to acquaint him- or herself with their creative output. Thus the linguistic barrier is invariably overcome with the help of influential individuals eager to assist those who

---

6   See Chapter 3.
7   Pavel, "Exile as Romance and as Tragedy," 27.

are worthy of such support and suffer injustice at the hands of native political regimes (for writers this means securing translations for their works and engaging good publishers). The names of Andrei Siniavsky and Joseph Brodsky immediately come to mind as examples from the twentieth century. For these individuals, widespread recognition helped to alleviate that which was lost. The poets of the New York Group represent a different paradigm. Since the exilic moment does not confront them at the point of their artistic maturity, but haunts them nonetheless as an afterthought, a trace or a shadow to be endured, the strategies employed to mitigate alienation and isolation are necessarily of a different kind.

First and foremost, instead of treading an individual path, they chose the support and comfort that comes with group activity. The feeling of solidarity and mutual understanding among the poets moved forward many joint projects like, for example, the publishing of the annual *Novi poezii,* and thereby contributed considerably to the initial cohesiveness of the group's creative platform. In this creative realm, Eros and exile can be perceived as strategies or coping mechanisms for internalizing the encroaching "elsewhere." Eros, laden with desire, offers a promise of a new beginning; exile, on the other hand, opens the door to a new freedom, and, possibly, a new home.

The idea of home in the poetry of the New York Group acquires various shapes and incarnations. It might refer to the poet's personal sphere, or it might entail his/her relationship to the lost homeland. In either case, the general tendency is to claim universality and to dispense with nostalgic sentiment. Bohdan Boychuk, for example, in his first collection *Chas boliu* (Time of Pain), reveals a considerable dose of skepticism as to the possibility of speaking about home in other than contingent terms:

> Так:
> Десь дім стояв—
>   а може не стояв.
> Була десь ціль—
>   а може не й було.[8]

---

8   Bohdan Boichuk, *Chas boliu* (New York: Slovo, 1957), 30.

Yes:

home stood somewhere,

    and, perhaps, did not;

the goal was somewhere,

    and, perhaps, was not.

The apparent pessimism of this poem very much stems from the poet's own personal experience. Captured by the Nazis and transported to Germany for hard labor in 1944, he witnessed human loss and the destruction of cities of unspeakable proportions. No wonder that in the aftermath of the horrors of World War II he distrusts the idea of a stable home. Boychuk often reminiscences about his childhood and peasant upbringing, but underscores the universal pain of being thrown into existence rather than the local specificity. Yet he is not a cosmopolitan poet. Implicit in his poetry is a longing for his native land, but it comes across more as a rational celebration of its rich tradition (e.g., in the poems "Stone Women" and "The Blind Bandura Players") than as homesickness. Also absent is a typically exilic tendency to turn the motherland into a lover.[9]

The paradigm of a homeland re-imagined as an erotic object of desire does not apply to the poetry of the New York Group. In fact, in the case of Bohdan Boychuk and Yuriy Tarnawsky we are dealing with an interesting reversal: it is the "elsewhere," the foreign land, that becomes a lover. In *Virshi dlia Mexiko* (Poems for Mexico), Boychuk personifies Mexico, makes it a woman, and then falls in love with her. Tarnawsky, on the other hand, displays his passion for things Spanish. In his *Bez Espanii* (Without Spain), the vision of Spain is internalized to the point that it dissolves into various parts of the lyrical hero's body.[10] The whole poem projects obsessive reminiscences about a farewell with a lover, which is Spain. She is beautiful, desirable, and very much missed.

One can only speculate on the provenance of this parallel approach. Personally, I think it has to do with some similarities in these two poets'

---

9   Irina Grigorescu Pana underscores the dynamics between the unloved Other country and the motherland, stating that "the elsewhere is adversarial to the motherland and, at the same time, its very *alibi*, for it voices the nostalgia for a home reimagined as an erotic object of desire, remembered only as lost." Cf. Pana, *The Tomis Complex*, 10.

10 Tarnawsky's preoccupation with the corporeal is analyzed quite thoroughly by Ihor Kotyk in his monograph *Ekzystentsiinyi vymir liudyny v poezii Iuriia Tarnavs'koho* (Lviv: NANU, L'vivs'ke viddilennia, 2009), 106-17.

biographies. Both lost their mothers at an early age, back home in Ukraine. Both left their native land in their teens. Therefore, the lost homeland would be re-imagined more as a mother figure than as a lover, and the feelings they have reserved for their own country cannot be erotic but filial. Interestingly, the Other, i.e. the adopted homeland, remains unmarked. It is occasionally thematized, but its relationship to the lyrical hero is that of neither a lover nor a son.

Yuriy Tarnawsky, despite his considerable efforts to project the image of a cosmopolitan, in the end does not avoid traps of exilic reality. As I pointed out in my earlier essay, his pronounced cosmopolitanism is but a consciously chosen mask, behind which we see the face of an exiled person who cares deeply about the fate of his native land. But his political concerns and passionate cry about the colonial status of Ukraine surfaced relatively late, mainly in the post-Chornobyl period of the second half of the 1980s, with the cycle "Dorosli virshi" (Adult Poems) and long poem *U ra na*, published on the eve of independence in 1991. True, we witnessed the first signs of his *engagé* approach to poetry as early as in the 1970s, but these were by and large isolated cases.[11] More common at the time was Tarnawsky's expressed desire to have his ashes spread over the sea in Santander, the Spanish city where he lived on and off in the mid-1960s. The contradictory nature of these responses points to the pervasive presence of exilic sensibility. Everything bears marks of being contingent, provisional, and polyphonic.

His first two collections, however, namely *Zhyttia v misti* (Life in the City) and *Popoludni v Pokipsi* (Afternoons in Poughkeepsie), seem unmarked by the exile factor in the thematic sense. The poetic tales presented there are fully grounded in the existential realities of everyday living, the poet's here and now so to say, though without references to specific events and locales. The poems foreground motifs of love, death, and the city, but at the center of it all we have a lyrical hero who is skeptical, dissatisfied, and struggling to overcome the apparent absurdity of life. Tarnawsky's next two collections, *Spomyny* (Memories) and *Idealizovana biohrafiia* (Idealized Biography), both published in 1964, constitute a turning point of sorts. *Memories* represents an attempt on the poet's part to reclaim the past in order to build the image of a lost home out of fragmented childhood memories. This painful recollection, conveyed as a series

---

11 See, for example, his poem "Russia" quoted earlier in Chapter 3.

of surreal narratives, conflates the vision of the homeland ravaged by war with that of a dying mother. The death of the poet's mother becomes a metaphor for his lost homeland and eventual displacement in time and space. *Idealized Biography* comes as an antipode to such a loss, not only thematically but formally as well. The dense, hermetic prose poems of *Memories* come as a stark contrast to the lyrical miniatures found in *Biography*. It is a collection of fifty love poems, in which the amorous and the erotic are fused into an indissoluble whole. Turning to love, however, does not compensate for the feeling of intense alienation. The initial optimism of Tarnawsky's lyrical hero is progressively superseded by existential angst and profound doubt. Eros, as it emerges in *Idealized Biography*, is perceived as a marked absence. Any relationship, it seems, is doomed at the outset because in the face of death each person stands alone.

Boychuk's Eros, on the other hand, comes across as more positive and radiant. The footprints of existentialism are still recognizable, like in Tarnawsky's oeuvre, but lovemaking in Boychuk's poetry acquires celebratory qualities. In fact, love alone is capable of alleviating loneliness and the anguish of death. It comes as a compensatory force, which also helps to overcome the feeling of not-belonging stemming from the exilic position. Moreover, Boychuk's images of women always represent the regenerative force, which seemingly neutralizes men's fear of imminent death, like in the poem "Usvidomlennia" (Self-Realization):

> Як дівчина
> розпустить
> трепет білих мушель
> і поглядом постелить
> дві дороги,—
> ти любитимеш її за те.
>
> І аж тоді,
> коли роки нагнуться над тобою,
> ти усвідомиш перший раз,
> що ти прийшов у ці сади
> з ріки
> такої дівчини.[12]

---

12 Bohdan Boichuk, *Virshi, vybrani i peredostanni* (New York: Suchasnist', 1983), 46.

When a girl
scatters
the trembling of white shells
and paves two roads
with her sight,—
you will love her for that.

And only when
years weigh down on you,
you'll realize
you came into this garden
from the river
of such a girl.

Mark Rudman, Boychuk's translator, put it succinctly: "His search for the girl [woman] could stand as a metaphor for all of his work. No answers are ever forthcoming, but Boychuk, refusing consolation, keeps the dialogue alive."[13] In the end, simply the ability to speak out, to have a voice, regardless of how limiting the circumstances are, creates a powerful therapeutic catharsis capable of undermining the impact of exilic marginality.

If for Boychuk and Tarnawsky the dynamic between Eros and exile reveals itself most conspicuously in the realm of space, both territorial and psychological, for Emma Andijewska and Patricia Kylyna it is rooted in the realm of language. Andijewska and Kylyna stand, of course, on opposite ends of the language spectrum. If the former is considered a master of the Ukrainian language (a credit often denied to the other members of the New York Group), the latter is a newcomer—in fact, a foreigner who fell in love with things Ukrainian and began writing poetry in a foreign language. Exile as such is not thematized in their poetry, but both poets display mental and emotional attitudes that bear traces of the exilic condition.

Kylyna's case is one of linguistic self-exile. Being an American, she consciously chose the status of the Other in her own country. She exiled herself

---

13 Bohdan Boychuk, *Memories of Love: The Selected Poems of Bohdan Boychuk* (Riverdale-on-Hudson: The Sheep Meadow Press, 1989), 14.

into the realm of a foreign language, de facto closing poetic channels of communication with her native audience. Andijewska's approach is less straightforward, but parallels Kylyna's in the importance of linguistic choices. Andijewska chose Ukrainian as her only medium of poetic expression.[14] The richness of her lexicon and the abandon of her imagination make her poetry hermetic, not easily translatable, and somewhat inaccessible even to Ukrainian readers. In other words, her poetic universe is so different and novel that it acts as if it were, metaphorically speaking, a foreign land. This is, of course, an outside perspective, but it also underscores one important aspect about Andijewska's oeuvre: the distance she insists on keeping between her self and her creation. But this relationship lacks the attributes of alterity, which is very much Kylyna's case.

There seems to be another connection between these two poets, and it has to do with homosexuality. Andijewska thematized it in her cycle "Dionisii" (Dionysia), Kylyna chose it as a way of life. Her departure from Ukrainian literature and transformation back to Patricia Nell Warren, triggered by her divorce from Yuriy Tarnawsky in 1973, coincides with her acceptance of gay identity. Kylyna's Eros is experiential, that is, inextricably linked to her personal choices with regard to sexuality. In her poetry, however, Eros is, by and large, a marked absence. Andijewska's private persona, on the other hand, is never exposed.

When one falls in love or leaves one's homeland, one abandons the forms of ordinary life and enters into an extraordinary mode of existence. The affinities between exiles and lovers are particularly manifested in the deep-seated longing to merge with an object of desire. Love can be directed toward another human being, toward a lost homeland, toward a language, and, for creative individuals, toward the Muse as well. Julia Kristeva once remarked, "Writing is impossible without some kind of exile."[15] And there is some truth in the idea that the exilic position can trigger a creative response for an individual with an artistic disposition. For example, poetry as refuge and the Muse figures quite strongly in the oeuvre of Bohdan Rubchak. In his collection *Divchyni bez krainy* (For a Girl Without a Country), he introduces the motif of homelessness, but

---

14 Born in Eastern Ukraine, in Donetsk (formerly Stalino), the poet recollects that she experienced considerable pressure at home to express herself in Russian.

15 Julia Kristeva, *The Kristeva Reader*, ed. Toril Moi (New York: Columbia University Press, 1986), 298.

only in order to reaffirm the possibility of finding a new home after a long journey of strife and uncertainty. Rubchak's "radiant home"[16] acquires a symbolic dimension and clearly points to the little world created especially for the space of writing. Rubchak does not dwell on alienation as much as Tarnawsky does. However, he thematizes the state of otherness. His lyrical hero is often a stranger, feeling awkward and misunderstood. But the sense of despair is absent and the balance and deliverance come from creativity. The poem "Poetovi" (For a Poet) sums up it beautifully:

> Душа твоя—паперу білий аркуш,
> Уважно складений між сторінками
> Твого ніколи не прочитаного тіла.
>
> Вночі,
> Перед собою на столі розклавши душу,
> На ній накреслюєш вдумливі пляни,
> І олівець твердий (не ніжний туш)
> Витискує твої рисунки раною.[17]

> Your soul—is the sheet of paper
> Carefully folded in-between the pages of
> Your never read body.
>
> At night,
> Spreading the soul on the table in front of yourself,
> You sketch thoughtful plans,
> And the hard pencil (not a gentle ink)
> Hurtfully impresses your drawings.

Creativity as home concerns Zhenia Vasylkivska as well. The act of writing preoccupied her as much as Rubchak. She has a number of verses addressing specifically poetry and poets. Her bard (Muse) is a highly intuitive

---

16 See his poem "Divchyni bez krainy," quoted in Chapter Three.
17 Bohdan Rubchak, *Kaminnyi sad* (New York: Slovo, 1956), 53.

being, who through words feels the presence of God. In fact, in one of her poems she makes it explicit. Addressing the poet, Vasylkivska says:

> Твої слова—це глибока стежка,
> Якою часом проходить Бог.[18]

> Your words are an inmost pathway,
> which God follows at times.

Hers is a world in which poetry and nature conflate seamlessly. She personifies nature and personifies poetry, turning to the latter as if to a living entity:

> Ти—як вінок насіння. Молот світла,
> що розіб'є луску, ще довго
> яснітиме слідами слів, і повінь
> не зірве сітей, не розділить зору,
> що в сутінках згрібає щедрі жнива.
> між молоком і м'ятою, на загорожах
> думок, твої зелені вени
> кільчаться глодом, чорнооким терном,
> загравою шипшини....[19]

> You are like a wreath of seed. A hammer of light,
> crashing the shell, will long glimmer
> after the traces of words, and the flood
> will not tear the nets and parcel out the sight
> that gathers generous harvest at dusk.
> Between milk and mint, hedged in
> thoughts, your green veins
> sprout with hawthorn, black-eyed thornbush,
> with the fire of wild rose....

---

18 Zhenia Vasyl'kivs'ka, *Korotki viddali* (New York: Slovo, 1959), 51.
19 Ibid., 57.

Vasylkivska rarely refers to contemporary reality; the density of her imagery and the abstract quality of her verse betray the exilic sensibility, mainly because they seem to act as protective shells against the encroaching realities of living outside the ordinary order of things. Poetry and nature become substitutive and compensating mechanisms. They also seem to alleviate the sense of loss brought on by displacement. The motif of homeland necessarily surfaces in this context, but her poem "Bat'kivshchyna" (Fatherland) is so detached from historical reality that, except for the title, one has hardly a clue to decipher its thematic strata. A subtle aura of nostalgia permeates the poem, all dressed up in imagery drawn from the world of nature. There is a reference to the "broken bridges," "rough roads," and "horizon of bones," all presumably pointing to the horrors of war, but overall the poem addresses the homeland as if it were an entity totally removed from the confines of time and space. What we have here is a construct of an imaginary home, defined solely by the poet's imagination.

The erotic in the poetry of Rubchak and Vasylkivska is implicit. It comes as a strong motivating undercurrent. Rubchak's reflections on love are marked by pessimism and betray existential underpinnings. Loneliness and alienation are so rooted in human existence that even a union between a man and a woman (no matter how passionate) cannot alleviate them. In the end, any physical relationship reveals transience and inherent frailty. So the poet turns his attention toward those things that have more sustainable power. Poetry takes a prominent place in this equation and becomes his object of desire. Rubchak's Eros, in other words, is touched and moved first and foremost by the creative impulse. For him, desire unfolds itself in the poetic word and conjures up his lover, his Muse.

Vasylkivska's poetry, on the other hand, is all about repressed desires, which resurface in images intimating libidinous subtext. As I have already alluded, nature plays a significant role in her oeuvre. It is often personified and eroticized; her poetry is rich in images suggesting the attributes of the male reproductive organ: images of tree trunks, poles, ribs, crescent moons, hard stones, swords, and piercing rays simply abound in her verse. Endowing nature with human eroticism is unique to Vasylkivska in the context of the New York Group.

In my attempt to elucidate the dynamic between Eros and exile, I have focused thus far on the New York Group's six founding members and paired them on the basis of three topoi, namely space (or territory), language, and the Muse. In the case of Boychuk and Tarnawsky, there is a discernable inclination on their part to neutralize the exilic position by turning foreign territories (rather than their homelands) into lovers and by questioning the efficacy of the concept of a stable home. Kylyna and Andijewska, on the other hand, direct all their creative energy toward language, transforming it into a battlefield of poetic ideas. Kylyna's linguistic choice underscores her desire to enter a voluntary exile of sorts; Andijewska's idiosyncratic poetic vision is best expressed through the language of hermeticism, which arguably engenders at least an illusion of a voluntary exile into the world of words. And, finally, in the case of Rubchak and Vasylkivska, we see an intricate interrelation between poetry as home and poetry as the Muse, that is, as a lover. None of these three paradigms fits the oeuvre of Vira Vovk, the seventh and last member of the New York Group I want to focus on.

The prevailing wisdom about exile is that, especially for an artist, it is a traumatic experience. It is not just because of pain caused by the physical separation, but also because so much of his or her creative vision is related to the cultural and linguistic realities of his/her country of origin. Vira Vovk's poetry displays her love for her lost homeland in a particularly pronounced way. Her early poems in particular, included in the first two collections, *Iunist'* (Youth, 1954) and *Zoria providna* (Guiding Star, 1955), evince feelings of nostalgia and abound in images drawing on childhood memories. In some sense, hers is the oeuvre reflecting the typical mode of exilic writing. That which is lost is desired and creatively re-imagined. There is no confusion regarding what her heart longs for: it is her native land, of course. And yet she manages, it seems, to strike a perfect balance between her affections for her country of origin and her adopted homeland of Brazil. Vovk has a number of poems that thematize the exotic beauty of Brazil and other countries of Latin America. Describing their atmosphere and local color, she always tries to find a trace that would reconnect her with the land she left behind. The poem "Nad morem" (Seaside) underscores this quite vividly:

> Як вечір котить зоряні лявіни
> На океану довгі береги,
> Душа співає з туги і нудьги
> За рідним морем, де біліші піни.[20]

---

20 Vira Vovk, *Zoria providna* (Munich: Molode zhyttia, 1955), 41.

When the evening triggers an avalanche of stars
Down onto the ocean's shore,
My soul sings out of longing and tedium
For my native sea, where the foam is whiter.

The lyrical heroine longs not for her "now," but for her "then," which in her imagination looks more alluring. The absence of her native landscape only reinforces her nostalgic sentiment. Surprisingly, Vovk's mature poetry, published in the last decade, also conveys the beauty of Ukrainian lands. She writes about her native Carpathian Mountains, wooden churches, and folk traditions. The mode is emotional, yet serene. Her love for the homeland is of agape rather than Eros. She loves her country regardless of its condition or circumstances. In fact, she was the only member of the New York Group to visit communist Ukraine in the late sixties as a tourist, even though some of her colleagues criticized that move and considered it as lacking an ideological stand on her part.[21]

However, Vovk's poetic oeuvre also takes up the theme of love between a man and a woman. Eros emerges in her love poetry as a transgressive force. As was discussed earlier, Vovk's collection *Liubovni lysty kniazhny Veroniky do kardynala Dzhovnnibattisty* (Love Letters of Princess Veronica to Cardinal Giovannibattista) tells the story of an unconsummated love affair between Princess Veronica, a proud and well-educated woman, and Cardinal Giovannibattista, a man of questionable integrity. But this transgressive relationship leads nowhere and ends with Veronica's exile to South America. For a noble heroine, this is the only logical outcome. After all, love and exile entail displacement and disorder of sorts. If anything, lovers and exiles have this in common: both treasure their perceived lack, both dwell in the Other's space, and both allow themselves to be governed by time.

Anne Carson makes an interesting comment: "The experience of eros is a study in the ambiguities of time. Lovers are always waiting."[22] I would add that exiles are waiting too. The poets of the New York Group, even though they reluctantly and rarely touched the subject of exile, nevertheless were all deeply entangled in the workings of time. Their poetic fascination with death is also a function of time. Death is central because it implies an ultimate loss. An exile

---

21 See Bohdan Boichuk, "Pro reliatyvnu absoliutnist' i navpaky," *Suchasnist'* 5 (1970): 104-7.
22 Carson, *Eros the Bittersweet*, 117.

has to reconcile himself to the thought of never seeing his native country again. Thematizing difference (linguistic and territorial) as well as estrangement and separation through the passage of time lies at the heart of the group's poetic output and clearly elucidates its exilic sensibility.

What I am trying to convey here is that even if one is somewhat in denial of his or her exilic condition, it will invariably strike from behind by exposing all the inconsistencies in the process of reconfiguring the topoi of identification. For Tarnawsky, it is a split in loyalties between enticing Spain and suffering Ukraine. Boychuk falls in love with Mexico, but cannot forget the images of his dying mother, who can be easily conflated with his lost homeland. Vira Vovk hesitates between the beauty of all-too-real Brazil and her left behind, re-imagined, native land. Kylyna and Andijewska transcend the territorial space altogether in order to dwell in the space of language. Kylyna's literary bilingualism contrasts with Andijewska's monolingual approach; however, both poets excel in building their own separate poetic universes. Rubchak and Vasylkivska, on the other hand, turn to ars poetica, the Muse, in order to overcome the linguistic and cultural periphery. Poetry is a portable home for them; they carry it like snails carry their own protective shells.

If exilic reality spurs a person to renegotiate the concept of home, Eros helps to move it through space and time. Anne Carson puts it as follows:

> The blind point of Eros is a paradox in time as well as in space. A desire to bring the absent into presence, or to collapse far and near, is also a desire to foreclose then upon now. As lover you reach forward to a point in time called "then" when you bite into the long-desired apple. Meanwhile you are aware that as soon as "then" supervenes upon "now," the bittersweet moment, which is your desire, will be gone. You cannot want that, and yet you do.[23]

In *Phaedrus*, one of Plato's dialogues on love, Socrates admits the importance of time in any evaluation of erotic experience. A lover should ask himself what it is he wants from time, because in the madness of desire he would want his beloved to remain unchanged, to remain in the "now" forever. Yet in his discourse Socrates goes well beyond the mortal confines of mere carnal pleasure. Platonic Eros is also known through the metaphor of wings. Socrates even resorts to a little verse to underscore this image:

---

23 Ibid., 111.

Mortals call him Eros (love)

But the immortals call him Pteros (fluttering dove),

Because fluttering of wings is a necessity to him.[24]

Hence Plato's Eros implies an upward movement; he is man's way to the Divine and the immortal. Love, in other words, is always a desire for the higher and more perfect. It is acquisitive because it aims at possessing an object perceived as valuable and egocentric because it centers on the individual self and its destiny. In the structure of Platonic Eros, there is also a hint of flight from the sense-world into the Ideal world. From this angle Eros itself acquires exilic attributes. He reifies exile and, at the same time, helps to alleviate its disorder.

To a varying extent and with varying success, Eros inspired all the poets of the New York Group. As I have discussed, following the devastation of World War II, which they witnessed either as youths or children, the poets turned to then-fashionable existentialism for answers. Erotic imagery became for them a vehicle for conveying existentialist views, especially the need for freedom and responsibility for each individual choice. The centrality of individualism in their poetry has some affinity with Platonic egocentric Eros. Moreover, they employed the erotic metaphor to probe the boundaries of the transgressive and the Other, be it an adopted homeland or a lover. As I have already pointed out, Eros is not only explicitly thematized in the group's poetic texts, but also emerges as a kind of 'behind-the-scenes' compulsion, inferred from the tension between images symbolically libidinal and their contextual exilic position. If Plato's Eros is striving for the immortal and the Divine, then the New York Group's Eros is longing for a new word, a new logos, a new poetic territory. In other words, the Divine is replaced by poetry. For the members of the New York Group, poetry has a power to overcome the exilic margin, and, in fact, constitutes for them a peculiar love affair, lived out in time and space. As with any love affair, a lover is full of hopeful anticipation. He or she yearns for the acknowledgement of all the wonderful attributes that his/her beloved is equipped with, and believes that the beauty and goodness emanating from him/her have a universal appeal. These were also the hopes of the poets of the New York Group with regard to their poetic output. Having worked within the confines of the

---

24 Plato, *Lysis, Pheadrus, and Symposium: Plato on Homosexuality*, trans. Benjamin Jowett (Amherst, NY: Prometheus, 1991), 70.

émigré audience for more than thirty years, they nonetheless expected that sooner or later their oeuvre would find a way to a wider readership.

The exilic condition for the New York Group began to dissipate in the late 1980s and lost its significance after Ukraine gained independence in 1991. Since then, the members of the group have made numerous trips back to their native land, and some (like Bohdan Boychuk) even decided to settle there semi-permanently. Their literary and publishing activity was necessarily transferred to Kyiv simply because the émigré readership shrank significantly. During the 1990s, the group managed to briefly influence the literary process by publishing the journal *Svito-vyd*. All this would indicate a considerable degree of acceptance and recognition by the center. In practical terms, however, the New York Group has never been truly incorporated into the contemporary literary scene. Despite publishing their works in Ukraine for the past two decades, the New York poets are by and large perceived there as outsiders. Their poetic innovations are acknowledged, but at the same time historicized; their version of modernism is studied, but again in historical rather than contemporaneous terms. And it appears that at least to some members of the group, still beaming with youthful energy and eager to argue, this attitude is somewhat wanting. Yet their desire to have a meaningful dialogue with the younger generations of Ukrainian literati has been left unfulfilled.

It is tempting to compare the New York Group's interaction with the literary center with that of a disappointed lover. After Ukraine gained independence, the poets' liaison with their native land has brought to the surface many ambivalent feelings. They yearned for a wholesale embrace there, but encountered for the most part a silent gaze. This, of course, has no bearing on their poetic logos. In the end, the members of the New York Group realized that their true embrace or satisfaction could only come from a word left on a page. Thus creativity itself became a center and a point of destination. The lover's only care is to be with his beloved. With their poetic art by their sides, the poets of the New York Group feel at home no matter where their physical presence takes them. As Plato's lovers, they "live in light always; happy companions in their pilgrimage, and when the time comes at which they receive their wings they have the same plumage because of their love."[25]

---

25   Ibid., 75.

CHAPTER 9

Patricia Nell (Kylyna) Warren's Constructed Alterities: Language, Self-Exile, Homosexuality

The distance between Kylyna's Ukrainian poetry and Warren's fiction in her native English, involving homosexual themes, is not unbridgeable if approached from an angle of alterity, understood as the condition of being on the margins, being the "Other," quite in line with Michel Foucault's conceptualization of the term.[1] The linguistic "Other" Warren chose for her poetic expression—the Ukrainian language spoken at the time by a stateless people—unquestionably bears all the attributes of a marginalized entity. Her thematization of homosexuality with a focus on injustices inflicted upon gay communities, as well as her own coming out in the early 1970s, betray the same bent toward the peripheral and the victimized. Yet the Foucauldian conceptualization of the Other, while no doubt valid and illuminating, turned out to be somewhat limiting in my attempt to read Warren's overall literary output. I discovered the applicability of the phenomenological perspective

---

1   In his works, he devotes much attention to those who are excluded from positions of power in Western society and are in some way victimized, as is often the case with homosexuals, women, the insane, and prisoners. Cf. especially his *Madness and Civilization: A History of Insanity in the Age of Reason*; *Discipline and Punish: The Birth of the Prison*; and *The History of Sexuality*.

proposed by Emmanuel Levinas, especially the ethical dimension underlying his construct of alterity. What follows is my reflection on Warren's poetry and fiction, drawing on Levinas's philosophical propositions, most notably his understanding of responsibility as "the essential, primary and fundamental structure of subjectivity."[2]

Born in 1936 and raised on a big ranch in Montana, Patricia Nell Warren is not by any measure a mainstream author,[3] be it in Ukrainian or in American letters. Judging by the choices she made in her literary career, it is doubtful that that has ever been her ambition. On the contrary, she has always betrayed a tendency to sympathize or identify with those who are excluded from positions of power and are in some way victimized or situated on the margins of society. Yet, regardless of the position she has gained in American literature, to any literary scholar specializing in Ukrainian literature, Kylyna most definitely represents an intriguing figure. In engaging herself in things Ukrainian in the America of the 1950s, she could not possibly have fallen more for the local and the marginalized. While there are quite a few Slavs who found literary fame in the West by writing in the language of an adopted country, Warren's self-conscious choice to express herself poetically in the Slavic language of a then-stateless nation is undoubtedly unprecedented. This fascination with alterity, with otherness, I argue, is what constitutes the main thrust of her entire oeuvre. Writing in the language of an oppressed nation, or writing about minorities (be it homosexuals, Native Americans, or mixed-blood people) whose political rights are either ignored or curtailed, is Warren's way of dealing with issues of identity, difference, and social injustice. It is also my assertion that adopting Ukrainian as a preferred medium of poetic expression during the period from 1957 to 1973 was a substitute (conscious or unconscious) for her closeted existence (as she herself labeled it), or to put it differently, her "closetedness" found an outlet in a linguistic self-exile.

In her 1995 autobiographical essay "A Tragedy of Bees: My Years as a Poet in Exile, 1957 to 1973," Patricia Nell Warren pays tribute to her sixteen-year

---

2   Emmanuel Levinas, *Ethics and Infinity: Conversations with Philippe Nemo*, trans. Richard A. Cohen (Pittsburgh: Duquesne University Press, 1985), 95.

3   She definitely has a strong following within the LGBT community both in the US and around the world, where her groundbreaking 1974 novel *The Front Runner* continues to sell well.

involvement in Ukrainian émigré affairs by acknowledging the impact that her
Ukrainian-language poetic output had on her subsequent literary endeavors.
She begins the essay by quoting a few lines from the poem "A Tragedy of Bees"
in her own English rendition:

> Like a tragedy of bees,
> Like a questing of beetles,
> The sun circles the bush of the sky....

and then professes:

> These were the first lines of the first poem—tentative, eager—that I wrote in
> the Ukrainian language. My struggle to escape from a tragedy of my own
> making would produce a couple hundred more poems, as well as a tentative
> first novel, before I finally came out in 1973 and wrote the novel that most
> people know me by, *The Front Runner*.
>
> Like any new Greek temple, *The Front Runner* stood on an older founda-
> tion of an older temple hidden deep beneath it. Every writer's work is a
> layered archeological site of personal anguish and growth. Mine was no
> different. Without that Ukrainian-language poetry, there would have been
> no *Front Runner*, nor the other novels I wrote. During the long years that I
> was a closeted writer, my poetry fed my hurting spirit in secret, and found its
> own secret code.[4]

The literary and personal evolution Warren alludes to in this opening para-
graph entails at least three transformations: that of a self-made Ukrainian poet
known as Patrytsiia Kylyna (or Patricia Kilina[5]); that of an American prose
writer publishing under the name of Patricia Nell Warren; and that of a
professed lesbian, actively involved in gay and lesbian issues and affairs. While
Warren (Kylyna) has always (and with much pride) underscored the conti-
nuity and complementarity of her hypostases,[6] the two literary personae

---

4   Patricia Nell Warren, "A Tragedy of Bees: My Years as a Poet in Exile, 1957 to 1973," *The
     Harvard Gay & Lesbian Review* 2:4 (1995): 17.
5   This is the spelling Warren herself used in her English writings whenever she referred to the
     period in which she wrote under this pen name.
6   Her English volumes, for example, list not only her English books published to date
     but her Ukrainian poetry collections as well. And more recently, in an interview with
     Kergan Edwards-Stout on Jan. 16, 2013, in the *Huffington Post*, she acknowledges her
     involvement in Ukrainian literature through her association with the New York Group. Cf.

invoked above could not possibly stand more apart, if measured by the receptive needs of the corresponding audiences. American readers appreciative of her fiction are only peripherally (if at all) aware of the writer's preceding rendezvous with Ukrainian letters. On the other hand, the Ukrainian readers and critics within the émigré community who in the 1960s acknowledged Kylyna's poetic contribution have not felt compelled to follow her prose writings in her native English once she decided to stop using Ukrainian for creative purposes. Hence this study is my attempt to reconcile Kylyna with Warren, or, in other words, to view her oeuvre inclusively, unmindful of the division that the two different linguistic realities necessarily impose on that oeuvre.

When Patricia Kylyna published her debut collection, *Trahediia dzhmeliv* (A Tragedy of Bees) in 1960, her émigré friends and critics greeted it with considerable enthusiasm. As I indicated earlier, her Ukrainian turn came as a result of events of a personal nature. Marrying Yuriy Tarnawsky, however, did not have to result in her writing poetry in Ukrainian. Yet the fact remains that Kylyna mastered the Ukrainian language within a remarkably short period of time, and, with a considerable degree of defiance against the mainstream American culture, chose it as her medium of poetic expression. She consciously assumed the status of the Other in her own country, as if celebrating her alterity: "Я, чужинка, розумію тільки по-водяному,/ по-часовому"[7] ("I am a foreigner, I understand only in watery,/ in temporal terms"), but she also admitted that her English poetry did not find sympathetic editors, and that is why she finally decided to write exclusively in Ukrainian: "... My style and themes were at odds with U.S. literary trends of the 50's and 60's. For a time, I faithfully mailed my works around to the little magazines, who always rejected them. Finally I said to myself, 'Screw you all,' and went into exile myself—writing seriously in a foreign tongue."[8]

Kylyna's Ukrainian output consists of four collections of poetry, three of which appeared as printed volumes: *Trahediia dzhmeliv* (A Tragedy of Bees), *Legendy i sny* (Legends and Dreams, 1964), and *Rozhevi mista* (Pink Cities, 1969). A number of poems from the fourth, unpublished collection, entitled "Horse with a Green Vinyl Mane," were published in the last three issues of

---

http://www.huffingtonpost.com/kergan-edwardsstout/patricia-nell-warren_b_2452879. html (accessed 25 Nov. 2013).

7   Patrytsiia Kylyna, *Trahediia dzhmeliv* (New York: NIH, 1960), 10.

8   "A Tragedy of Bees: My Years as a Poet in Exile," 18.

Novi poezii. Her English works include eight novels, two anthologies, works of non-fiction, and numerous articles. With the exception of two novels (her debut volume, entitled *The Last Centennial* [1971], and *One Is the Sun* [1991], chronologically her fifth book), all her fiction deals with the lives and issues of gay men, and only peripherally touches on the concerns of lesbian women.[9]

As I mentioned at the outset, in Emmanuel Levinas's philosophy, responsibility, or ethical dimension, is the most essential part of subjectivity's structure. The French philosopher approaches responsibility as responsibility for the Other; he states: "… Since the Other looks at me, I am responsible for him,"[10] and further elaborates: "I analyze the inter-human relationship as if, in proximity with the Other—beyond the image I myself make of the other man—his face, the expressive in the Other (and the whole human body is in this sense more or less face), were what *ordains* me to serve him."[11] These statements foreground the ethical underpinnings of human interaction; moreover, there is no demand for reciprocity. In fact, Levinas underscores that "the inter-subjective relation is a non-symmetrical relation"[12] and points to the necessarily dialogic nature of subjectivity. The ethical and the dialogic are the two angles through which I want to analyze the Ukrainian poetry of Patricia Nell Warren.[13] In this framework, the adopted language becomes the site of alterity precisely because it is the Other's language, and at the same time it provides the poet with a unique opportunity to access her own subjectivity through the responsibility for the Other.

---

9   In the *Huffington Post* interview, she admits that this choice was at first controversial: "I was completely shocked when I found myself being criticized from some in the gay community who felt that I had somehow broken the rules, being a woman and writing about men" (cf. Edwards-Stout).

10   *Ethics and Infinity*, 96.

11   Ibid., 97.

12   Ibid., 98.

13   I have to acknowledge the inspiration found in Michael Eskin's book *Ethics and Dialogue in Works of Levinas, Bakhtin, Mandel'shtam, and Celan* (New York: Oxford University Press, 2000). Eskin believes that poetry "provides a particularly unobstructed view of the complex enmeshment of the dialogic and the ethical" (2), but in his analysis of two theorists (Levinas and Bakhtin) and two poets (Mandelshtam and Celan) he does not dwell on the issues of language as alterity, which is very much my focus. Rather, he seeks parallels between Levinas and Bakhtin and then insists that Celan's texts (and indirectly Mandelshtam's as well) can be read "as poetalogically complementing and poetically staging and illuminating both Levinas's correlation of Saying and Said and Bakhtin's claim that dialogic-existential relations 'pervade utterances from within'" (11-12).

In her sixteen-year liaison with Ukrainian letters, Warren produced poems that project a world in which nature and civilizations are not opposed but intertwined, a world in which humans live at the intersection of both realities and mediate the truce between them, though not always successfully. Kylyna's nature, powerful and eternal vis-à-vis human fragility, never stands on its own—it always entails the human dimension. People, with their mundane affairs and artifacts, coexist and uncannily interact with animals, trees, and landscapes:

> Коло автостради крутяться верби,
> чорнолиці, чорно-одягнені;
> вони танцюють коло ставка,
> на якім, на льоду, стоїть машина до прання:
> старий зразок, що має чотири ноги.
>
> Навкруги пильно дивляться верби,
> як плакальниці або фурії, не знати,
> і машина напевно поранена:
> її боки червоні іржею;
> двоє ніг спускаються у лід,
> і машина хилиться.
>
> Може за тисячу років археолог
> її знайде в чорнім болоті,
> і немов на саркофаг славної королеви
> він ніжно подивиться на неї і скаже:
> «Колись це була машина до прання.»
>
> Коло автостради верби ладнаються в ряд;
> авта, думаючи, що чорно-одягнені дипломати
> чекають на когось важливого,
> весело трублять.[14]

---

14 *Trahediia dzhmeliv*, 30.

Near the highway the willow trees are spinning,
black-faced, dressed-in-black;
they dance near the pond,
on which, on ice, a washer stands:
an old model that has four legs.

Around the willows diligently watch
like weepers or Furies, who knows,
and the washer is surely wounded;
its sides are red with rust;
two legs descend into the ice,
and the washer bends over.

Perhaps in a thousand years an archeologist
will find it in the black mud,
and as if looking at the sarcophagus of a famous queen
he'll gently take a glance and say:
"A long time ago it was a washer."

Near the highway the willow trees form a row;
cars, thinking that these diplomats dressed-in-black
are waiting for someone important,
merrily honk.

An archeologist, mentioned in this poem, is the role that the poet herself assumes; the motif of digging out the things of the past is quite pervasive in the first two collections, whether it be a wooden spoon left by a great-grandmother or a cow's skull found in the ground, as in the poem "Case History":

Дочка принесла щось у фартусі;
в її волосся заплутався листок.
Вона прийшла в кухню, де сиділа сім'я
                        при столі,
і відкрила фартух, щоб сім'ї показати
череп корови з роздавленим носом.[15]

---

15 Ibid., 23.

The daughter brought something home in her apron;
leaves were tangled in her hair.
She came in the kitchen, where the family were sitting around the
table,
and opened the apron to show them what she had:
a cow skull with shattered nose.[16]

Kylyna's poetic juxtapositions, often unusual and wrapped in metaphors that commingle human objects with the phenomena of the natural world, underscore the surrealist way of perceiving the world. Surrealist reality embraces visible reality, but mixes it with the contradictory realities of the oneiric and the fantastic. Ideologically, her work is firmly situated in the existentialist camp. Her obsessive preoccupation with death, with the passage of time, temporality, and eternity, indicate the poet's intellectual preferences, all grounded in the philosophy of existentialism. Kylyna's three slim volumes, all published in the 1960s, offer poetry that is fresh and different not only because of her peculiar poetic vision, but also because of the occasional oddities in language usage. Her poetic beginnings were marked by frequent praise from her group colleagues[17] and the older generation of literary critics, especially for her remarkable and expeditious acquisition of the Ukrainian language.[18] However, there were also those who made an issue out of her nonstandard usage and chastised her for grammatical trespasses.[19]

---

16 Translated by the author. Published online at: http://lodestarquarterly.com/work/113/ (accessed 25 Nov. 2013).

17 The most notable interpretation of her poetry from within the group was published by Bohdan Rubchak. His extensive essay, entitled "Mity chuzhynky" (The Myths of a Foreigner), focuses upon the mythopoetic, archetypal nature of her poetry. According to Rubchak, myth plays a central role in Kylyna's poetic output. He differentiates between two types of myth in her oeuvre: "open" myth, which is based on references to the known sources, and "hidden" myth, which is solely the product of the poet's imagination. This thesis was vigorously denied by George Grabowicz in his 1969 polemical essay "Vid mitiv do krytyky" (From Myths to Criticism). See also Footnote 19.

18 See Iurii Dyvnych, "Z rodu Mavok i Kassandr," *Lysty do pryiateliv* 13.8-10 (1965): 21, and Vadym Lesych, "Andiievs'ka, Kylyna, Tarnavs'kyi: krytychni notatky," *Lysty do pryiateliv* 9.11-12 (1961): 28.

19   It is noteworthy to mention that less tolerant of Kylyna's language imperfections were critics of the younger generation. See Marko Tsarynnyk, "Mitotvorcha spadshchyna," *Suchasnist'* 12 (1965): 106-8, and Hryhorii Hrabovych, "Vid mitiv do krytyky: deshcho pro analizu Rubchaka ta poeziiu Patrytsii Kylyny," *Suchasnist'* 5 (1969): 84. The latter's criticism came as

It is true that Warren's poetry is spattered by occasional language idiosyncrasies:

О, сонце, сонце, куди ти ідеш?
До котрого озера меду і тиші
ти летиш? Чи ти не чуло про озера,
що ВОНИ лежать під льодом?[20]
(My emphasis—MGR)

O sun, sun, where are you going?
To which lake of honey and stillness
are you destined? Haven't you heard of lakes
that lie under ice?

But the question remains whether or not they are deliberate. Here, for example, the personal pronoun "vony" (they) in the last line of this stanza from the poem "A Tragedy of Bees" is clearly redundant if it refers to "lakes" in the preceding line, which has already been replaced by a relative pronoun "shcho" (that), unless, of course, the pronoun "vony" (they) refers to "honey and still-ness" but that would demand a different phrasing. Such an ambiguity could have been easily avoided, if Kylyna truly aimed at language purity. That, however, was never the case. My contention is that the departures from the standard usage are not oversights on her part, but deliberate reminders of her otherness and foreignness; hence, she unsurprisingly begins one of her poems with: "Я чужинка" (I am a foreigner). Kylyna's lyrical heroine, aware of her own displacement, embraces contingency and tentativeness:

Самітна, я сиджу під рожевим муром
і ні думаю, ні шаную, ні молю,
бо, народившись, не існую.[21]

---

a response to Bohdan Rubchak's study on Kylyna published in *Suchasnist'* in 1968. See his "Mity chuzhynky," *Suchasnist'* 1-2 (1968): 10-29; 33-60.

20 *Trahediia dzhmeliv*, 5.
21 *Legendy i sny*, 56.

Alone I sit at the rose-colored wall
and neither do I think, nor honor, nor pray
for, having been born, I do not exist.

Yet in her loneliness she discovers the Other:

Раптом—хто це?
Чужинець, чужіший від мене,
мандруючи через моє місто.[22]

Suddenly—who's that?
A stranger, more foreign than myself,
walks through my city.

Warren populates her poems with protagonists who are clearly different and who are, one might almost say, carriers of alterity. Their otherness engenders detachment, but in that detachment there is an awareness of the Other's presence and the inevitability of interaction. This brings me back to Levinas and to the dialogic and ethical aspects mentioned at the outset.

I discern two kinds of dialogues in Kylyna's poetry: a dialogue with the Self and a dialogue with the Other. The first dialogic relation refers to the poet's own alterity, or, to put it differently, to the exchange between Warren and Kylyna that takes place in the realm of language, and the second dialogic relation encompasses the offering made to the Other in the form of the language chosen for poetic expression, i.e. Ukrainian. In other words, by making that particular choice, Warren simultaneously thematizes and elevates the people who speak that very language. Levinas puts it succinctly: "To say is to approach a neighbor, 'dealing him signifyingness.'"[23] He also believes that "the *said* (le dit) does not count as much as the *saying* (le dire) itself. The latter is important [...] less through its informational contents than by the fact that it is addressed to an interlocutor."[24] I argue that "saying" (using Levinas's term) or offering

---

22 Ibid.

23 Emmanuel Levinas, *Otherwise than Being or Beyond Essence*, trans. Alphonso Lingis (Pittsburgh: Duquesne University Press, 1998), 48.

24 *Ethics and Infinity*, 42.

poetry to the Ukrainian people in their own native language is a profoundly ethical gesture on Warren's part. It is as if the poet, paraphrasing Levinas, says to her interlocutor: "Here I am!," bearing a witness to your injustice, my-Self taking on responsibility for you, ready to serve you, expecting nothing in return, for "this 'Here I am!' is the place through which the Infinite enters into language, but without giving itself to be seen."[25]

Metaphysical concerns do not figure prominently in Warren's poems, although one should admit that there is much preoccupation with such themes as death, time, and existence. She rejects the centrality of Logos; according to her, "words are picturesque but untrue."[26] For Kylyna, the truth unfolds itself in the process of "saying" (le dire), and through this unfolding, which is life itself, one might find the glimpse of the Infinite. She ends her first volume of poetry, A Tragedy of Bees, with the following:

> Для нас живеньких, життя є єдиною правдою,
> а поезія найкращою брехнею.[27]

> For us, still living, life is the only truth,
> and poetry the best lie.

The imperative of responsibility for the Other reveals itself in the most pronounced way in Kylyna's third collection, Rozhevi mista. Most of the poems included in this volume were written in Spain, where she had spent considerable time after buying an apartment with her husband Yuriy Tarnawsky in Santander. It is a well-known fact that both she and Tarnawsky have become fluent in Spanish, yet she has never been tempted (unlike her husband) to try her hand at writing poetry in Spanish. What I am trying to convey here is that choosing Ukrainian for poetic expression was for Warren more than just a demonstration of her proficiency in a given language. She has developed a deep bond with the Ukrainian language and its people that goes well beyond mere language acquisition. Here we have a situation in which an American lives in Spain and speaks Spanish but continues writing

---

25 Ibid., 106.

26 In the original: "Мої слова є мальовничі, та неправдиві." See Trahediia dzhmeliv, 31.

27 Ibid.

poetry in Ukrainian.[28] This choice, I contend, involves ethical considerations and corresponds to what Levinas coins as "responsibility for the Other."

Warren's poetry evinces a sense of personal responsibility for the plight of all the downtrodden and marginalized. For example, in *Rozhevi mista*, which by and large describes the beauty, mood, and character of Spanish cities, there is a poem titled "San Juan de la Peña" which reads like a duma, one of the genres belonging to the Ukrainian oral tradition, depicting the Cossacks' captivity and struggles with the Tatars and the Ottoman Empire.[29] However, as much as Warren wants to fully identify with the Other through his/her language, culture, and history, she still insists on preserving her alterity; hence her identity is rooted in otherness. The motif of foreignness continues in this volume as well:

> Нарешті я приїхала до міста, в якім народилася,
> хоч у нім я чужинка.
> Перед собором я дивилася в тихий фонтан,
> та не бачила свого лиця.[30]

> At last I've arrived in the city, in which I was born,
> even though I'm a foreigner here.
> In front of the cathedral I was looking at the silent fountain
> but did not see my face.

The seeming contradiction between what happened in the past (being born in a certain place makes that place a hometown) and the present (being a foreigner implies being there for the first time) is neutralized if one makes the condition of time irrelevant. Once linearity of time is rejected, events do not necessarily have to adhere to chronology. And this is the case throughout

---

28 In her short memoir "A Tragedy of Bees," she actually mentions writing a novel in Spain, but is not very specific about it: "In Spain I had actually began writing a novel whose characters wrestled with homosexuality; this book was kept in the bottom drawer, so my spouse didn't see it" (20).

29 Kylyna and Tarnawsky actually worked on the first English translation of dumy. Clearly this work had some impact on her poetry. This translation project resulted in the publication of *Ukrainian Dumy*, published jointly by the Canadian Institute of Ukrainian Studies and the Harvard Ukrainian Research Institute in 1979.

30 *Rozhevi mista*, 18.

Warren's Ukrainian oeuvre. The poet deliberately undermines the prerequisites of time, moving freely from the present to the past and on to the future, denying the logic of temporality. The poem from her second book, *Legendy i sny*, illustrates these shifts quite vividly:

Між століттями

Я молодша від молока,
старша від каменя.
Я мудріша від гриба,
дурніша від води.
Сімсот казок я знаю,
і сімсот ще не чула.
Я напівнародилася,
і теж напівумерла.
Я Цезаря знала добре,
познайомлюся з Цезарем завтра.
Я вільна від часу,
Я—полонена години.
Говоріть до мене вчора,
говоріть про мене сьогодні.
Я напевно не існую,
бо забагато думаю.[31]

Between Centuries

I am younger than milk,
older than a stone.
I'm wiser than mushroom,
sillier than water.
I know seven hundred fairytales,
and seven hundred more haven't heard yet.
I'm half-born

---

31 *Legendy i sny*, 30.

and also half-dead.

I knew Cesar well,

I will meet Cesar tomorrow.

I am free of time,

I'm an hour's captive.

Talk to me yesterday,

talk about me today.

I certainly do not exist

because I think too much.

Questioning the pillars of the metaphysical discourse, as is in the above poem, is quite in line with Levinas's propositions in which ontology, the philosophy of Being, is replaced by the ethical relationship. Ethics, he says, "does not supplement a preceding existential base; the very node of the subjective is knotted in ethics understood as responsibility."[32] And responsibility is, as I have tried to indicate all along, at the center of Warren's alterity, rooted in the language of the Other. Interestingly, there is also a remarkable correspondence between Warren's poetic musings on time and what Levinas has to offer on the subject:

> Relationship with the future, the presence of the future in the present, seems all the same accomplished in the face-to-face with the Other. The situation of the face-to-face would be the very accomplishment of time; the encroachment of the present on the future is not the feat of the subject alone, but the intersubjective relationship. The condition of time lies in the relationship between humans, or in history.[33]

The dialogic relationship with the Self, to which I alluded earlier and which stands for an internal dialogue between Warren and Kylyna, two different linguistic personae of the same individual, first and foremost foregrounds alterity. The poet makes a conscious effort to preserve her "foreignness" in the adopted language and rejects calls for hiring an editor to help her achieve a more standard version of the Ukrainian language, as some critics suggested.[34]

---

32 *Ethics and Infinity*, 95.

33 Emmanuel Levinas, *The Levinas Reader*, ed. Seán Hand (Cambridge, MA: Blackwell, 1989), 45.

34 Ihor Kostets'kyi was the most vocal in this respect. See his review of *Trahediia dzhmeliv* in *Ukraina i svit* 25-27 (1963-65): 113.

The dialogic relation with the Other, on the other hand, is grounded in respon-sibility and is ethical in its provenance. Kylyna exudes a deep, though implicit, conviction that her involvement in Ukrainian letters will not be forgotten, even though she herself does not expect immediate returns. The ending of the poem "Opys maina" (Estate Description) sums up this beautifully:

> Отже я зреклася пам'ятки й начиння,
> навіть гребенів і дзеркал,
> і переношуся з будинку до будинку,
> з міста до міста, надіючись на кімнату,
> де можна було б жити просто, без меблів –
> сказати б, аскетичне життя.
> Та ті, кому я довірила мої покинуті речі,
> ніколи мене не забудуть.[35]

So I've given up memorabilia and flatware,
even combs and mirrors,
and move from building to building,
from one town to another hoping for a room
where I could live a simple life, without furniture—
an ascetic life so to say.
But those in whose care I left my abandoned belongings
will never forget me.

Warren's fiction published to date deals by and large with homosexual issues. Her most celebrated novel, *The Front Runner*, a gay love story, has thus far yielded two sequels: *Harlan's Race*, published in 1994, and *Billy's Boy*, published in 1997. This is how she introduces the latter in the Author's Foreword:

> *Billy's Boy* is the third novel in my series that began with *The Front Runner* in 1974. There has never been a saga about gay family life, or gay generation passing. As a young book reader and writer-to-be, I was nurtured on Classic dynasty literature like *The Forsythe Saga*. Today I want to be the one to write the first saga focusing on a gay, lesbian, bisexual and transgendered family.[36]

---

35   *Legendy i sny*, 33.
36   Patricia Nell Warren, *Billy's Boy* (Beverly Hills: Wildcat Press, 1997), 3.

Two other novels about homosexual life and love, written in the 1970s, are *The Fancy Dancer* and *The Beauty Queen*, published in 1976 and 1978 respectively. Her last novel to date, *The Wild Man* (2001) also deals with gay life, but transfers the story first to Franco's Spain of the late 1960s and then back to the US. Through the lives of two homosexual couples, gays and lesbians, Warren shows the broad range of evolution among Americans with regard to attitudes toward open gay relationships.

This brief enumeration of Warren's English output indicates how narrow the thematic scope of her prose really is. However, as with her Ukrainian poetry, her fiction reveals her preoccupation with alterity. In fact, it is possible to talk about two kinds of alterities, or two different "Others" in Warren's oeuvre: a self-exiled and a homosexual, both contextual, both historically and culturally specific. Thus, I contend that Levinas's phenomenological perspective constitutes a key, opening the door not only to Kylyna's poetry but also to her fiction, especially her first novel, *The Last Centennial* (1971). Rooted in existential philosophy, Levinas's Other becomes a transcendent category.

In a poem "Antypora" (Anti-Season), Kylyna says: "Я абсолютно нічого не знаю про смерть"[37] (I know absolutely nothing about death). This line from the last poem in *Trahediia dzhemeliv*, a collection obsessed by motifs of death, resonates particularly well with the concept of alterity advanced by Levinas. According to him, a true encounter with the Other is an experience of something that cannot be conceptualized or categorized: "If one could possess, grasp, and know the other, it would not be the other."[38] In one of his interviews, he reiterates: "Death is the most unknown of unknowns."[39] Yet this total and absolute alterity, the Other which evades comprehension, does not preclude for Levinas the existence of purely formal types of alterity, i.e., the alterity of the world and the alterity that can be found internally in the self. Levinas insists that worldly entities are all characterized by a certain alterity, but the subject constantly transforms the foreign and different into the familiar and the same, and thereby makes them lose their strangeness. Therefore, the relationship

---

37 *Trahediia dzhmeliv*, 31.
38 Emmanuel Levinas, *Time and the Other*, trans. Richard A. Cohen (Pittsburgh: Duquesne University Press, 1987), 90.
39 Emmanuel Levinas, *Alterity and Transcendence*, trans. Michael B. Smith (London: Athlone, 1999), 153.

with the Other self (i.e., not me) becomes of paramount importance in deter-mining one's own identity and invariably entails the ethical dimension.

The interplay between the alterity of death and the alterity of the Other person comes to the surface in a particularly pronounced way in *The Last Centennial*. This novel, set in a ranching area of Montana, uses the centennial of the town of Cottonwood as a background against which the personal drama of three different characters unfolds. *The Last Centennial* is structured as a set of three novellas, each presenting a different protagonist and a different point of view. These stories of three very different people, however, have much in common: all point to the contingency of identity and kinship, all underscore ethical responsibility in the face of the Other, and all grapple with the ultimate alterity of death.

The first story is that of Johnny Chance, a full-blooded Cheyenne Indian who was raised as part of a white rancher's family. Johnny's sense of belonging is severely undermined because his American Indian kin have rejected him and the white world has not accepted him fully. The relationship with his adopted family comes to an abrupt end during the festivities organized for the centennial, following the discovery that he has carried on a sexual relationship with his white sister Kitie. A misfit in her own right, Kitie returned home after years of prodigal hippie existence and was attracted to Johnny's otherness. She even dreamed of having his baby, despite the fact that such a union would have an appearance of being incestuous. In the end, Johnny not only rejects Kitie but also all ties to his white past. He joins a camp of Native Americans who have come to celebrate the centennial, fights for their rights with the organizers of the festivities, and feels redeemed in taking responsibility for his own self and the selves of his blood kin. Johnny's story is the longest, but at the same time the most straightforward. His initial split identity eventually becomes whole again and finds solace in helping the Other in need.

There is no redemption for Beth Stuart, the main protagonist of the novel's second story, who in the end, at a very young age, is forced to face the death of the other man. She is the only daughter of a successful rancher, and falls in love with a Mexican jockey boy, Speedy Gonzalez. They share a love for horses and meet at a little Cottonwood fair a year prior to the centennial cele-bration. Beth, a high-school senior, defies traditional gender roles. She behaves more like a boy than a girl, and, seemingly ignorant of erotic matters, is unresponsive to the sexual advances of Speedy Gonzalez. He wants to marry her, but she insists on more time. To boost Beth's feminine side, her mother decides to send her daughter to a private college in the suburbs of New York City. Eventually, the mother, an East-Coast socialite who by a whim of fate ended up on a ranch in Montana with a man she hardly feels compatible with, leaves Cottonwood and the family, and moves to New York herself. Beth struggles with her loyalties and the identities imposed upon her by her parents' split and different agendas. When at last she decides on a course she wants to pursue—to reunite with Speedy Gonzalez—she learns that he has died of leukemia in a hospital, completely alone, abandoned by his mother and stepfather. His pride prevented him from contacting her. She realizes that his death is very much her own, and that realization makes her ill.

Beth's story reifies Levinas's position about the responsibility vis-à-vis the face of the Other:

> ... that face facing me, in its expression—in its mortality—summons me, demands me, requires me: as if the invisible death faced by the face of the other—pure alterity, separate, somehow, from any whole—were "my business." ... The death of the other man puts me on the spot, calls me into question, as if I, by my possible indifference, became the accomplice of that death, invisible to the other who is exposed to it; and as if, even before being condemned to it myself, I had to answer for that death of the other, and not leave the other alone to his deathly solitude.[40]

This appeal to the responsibility for the Other's well-being is what the third character of *The Last Centennial* experiences. Pinter Brodie is an old man, a loner keeping his distance both from the people and from the town's activities. He does not participate in the centennial celebrations and resents the intrusion of modern ways of life—new highways and corporations acquiring more and more land—because they interfere with the old ways of the ranching business. Fear for the death of the Other has a firmer grip on him than the fear of his own death. In fact, he intends to commit suicide once he brings his cattle down from their summer range. However, an accident that happens to his cowboy assistant, Vin, forces the reluctant, asocial Brodie to face the man in need and compels him to help him. He cannot face the

---

40 Ibid., 24-25.

Other's death, although he does not fear it for himself and is resolved to end his life. In the end, however, the moment of the rifle does not come to him. As Levinas put it: "Death is the impossibility of having a project,"[41] and Brodie realizes that he still has a lot of unfinished business to attend to:

> Now that he was free of Vin, he could obliterate his holdings as he saw fit. He would sell the cattle this fall, because he couldn't be sure he'd have a range to run them on next year. He would sell the antiques, too, down to the last old saddle and buggy, not because he was no longer sentimental but because they were worth a lot of money. He would put the land in perpetual trust as a wildlife sanctuary. No one would ever touch that land, even if they built glass skyscrapers on every other square foot of the Cottonwood Valley. The old ranch papers he would turn over to the Montana Historical Society.[42]

Interestingly, it is through Pinter Brodie, a passive old man turned activist, that the reader learns that Johnny Chance joins his tribe and that Beth Stuart is in the hospital. Thus, all three stories come to a closure.

I have focused so much on this first novel because in many ways it stands as a metaphor for Warren's own metamorphosis. She considers *The Last Centennial* a tentative novel, yet this novel does not neglect the formal aspects of the genre. Far from being experimental, it nevertheless fragments the narrative, appears opaque without losing introspective qualities, and manages to bring to the forefront existential dilemmas from different points of view. In Warren's literary biography, *The Last Centennial* occupies a liminal space: it coexists with her Ukrainian poetic activity, yet simultaneously signals new beginnings. Like Pinter Brodie, she sheds her passivity, rejects self-exile, and finds a new cause for activism:

> On these works [i.e. poetry], and on my first English novel, I used the pen name Patricia Kilina. I had desired to have a literary identity independent of my spouse. Ultimately my surge toward "identity" provoked his heterosexual frown, when I finally told him I am gay. ...

---

41 *Time and the Other*, 74.
42 Patricia Kilina, *The Last Centennial* (New York: Dial Press, 1971), 312-13.

The tragedy was over. Tragedies always end in defeat and death. I'd decided I was more interested in victory. Kah-Lee[43] wanted to live.[44]

Warren's homosexual novels are straightforward narratives, adhering to the traditional patterns of a realistic novel. Not free of occasional publicist rhetoric, these narratives visibly subordinate artistry of form to the ideological cause. And the cause is, of course, fighting for an end to discrimination based on sexual orientation. Beginning with *The Front Runner*, Warren's most commercially successful book, the philosophy of identity so prominent in *The Last Centennial* is increasingly replaced by the philosophy of difference. Her protagonists embrace their different sexual dispositions gradually but steadily, despite the overall hostile attitudes of the social milieus in which they are forced to function. The themes of certain victimization, homophobia, marginalization, and pure injustice are abundant and deeply permeate all Warren's novels that deal with gay issues. For example, *The Front Runner* is the love story of a track coach, Harlan Brown, and his best runner, Billy Sive. They are hated in athletic circles because they are openly gay and refuse to compromise. Ultimately, this refusal of closeted existence costs Billy his life: he is shot dead by one such hatemonger while competing at the Olympic Games. *Harlan's Race*, the sequel to *The Front Runner*, portrays Brown's coping with the fear spurred by stalking and threats of an accomplice to Billy's murderer still at large. *Billy's Boy*, the last volume of the saga, focuses on gay youths and their struggle to be accepted either by their peers or by their parents who, as a rule, have a difficult time accepting their children's queer natures.

In Warren's fiction dealing with homosexuality, there is no doubt a great focus on injustices inflicted upon gay communities and their disadvantages vis-à-vis the heterosexual world. It seems to me that this atmosphere of gloom and oppression that Warren's novels invariably evince has some correlation to the circumstances in which she and her émigré colleagues began to write in the 1950s. The young poets not only had to struggle with the conservatism of their immediate milieu, but also were truly concerned about the survival of Ukrainian culture under the oppressive communist regime. There is no doubt

---

43   This is the name of an androgynous figure from Kylyna's unpublished English poetic drama
     "The Horsemen."
44   "A Tragedy of Bees: My Years as a Poet in Exile," 21.

that émigrés and gay people share an impetus towards marginalization and indefinability. These two groups occupy peripheral positions vis-à-vis their respective centers. Julia Kristeva writes: "Our present age is one of exile. How can one avoid sinking into the mire of common sense, if not by becoming a stranger to one's own country, language, sex and identity? Writing is impossible without some kind of exile."[45] Linguistic barriers aside, what I have tried to convey throughout this chapter is that the distance between Kylyna's Ukrainian poetry and Warren's homosexual fiction is not as overwhelming as it might otherwise appear.

---

45 Julia Kristeva, *The Kristeva Reader*, 298.

CHAPTER 10

Literary New York:
The New York Group
and Beyond

The trajectory of Ukrainian émigré literary centers in the twentieth century begins in Prague and Warsaw in the interwar period and ends in New York after World War II. While the former two centers are best represented by the activities of the Prague School, the latter found its most vivid embodiment in the poetic phenomenon of the New York Group. As indicated at the outset, it is indeed in New York City where, in the mid-1950s, the group originated, and even though some of the group's members lived elsewhere the city itself has become for them a symbol of innovation and avant-garde spirit. The seven founding poets, Boychuk, Tarnawsky, Rubchak, Vasylkivska, Kylyna, Andijewska, and Vovk, influenced by surrealism and existentialism, all aimed at making novelty part of their poetic craft.

Taking into account how important New York appears to be in the group's artistic evolution (after all, the group's name references the metropolis), it is surprising how little, if at all, the place itself is thematized in the poets' works. It is not that urban motifs are absent, but that they are by and large abstract, not referring to a concrete locality. Or, as it happens in quite a few cases, other cities than New York usurp the right to be poetically embraced.[1] This comes as a stark contrast to what Vasyl Makhno, a Ukrainian poet who settled permanently in New York in 2000, proposes in his *Cornelia Street Café*, published in 2007, which in addition to his new poems also includes a previously published collection titled *38 virshiv pro N'iu-Iork i deshcho inshe* (38 Poems about New York and a Few Other Things, 2004). Makhno celebrates New York with all its ups and downs, even if at first with a dose of considerable hesitation, if not outright reluctance. His New York comes across as a site of archaeological importance, a site in which he digs up layer upon layer of textual deposits left by his predecessors and contemporaries alike.

This chapter examines the extent of the New York themes in the poetry of the New York Group, elucidates the reasons behind its scant treatment, and then compares it to Vasyl Makhno's poetic contribution. I argue that the crux of the difference in the manner of New York's thematization then and now is best explained by the aesthetic shift from modernism (with its preference for the universal and the cosmopolitan) to postmodernism (with its preference for the local and the particular).

Among the poets of the New York Group, the most explicit presence of the city is found in the poetry of Bohdan Boychuk. Perhaps this is because he is the only poet who lived permanently in New York City, though he moved from there in 2001. Yet the theme of the metropolis, a concrete reference to New York, arrives rather late, in his fourth collection, *Spomyny liubovy* (1963). In the poem "Virshi pro misto" (Poems about the City) the lyrical hero states:

2.

Я чекаю, поки
стопляться під місяцем
дахи
на Bleecker Street
і пам'ять набубнявіє
від мітів.[2]

---

1   For example, Kylyna's third collection, *Rozhevi mista*, represents poetic descriptions of Spanish cities which she visited in the 1960s.

2   Bohdan Boichuk, *Virshi, vybrani i peredostanni* (New York: Suchasnist', 1983), 32.

I wait until
the roofs
on Bleecker Street
melt under the moon
and memory swells
from myths.

Here the reference to Bleecker Street indicates that the lyrical hero is in New York's bohemian Greenwich Village, but the picture of the city that emerges is anything but enticing: "місто/ затягнулось каменем" (the city/ gloomed by stone), and he expresses loneliness: "і я лишаюсь сам" (and I'm left alone). Moreover, this is the city in which there is no love and sex is cheap:

4.

Мури
тиснуть тих,
які кохаються
вночі,
розшарпані
гарячим саксофоном;

по коханні
хлопець кидає в горнятко серця
тридцять срібняків[3]

The walls
press those
who make love
at night
torn by
a hot saxophone

---

after sex
a young fellow
drops thirty silver coins
into the cup of heart

Boychuk's image of New York is monothematic. It is a city that curses love and deems finding the loved one impossible. In the same collection, *Spomyny liubovy*, the poet narrates in one of the "Letters," dated September 11: "I was looking for you on the streets of New York. A hopeless search. The streets choked with faces, swollen with weariness, boredom, stale loves. Time smeared the faces with sweat and wrinkles, drove them closer to the end of the street. You were not there."[4]

    The poet returns to the theme of New York again in his long poem "Liubov u tr'okh chasakh" (Three-Dimensional Love), but the city is depicted in corrupted and dark paint, marred by prostitution and cheap love. Each poem in this cycle is measured by time: future, present, and past. The future represents an idealized love in the form of a song; the present tense is the vers libre of everyday existence in the metropolis, and the past is a prose narrative about the lyrical hero's first love, buried deep down in memory and torn by guilt from surviving the horrors of the war. As Boychuk puts it, referring to the present, there is nothing exciting about living in the city, where "до тебе простягаються/ побиті вікна/ мов проколені долоні/ якими затікає сажа"[5] (the broken windows/ stretch toward you/ like pierced hands/ through which/ the soot sifts in.")[6] There is a certain inevitability about fallen acts in the fallen city: "зашморгуєшся/ в довгих вулицях" (you're strangled/ by long streets) or "обліпаєш .../ голими грудьми/ ховзькими бедрами/ набряклими устами"[7] ([you are] "plastered by/ naked breasts/ sweating hips/ swollen lips"[8]). The

---

4   Bohdan Boychuk, *Memories of Love: The Selected Poems of Bohdan Boychuk* (Riverdale-on-Hudson: The Sheep Meadow Press, 1989), 60. Translated by Mark Rudman. The original reads: "Я шукав тебе на вулицях Нью-Йорку. Та дарма, дарма. Вулиці душилися втомою, нудьгою, перестояним коханням, шмінкою, роздертими устами. Час розмазував обличчя зморшками і потом,—гнав людей до кінця однієї вулиці. Там тебе не було" (*Virshi, vybrani i peredostanni*, 40).

5   *Virshi, vybrani i peredostanni*, 140.

6   *Memories of Love*, 16. "Three-Dimensional Love" was translated by Mark Rudman.

7   *Virshi, vybrani i peredostanni*, 144.

8   *Memories of Love*, 20.

metropolis is like a labyrinth that ensnares men and compels them into the embraces of prostitutes:

> роздерши на грудях перкаль
> вона переходить times square
> і віддається кожному
> хто прагне кохання
> за гроші[9]

> tearing apart her cotton dress
> she crosses Times Square
> and gives herself to everyone
> who hungers for flesh
> and pays[10]

Unlike in Boychuk's oeuvre, there are no explicit references to New York in Yuriy Tarnawsky's poetry. However, in his 1956 debut collection, *Zhyttia v misti*, New York is implicit. Tarnawsky's city, like Boychuk's, is not a place in which one feels comfortable, although different aspects are underscored. In the collection's opening poem, "Mis'kyi noktiurn" (City Nocturne), the personified moon, looking for inspiration in the city landscape, finds only "the naked dirty truth":

> а місяць
> (самітний пустельник
> блукає в просторі)
> розсуває руками хмари,
> як спомини,
> і шукає надхнення
> серед бруду
> міських смітників:
> гляне на землю
> і сховає лице в хмарах,

---

9   *Virshi, vybrani i peredostanni*, 160.
10 *Memories of Love*, 36

вражений голою,
брудною правдою.[11]

and the moon
(a lonely hermit
drifting in space)
pushes clouds away
as if they were memories
and looks for inspiration
in the dirt
of city garbage containers:
he looks down
and hides his face in the clouds
struck by the naked
dirty truth

An even more accusatory tone is struck in the poem "Himn mistu" (Hymn to the City). Here the city is described as deceitful and likened to a prison, and the lyrical hero singing a hymn is no longer sure if in the long run he would not curse the city, because:

... ти зібрало
в невидимі мури своєї в'язниці
мільйони світів,
мільйони тіл,
які горять,
які кричать,
підсвідомим бажанням,
за те,
що ти довгими роками
дуриш їх надією,

---

11   Iurii Tarnavs'kyi, *Zhyttia v misti* (New York: Slovo, 1956), 5.

за те,
що робиш їх рабами,
о, велике місто
рожевих пірамід
на синіх пісках неба[12]

... you gathered
into the invisible walls of your prison
a million worlds
a million bodies
which burn
which cry
with unconscious desires
because
for many years
you deceive them with hope,
----
because you make them into slaves
you, oh, great city
of pink pyramids
on the blue sand of sky

In *Zhyttia v misti*, Tarnawsky continues to express his feelings about the city in abstract terms, occasionally even confusing the reader with unexpected images, like "pink pyramids" in the above excerpt, which undermine the understanding of the setting. For if the implicit city in this collection is New York, why "pink pyramids?" Where does this image come from? The poet does not provide a clue. The extent of abstractness is even more apparent in the poem "Oda do kafe" (Ode to Café). Knowing the history of the New York Group and its early habit of spending time in Greenwich Village cafés discussing poetry and much more, it is safe to assume that it is one of those places Tarnawsky chose for his poem. Yet there is not a shred of recognizable description in this poem. There is absolutely nothing that allows specificity

12 Ibid., 30.

and puts the café into identifiable context. On the contrary, Tarnawsky's café is praised and "sung" about only because it provides: "тепле місце відпочивання тіла,/ де можна розвісити мокрі полотна шкіри,/ висушити на вітрі сухих але ласкавих хвиль/ піт втоми, ноги поставити, чекаючи/ аж біль стече на долівку тихим скимлінням ножа"[13] (a warm place for the body's rest/ where one can hang wet canvas of skin/ and dry fatigue's sweat with the wind of dry and kind waves/ where one can put down the legs waiting/ until pain flows down to the floor with a knife's quiet whining). In fact, it does not take long to grasp that the café is important only to the extent that it provides a haven for the subject to experience pleasurable moments. It is a place where the lyrical hero escapes from the weariness imposed by the city. The poem focuses first and foremost on the subject, and the specificity of the background becomes secondary.

Vasyl Makhno's treatment of the same theme could not have been more different. His café, whether it is Cornelia or Starbucks, is immersed in utmost specificity. The poet strives to place it not only in space but in time as well. Moreover, Makhno thrives on being a *flâneur* of sorts who observes the city and leaves behind a poetic record of New York's here and now, like in the poem "Na kavi u Starbucks" (Coffee in Starbucks):

у грудні—у долішньому нью-йорку—
            п'ючи каву в "Starbucks"—спостерігаю
як два мексиканці вкладають мармурові плити
            до парадного входу в будинок

у кав'ярні крутять нав'язливий Jingle bells
вулицями миготять нью-йоркці
            з різдвяними подарунками й авта
вуличні торговці розпродують туристам усілякий
   непотріб
поліціянти мирно дрімають у теплому авті[14]

---

13 Ibid., 44.
14 Vasyl' Makhno, *Cornelia Street Café* (Kyiv: Fakt, 2007), 132.

in december—in downtown new york—
    drinking coffee in Starbucks—i watch
two mexicans laying marble wall slabs
    in the entrance to the building

an irksome Jingle Bells keeps playing in the café
new yorkers shimmer with their Christmas gifts and cars
street peddlers sell the tourists all kind of crap
the policemen snooze peacefully in their warm car[15]

This poem gives a poetic snapshot of a particular moment in New York. We are told at the outset that it is December and the café is in downtown New York. We observe what is happening through the poet's eyes, yet he himself is almost invisible. Only in the middle of the poem does he reemerge with his own reflections about the passage of time, the community of other poets, and ars poetica, but not for long, because the poem ends as it begins: with the observation of two Mexicans working with stone on the entrance to the building.

Makhno's New York is concrete and alive, a quality that is simply missing in the poetry of the New York Group. In some ways he has more in common with the group's older émigré colleagues, Iurii Kosach (1909-1990)[16] and Vadym Lesych (1909-1982), who, writing about New York, present it to the reader much more concretely than their avant-garde contemporaries.[17] Both

---

15 Translated by Michael Naydan. Taken from the site: http://ukraine.poetryinternationalweb. org (accessed 26 Nov. 2013).

16 According to Boychuk and Rubchak in their anthology *Koordynaty*, Iurii Kosach published a collection titled *Manhattans'ki nochi* (Manhattan Nights, 1966) in Kyiv. Kosach was accused by the émigré community of collaboration with the Soviet regime. However, regardless of how one evaluates his ideological stand, it would be extremely interesting to examine this poetry book. Unfortunately it is not available in any North American research libraries. I was unable to verify if such a publication indeed exists. Vira Aheieva's edition of Kosach's works, published in Kyiv, focuses on his prose output, and there is no reference to this collection. Cf. *Proza pro zhyttia inshykh: Iurii Kosach, teksty, interpretatsii, komentari* (Kyiv, 2003).

17 It is noteworthy to mention that a prominent member of the Prague School, Evhen Malaniuk, also has a few poems about New York. But unlike Kosach and Lesych, Malaniuk does not thematize New York for its own sake. His New York emerges only as a background to the poet's own reflections about his émigré life, dominated by nostalgia and a sense of finality. Malaniuk presents New York in abstract terms, similarly to the manner in which the New York Group poets approach the theme.

Kosach and Lesych have poems about black New York, a theme completely absent in the poetry of the group, but immensely thematized by Federico García Lorca in his *Poet in New York*, written in 1929-30. Kosach's poem "Manhatten, 103-tia vulytsia" (Manhattan, 103-rd Street), for example, captures the dynamism of the black girl's dance movements. It is a somewhat obscure poem with a surreal coloring reminiscent of Lorca, free of commentary but with hints of compassion:

Дівчина—голубе торнадо
вухом її біси вповзають
щоб вповзти в живіт
і вертіти ним як одурілим
сонцем
зуби зуби зуби
цокотом перлистого граду
зуби зуби зуби
фіолетні риби
піймані в глибах місячних рель
наситять не одного
тисячі
чорних людей.[18]

A girl—blue tornado
through her ear demons crawl in
to settle in her belly
to turn round it as if the maddened
sun
teeth teeth teeth
with chattering pearl hail
teeth teeth teeth
violet fish
caught in the depths of moon's lyre
will feed not one

---

18 Iurii Kosach, "Manhatten, 103-tia vulytsia," in *Koordynaty: antolohiia suchasnoi ukrains'koi poezii na zakhodi*, vol. 2, ed. Bohdan Boichuk and Bohdan Rubchak (Munich: Suchasnist', 1969), 101. The poem was originally published in Kosach's book *Kubok Hanimeda* (New York: Lesyn dim, 1958).

but thousands
of black people.

Lesych, on the other hand, does not shy away from politically charged comments, and in his poem "Harlem" he implicitly calls for social justice. Taking into account that the poem was included in his collection *Kreidiane kolo* (Chalky Circle), published in 1960, it says a lot about the author and his political stand regarding the Civil Rights movement. Lesych, himself an émigré poet, seems to understand the predicament in which African-Americans of the time found themselves:

> Там бродять в білий день
> від вулиці до вулиці—
> порожні і зажурені,
> волочать чорну іншість,
> такі самі, як ми
> —роззяви і поети і комедіянти,
> і ті, що із тривогою
> очікують важкого материнства.
> Усі такі, як ми,
> але ще більш людські,
> ще правдивіші[19]

On a light sunny day
the empty and worried
roam from street to street
and drag their black otherness
the same as us
—gaping fools and poets and comedians,
and those who with anxiety
expect difficult motherhood.
All of them like us,
but even more human,
more real.

---

19 *Koordynaty*, vol. 2, 117-18.

Lesych's immigrant alterity allows him to embrace the alterity of the black America, the one that still remembers the hardship of slavery: "Їм сняться часом ще:/ канчук цукрової плянтації" (118) (They still dream from time to time/ about the whip of a sugar plantation). Writing a poem about New York's Harlem provided the poet with a powerful tool to express his sympathy and support for people of color.

In strange ways, traces of Lorca's *Poet in New York* are found in the output of all the poets discussed here. In the case of Boychuk and Tarnawsky it is most conspicuous in the general mood of gloom, decay, and death. Lorca's New York comes across as a symbol of universal unfulfillment; Boychuk's and Tarnawsky's city becomes additionally a symbol of impediment, and, at the same time, a powerful source of inspiration. Many critics have pointed out a prophetic quality in *Poet in New York*, found mainly in Lorca's ability to express the general pessimistic mood of the 1930s, which eventually culminated in World War II, the worst calamity the human civilization had ever experienced. The poets of the New York Group experienced the horrors of the war, and the existential angst caused by it is either directly or indirectly reflected in their poems. Lorca, however, is never explicitly invoked in the poetry of either Boychuk or Tarnawsky, at least not in connection with the theme of New York City. Yet Tarnawsky's *Zhyttia v misti* shares a few poetic forms with *Poet in New York*: a nocturne and an ode. There is also a tendency in both poets to convert the concrete into the abstract and to create metaphors based on distant and inconceivable associations.

In Makhno's poems about New York, Lorca becomes a central literary figure. In *Poet in New York*, the creative elements are based on direct impressions, which in many cases can be easily localized. Makhno goes even further: his direct impressions (often named and specified) indeed play a role, but so do his textual appropriations. Not only are Lorca's images invoked (e.g., the poem "Pro Asyriis'koho psa" [About Assyrian Dog]), but the Spanish poet himself becomes a protagonist in Makhno's poetic world. Bohdan Rubchak rightly notes that Lorca, in Makhno's poetry assumes the same role as Virgil in Dante's *Inferno*.[20] Where the critic errs, however, at least in my view, is in his claim that Makhno, through his tone and imagery, attempts to shift the

---

20 Bohdan Rubchak, "Mandrivnyk, inodi ryba," in Vasyl Makhno, *Cornelia Street Café* (Kyiv: Fakt, 2007), 13.

New York of today back to the modernism and surrealism of the 1930s.[21] Nothing could be farther from the truth. Makhno's metropolis reflects contemporary New York to the minutest detail, but his New York is first and foremost a textual New York. The poet actively seeks all literary traces left on the many surfaces of the city. He becomes an archaeologist of sorts who patiently digs and reveals all poetic layers imprinted on New York's walls. In that sense, it is not only Lorca that he embraces but also the poets of the 1960s, including the New York Group, as well as Americans Walt Whitman, John Ashbery, and Frank O'Hara. In fact, Makhno's textual New York is simply a community of poets of all generations and many different nationalities. They are present in his poetic texts either through his memory, which resurrects them to life in his imaginary New York, or through their own association with the city, which the poet then conscientiously rediscovers and textualizes anew.

As I already intimated, Makhno celebrates New York in all its literary, historical, and ethnic peculiarities. It is "a recurrent character" in his poems ever since the poet settled in the city, as Oksana Lutsyshyna rightly assessed.[22] From the Jewish Brooklyn to Manhattan's Chinatown, specificity and local flavor dominate the tones and images of all his New York poems. In "Bruklins'ka elehiia" (Brooklyn Elegy), the poet's own persona retreats to the shadows, becoming almost inconspicuous; only his gaze, his detailed observation, counts:

> щоранку пекарні єврейські відчиняють з пітьми
> перше що добігає—схожий на прудкість лисиць—
> запах цинамону—розтертих із цукром яєць—
> до цегляних синагог—і це є початком зими
> бо тісто пахне сосною і зірваний вчора жасмин
> разом із часником і цибулею сиґналить тобі з
> полиць[23]

---

21 Ibid., 14.

22 See her review *"Winter Letters* across Time and Space," in *The Ukrainian Weekly*, 10 June 2012, 10.

23 *Cornelia Street Café*, 111.

each morning the Jewish bakeries open up while it's still dark
the first thing that runs up to you—quick as a fox—
is the scent of cinnamon—beaten eggs with sugar—
to the brick synagogues—and this is the beginning of winter
because the dough smells of pine and jasmine picked yesterday
together with garlic and onions beckoning to you from
       the shelves[24]

Occasionally, the ethnic coloring implies bias, and the poet's commentary is anything but flattering. Consider, for example, the poem "Chinatown: Rybna kramnytsia" (Chinatown: Seafood Store):

вони ґелготять як пекінські гуси
ну от Пекінська опера задурно

коли вибирають у рибній крамниці
заморожену чи свіжу рибу

рибу китайці купують щодень

продавці у ґумових чоботях
—наче сірі чаплі—
витирають в засмальцьовані білі фартухи
змащені риб'ячим жиром руки[25]

they cackle like Peking geese
here it is—Peking opera for free

when in the store they select
frozen or fresh fish

the Chinese buy fish everyday

---

24 Translated by Michael Naydan. Taken from the site: http://ukraine.poetryinternationalweb.
    org (accessed 26 Nov. 2013).
25 *Cornelia Street Café*, 55.

vendors in rubber boots
—like gray herons—
wipe their hands greasy with fish oil
on dirty white aprons

Yet, I contend, the poet's seeming criticism is free of malice. He embraces difference and locality with the typical postmodernist acceptance. His New York, deeply rooted in the specific, reflects diversity, history, and allegiance to multiculturalism. Makhno's community of Others includes not just poets but also ordinary men and women he observes while walking or merely drinking coffee in one of the city's cafés. This egalitarian approach to life invokes Walt Whitman, a poet who is also included in Makhno's poetic pantheon (cf. his "Chytannia virshiv—Svitlani" [Poetry Reading—To Svitlana]). Perhaps it is this embracing attitude with a personal touch that prompted one critic to conclude: "Makhno is at his best when he speaks of personal pains, of sorrows and suffering."[26] I would interject here that while the poet at times does share his life's painful moments, he more frequently describes and dwells on the lives of others.

Discussing the poetics of exile in the New York Group's output, I pointed out that one of the characteristics of exilic sensibility is the tendency to put the personal experience in universal terms. But I would also add at this point that the inclination toward the abstract and the general stems from the modernist belief in the universality of human progress and evolution. The sense of belonging to a community of like-minded individuals happens through the encompassing values of general validity rather than through the acceptance of difference. The fact that the majority of the poets of the New York Group have not thematized New York in their poetry could be explained first by distance (not all the members of the group permanently resided in New York), second by exilic sensibility, and finally by the modernist conceptualization of artistic imperative in which the self, or each individual subjectivity, takes precedence over any concrete locality. Makhno, on the other hand, a postmodernist by inclination and practice, revels in the idiosyncrasies New York offers with all its local color, charm, and incongruity.

---

26 Leonid Rudnytzky, "A Poetical Voice of the Ukrainian Diaspora: Random Notes on the Poetry of Vasyl Makhno," *The Ukrainian Quarterly* 67 (2011), 162.

By the time Vasyl Makhno settled in New York in 2000, almost none of the poets of the New York Group was firmly based in the city. Yuriy Tarnawsky—the only poet whose White Plains residence in the Westchester, New York, suburbs remains the same now as it was some fifty years ago—still visits the city regularly, but Bohdan Boychuk now spends most of his time in Kyiv, Ukraine, and comes to the US only during the summer months. Patricia Nell Warren lives in Glendale near Los Angeles; Vira Vovk and Emma Andijewska continue residing in Rio de Janeiro and Munich, respectively; Zhenia Vasylkivska lives in Washington, DC; and Bohdan Rubchak lived in Chicago until 2005, and then moved to Boonton, NJ. Despite the fact that they are now scattered around the globe and in their seventies and eighties, they are still creatively active, with the sole exception of Vasylkivska.[27] In the past few years, Tarnawsky has been concentrating his energies on writing fiction in English,[28] and Warren has continued to focus on the issues facing the LGBT community, as both a writer and an activist. Boychuk, Andijewska, and Vovk, on the other hand, carry on publishing in Ukrainian in Kyiv or Lviv. Paradoxical as it sounds, the legacy of the New York Group in New York proper is kept alive by a younger generation of Ukrainian diaspora literati; among them Makhno is arguably the most ingenius. Not only does he fill the thematic gap left unexplored by the New York Group by taking up New York motifs, but he also celebrates the lives of his older colleagues poetically. He could not possibly compose a book of poems about New York City without acknowledging the traces left there by the group. He has done this with a smile, somewhat offhand, but not without a dose of admiration and a slight hint of nostalgia. I could not find a better way to conclude my story about this enduring poetic phenomenon than to quote Makhno's poem on the group in its entirety:

---

27 Vasylkivska stopped publishing a long time ago, but in a recent conversation with me she admitted that she is working on a bilingual poem. Rubchak no longer publishes any belles-lettres, but in 2012 he authored a collection of essays in Ukrainian, published by Piramida House in Lviv. (See his *Mity metamorfoz abo poshuky dobroho svitu: eseï*.)

28 See his *Like Blood in Water* (2007) and *Short Tails* (2011), and more recently *The Placebo Effect Trilogy* (2013).

Нью-Йоркська Група

порожній East Village—заросла щока
Тарнавського—Бойчука й Рубчака
Немає—вони в 60-тих
в каварні сидять попиваючи drink
забули про час і сидять отак рік
а може століття—спитати?

але їх не викличеш з кнайпи сюди
бо їм там цікаво там пиво і дим
там перші дружини і треті коханки
вони розмовляють неначе брати
викликують Лорку—як їх тепер—ти
й чарують підпилу еспанку

ну знаєте—каже Богдан-і-Тиміш
(Ortega-i-Ґасет)—він каже сумніш
пора забиратись додому
бо чути повсюди оте не пора
вони усвідомлюють: чорна діра
їх може втягнути—й по всьому

посидьмо—відказує тихо Б.Б.
та хто там чекає удома тебе?
а тут хоч ці вірші й Антонич
зелений стримить у зеленім вікні
—мов ключ у замку—наче корок на дні
який хоч-не-хоч не потоне

куди це додому?—питає Ю.Т.
він в светрі червонім—як кактус—цвіте
не бачить він дому—пустеля
Еспанії без і найменшя Міґель
що схоже на хрипи шахтарських легень
й католицькі шпилі костелів

отож порішили посидіти ще
трикутні трапеції гострих плечей
і повні бокали тріпочуть по стінах
Богдан-і-Тиміш і Ю.Т. і Б.Б.
мов змій триголовий вогнями сопе
а далі—Харибда і Сцилла

під ранок вони—посварившись—мовчать
і пиво і сеча й дружини сичать
а далі ще старість по різних містах
усіх розведе—а при цьому столі
ще легко пропити образи старі
і марку приклеїти на листа[29]

The New York Group

an empty East Village—stubbles on the cheek
where are you Tarnawsky—Boychuk and Rubchak?
they're gone—back to the sixties where their hearts belong
in their favorite café sipping wine and beer
having lost track of time sitting there for a year
perhaps for century—dare one ask how long?

but from that hangout you can't call them back here
they prefer that place—with the smoke and the beer
where their first wives and third lovers they'd meet
that's where they can converse like brothers
reciting Lorca among others
and romance a tipsy señorita

well you know—says Bohdan-y-Tymish
(Ortega-y-Gasset)—as much as I wish
to stay here with you—it is time to go home
for the words *Now's Not the Time*[30] are heard by us all

---

29 Vasyl' Makhno, *38 virshiv pro n'iu-iork i deshcho inshe* (Kyiv: Krytyka, 2004), 40-41.

30 Translation of the Ukrainian original "Ne pora," which is the title of a patriotic Ukrainian song based on the words of Ivan Franko.

and we realize now that a deadly black hole
can pull us inside—and then all will be gone

let's stay longer—whispers B.B. in response
there is no one waiting for you at the house
here at least there's poetry and drink
and stuck in a green window is the green Antonych
—like a key in a lock—or a cork at the bottom—which
like it or not will float and not sink

asks Yuriy Tarnawsky—and go home to whom?
in his red sweater—like a cactus—in bloom
for him there is no home—only a wasteland
Without Spain and the name of Cervantes—Miguel
resembling the cough that coalminers' lungs expel
and the church spires of that Catholic land

and so they decided to stay even longer
triangular shadows of their pointed shoulders
and the full decanters dance all over the wall
Bohdan-y-Tymish and Yu. T. and Boychuk Bóhdan
who's puffing smoke and fire like a three-headed dragon
until—between Scylla and Charybdis they fall

by dawn all arguments dissolve into silence
only full bladders and the wives try their patience
soon with old age to different towns they'll scatter—
while the comfort this table still brings
is to drown the old insults in drinks
and to glue a postage stamp on a letter[31]

A citizen of the world, Makhno pays tribute to the New York Group in a very witty, humorous, observant, sophisticated, and simultaneously down-to-earth manner. And the group's legacy lives on.

---

31 Vasyl Makhno, *Thread and Selected New York Poems*, trans. Orest Popovych (New York: Meeting Eyes Bindery, 2009), 40-41.

Conclusion

The phenomenon of the New York Group of Ukrainian émigré poets provides an engaging case study for exploring the cultural and aesthetic ramifications of exile. Political expulsions, forced or voluntary, engender states of living in-between, living in the interstices of different cultures, different linguistic realities, and different ideological premises. The twentieth century lends itself particularly well to studies of exilic and liminal circumstances—after all, it witnessed two horrific world wars in which millions perished, and which resulted in millions of refugees and displaced persons. These people, for whom the concept of home lost its stability and changed meaning, invariably became "Others" in their adopted countries. The state of alterity, or the state of radical otherness, applies equally to everyday existence and to the realm of aesthetic production. The artistic manifestations put forth by the poets of the New York Group fit these parameters especially well. Having settled mostly in the United States, they accepted their exilic condition with no grudges—one could even say they welcomed it, but continued, nonetheless, to cherish their link with their homeland via poetry written in the mother tongue. This was their way of paying tribute to the poetic tradition of their ethnic kin, at the same time infusing it with formal and thematic innovations spurred by their intimate knowledge of the achievements in the arts of the Western world.

The poets of the New York Group considered themselves the only genuine modernists in Ukrainian literature, even though modernist movements in Ukraine had their beginnings in the late 1890s. However, being part of modernism, especially in its international hypostasis, meant a great deal to them. The poets cultivated this connection with utmost care, sometimes through numerous translations of iconic modernist texts into Ukrainian, at other times through critical writings, and it would not be an exaggeration to conclude that they were indeed the first self-consciously modernist literati in Ukrainian letters.

The New York Group's most active period spans approximately fifteen years, from the mid-1950s through the early 1970s. This period coincided with the publication of its annual poetry almanac *Novi poezii* and witnessed the publication of its members' most significant poetic books. The poets were not only very productive aesthetically during that time, but were also discursively vocal. In their dealings with the Ukrainian émigré milieu (periphery) and Ukraine (center) they engendered three distinct discourses, each touching on a different aspect of their activity and pertaining to a specific time interval. The first discourse pertained to the issue of establishing the group's authority. During the formative years of the group's existence (roughly 1955-1962), the forging of power relations and the acquisition of recognition were at the forefront of their discursive practices. Consolidating into the poetic avant-garde faction of seven and assuming the label "New York Group" allowed its members to gain considerable authority within literary circles and rather quickly paved the way to their further development.

Yet the emergence of a new wave of writers in Ukraine in the 1960s, thanks to Nikita Khrushchov's policy of liberalization following Stalin's death, created a situation in which the New York Group was forced to compete for an audience with the "Sixties" (*shistdesiatnyky*) generation in Ukraine. Hence, the second discourse was all about the issues of reception and sufficient access to the reading public, replacing the previous concerns of building power relations to effectively impact the émigré literary process. The discourse on reception and on possible collaboration with the literati from Ukraine lasted more or less from the mid-1960s through the early 1970s. The New York Group's hopes of visiting Ukraine on an official invitation from the Writers' Union after establishing personal contacts with the poets Dmytro Pavlychko and Ivan Drach of Kyiv (the leading *shistdesiatnyky*) were not fulfilled: the New York Group had to wait for such invitations until the period of glasnost and perestroika in the late 1980s. The discursive encounter with the Kyiv poets initiated a desire among some members of the New York Group to be recognized and accepted also by the center, that is, by their homeland.

The third and final discourse hovers around the issues of the group's legacy and acceptance by literary Ukraine. This period coincided with the publication of the journal *Svito-vyd* (1990-1999), which was a joint publishing venture of the New York Group and the Writers' Union of Ukraine. Publishing the journal was one way the group was able to influence its own legacy, at the same time shaping the reception of its output in Ukraine shortly after independence. Another way to influence its image was to publish books in Ukraine rather than in the United States. And, indeed, all creatively active members of the group have had their poetry books published exclusively in Ukraine since 1991.

Philosophically and aesthetically, the poets of the New York Group are firmly anchored in existentialism and surrealism. In a way, these two signposts point equally to the importance of freedom, and both project something unsettling about the human condition. In the case of existentialism, being condemned to be free puts an enormous burden upon an individual to use this freedom wisely and responsibly; in the case of surrealism, the desire to transcend rationality and reach a place in which opposites are no longer contradictory is arguably utopian. In either case, a world with no a priori given moral values, as professed by existentialists, reverberates somewhat with surrealists' dreams of unharnessed creative forces lying deep in the human unconscious. A belief in the power of startling images lies at the core of the group's poetic activity. The reliance on metaphor and unusual verbal juxtapositions makes the poets' oeuvre uniquely fresh and exciting.

Thematically, the New York Group also offered new paradigms. Despite the fact that New York City as a metropolis does not figure prominently in the group's texts, the poets do not shy away from urban motifs. In fact, the city in its abstract accoutrement, often depicted in opposition to nature, is overwhelmingly present throughout the poetic landscape put forth by the group. The most iconic thematic innovations introduced by the New York Group comprise the utilization of Spanish and/or Latin American material and the incorporation of a play element and erotica. The latter was employed not only to stir controversy by debunking sexual taboos, but also to convey existentialist views—the need for freedom and responsibility for each individual choice. The poets' shared preoccupation with death as an existential predicament unquestionably has its roots in the philosophy of nothingness. The ludic and Spanish motifs, on the other hand, constitute the masks behind which looms the New York Group's profound connection to the internationalist tendencies inherent in the modernist movements. The poets' rapture with eroticism, death, "Spanishness," and the ludic betrays their cosmopolitan stance, which many a time antagonized their potential émigré readers.

While being popular was never the group's goal, the New York poets yearned nonetheless for an appreciative reader. Despite occasional controversies instigated by those who found the poets' oeuvre too pessimistic or "un-Ukrainian," by and large the New York Group always had a loyal audience. However small this audience was, it did not lack in enthusiasm. Thanks to those devoted readers, the group could establish its own publishing venture, supporting first the publication of *Novi poezii* and then some twenty years later that of *Svito-vyd*, as well as managing the publication of a number of poetry collections for both its own members and other poets.

In many ways, the longevity of the New York Group's existence and activity is intriguing. None of the known modernist groupings managed to persist for such a long span of time. Despite the fluidity of its membership and periods of creative quietude, the group has no doubt influenced the path of the native poetic tradition over the course of half a century, and inscribed itself permanently in the history of Ukrainian literature. Yet, even though individual poets of the New York Group are studied in Ukraine, with Emma Andijewska and Yuriy Tarnawsky leading the charts, the phenomenon of the group as a singular aesthetic entity still awaits its comprehensive treatment by Ukrainian literary scholars. This book of essays touches on many different aspects of the group's artistic achievements, viewed from many angles—discursive, aesthetic, thematic, and even historical—but in the end provides just one possible reading of its creative output, far from exhaustive and undeniably subjective. Thus, my interpretation invariably constitutes an invitation to a further conversation.

Selected Bibliography

Agosin, Marjorie. *Pablo Neruda*. Translated by Lorraine Roses. Boston: Twayne, 1986.

Andiievs'ka, Emma. *Arkhitekturni ansambli*. Munich: Suchasnist', 1989.

——. *Kavarnia*. Munich: Suchasnist', 1983.

——. *Kuty opostin'*. New York: V-vo N'iu-Iorks'koi hrupy, 1962.

——. *Mezhyrichchia*. Kyiv: Vsesvit, 1998.

——. *Narodzhennia idola*. New York: Slovo, 1958.

——. *Nauka pro zemliu*. Munich: Suchasnist', 1975.

——. *Pervni*. Munich: Suchasnist', 1964.

——. *Pisni bez tekstu*. Munich: n.p., 1968.

——. *Poezii*. N.p.: Ukraina, 1951.

——. *Ryba i rozmir*. New York: V-vo N'iu-Iorks'koi hrupy, 1961.

——. *Spokusy sviatoho Antoniia*. Munich: Suchasnist', 1985.

——. *Znaky. Tarok*. Kyiv: Dnipro, 1995.

Astaf'iev, O. H., and A. O. Dnistrovyi, eds. *Poety N'iu-Iorks'koi hrupy: Antolohiia*. Kharkiv: Ranok, 2003.

Barth, John. "The Literature of Exhaustion." *The Atlantic* 220.2 (1967): 29-34.

———. "The Literature of Replenishment: Postmodernist Fiction." *The Atlantic* 245.1 (1980): 65-71.

Bataille, Georges. *Erotism: Death and Sensuality*. Translated by Mary Dalwood. San Francisco: City Lights, 1986.

Bauman, Zygmunt. "Assimilation into Exile: The Jew as a Polish Writer." In *Exile and Creativity: Signposts, Travelers, Outsiders, Backward Glances*, edited by Susan Rubin Suleiman, 321-52. Durham and London: Duke University Press, 1998.

Berman, Art. *Preface to Modernism*. Urbana: University of Illinois Press, 1994.

Bila, Anna. *Ukrains'kyi literaturnyi avangard: poshuky, styl'ovi napriamky*. Kyiv: Smoloskyp, 2006.

Boichuk, Bohdan. *Chas boliu*. New York: Slovo, 1957.

———. "Dekil'ka dumok pro N'iu-Iorks'ku hrupu i dekil'ka zadnikh dumok." *Suchasnist'* 1 (1979): 20-33.

———. "Iak i poshcho narodylasia N'iu-Iorks'ka hrupa: Do bil'sh-mensh desiatylittia." *Terem* 2.2 (1966): 34-38.

———. *Mandrivka til*. New York: V-vo N'iu-Iorks'koi hrupy, 1967.

———. *Memories of Love: The Selected Poems of Bohdan Boychuk*. Translated by David Ignatow and Mark Rudman. Riverdale-on-Hudson: The Sheep Meadow Press, 1989.

———. *Podorozh z uchytelem*. New York: V-vo N'iu-Iorks'koi hrupy, 1976.

———. "Pro reliatyvnu absoliutnist' i navpaky." *Suchasnist'* 5 (1970): 104-7.

———. *Spomyny liubovy*. New York: V-vo N'iu-Iorks'koi hrupy, 1963.

———. *Tretia osin'*. Kyiv: Dnipro, 1991.

———. *Virshi dlia Mekhiko*. Munich: V-vo N'iu-Iorks'koi hrupy, 1964.

———. *Virshi kokhannia i molytvy*. Kyiv: Fakt, 2002.

———. *Virshi, vybrani i peredostanni*. New York: Suchasnist', 1983.

———. "Zatemnena storona misiatsia." *Krytyka* 4.10 (2000): 27-28.

———. *Zemlia bula pustoshnia*. New York: V-vo Ukrains'koi students'koi hromady, 1959.

———. *Zibrani tvory*. 2 vols. Kyiv: Fakt, 2007.

Boichuk, Bohdan, and Bohdan Rubchak, eds. *Koordynaty: Antolohiia suchasnoi ukrains'koi poezii na Zakhodi*. 2 vols. Munich: Suchasnist', 1969.

Bradbury, Malcolm, and James McFarlene, eds. *Modernism, 1890-1930*. 1976. Harmondsworth: Penguin, 1991.

Breton, André. *Manifestoes of Surrealism*. Translated by Richard Seaver and Helen R. Lane. Ann Arbor: University of Michigan Press, 1969.

Brodsky, Joseph. "The Condition We Call Exile." In *Altogether Elsewhere: Writers on Exile*, edited by Marc Robinson, 3-11. Boston: Faber, 1994.

Bürger, Peter. *Theory of the Avant-garde*. Translated by Michael Shaw. Minneapolis: University of Minnesota Press, 1984.

Burke, Ruth E. *The Games of Poetics: Ludic Criticism and Postmodern Fiction*. New York: Lang, 1994.

Caillois, Roger. *Man, Play and Games*. Translated by Meyer Barash. London: Thames & Hudson, 1962.

Calinescu, Matei. *Five Faces of Modernity: Modernism, Avant-garde, Decadence, Kitsch, Postmodernism*. Durham and London: Duke University Press, 1987.

Carson, Anne. *Eros the Bittersweet: An Essay*. Princeton: Princeton University Press, 1986.

Dyvnych, Iurii [Iurii Lavrinenko]. "Mekhikans'ko-ukrains'ke vydyvo v poezii Bohdana Boichuka." *Lysty do pryiateliv* 13.5-7 (1965): 49-55.

———. "Z rodu Mavok i Kassandr." *Lysty do pryiateliv*. 13.8-10 (1965): 21-25.

Edwards-Stout, Kergan. "Legendary Author Patricia Nell Warren: Ever the Front Runner." *The Huffington Post*. 16 Jan. 2013. Web. http://www.huffington-post.com/kergan-edwardsstout/patricia-nell-warren_b_2452879.html (accessed 25 Nov. 2013).

Efimov-Schneider, Lisa. "Poetry of the New York Group: Ukrainian Poets in an American Setting." *Canadian Slavonic Papers* 23 (1981): 291-301.

Ehrmann, Jacques. "Homo Ludens Revisited." Translated by Cathy and Phil Lewis. In *Game, Play, Literature*, edited by Jacques Ehrmann, 31-57. Boston: Beacon, 1968.

Eskin, Michael. *Ethics and Dialogue in the Works of Levinas, Bakhtin, Madel'shtam and Celan*. New York: Oxford University Press, 2000.

Eysteinsson, Astradur. *The Concept of Modernism*. Ithaca, NY: Cornell University Press, 1990.

Fizer, Ivan. "Interv'iu z chlenamy N'iu-Iorks'koi hrupy." *Suchasnist'* 10 (1988): 11-38.

Foster, Hal, ed. *Anti-Aesthetic: Essays on Postmodern Culture*. Port Townsend, WA: Bay, 1983.

Foucault, Michel. *Discipline and Punish: The Birth of Prison*. Translated by Alan Sheridan. 2ⁿᵈ ed. New York: Vintage Books, 1995.

———. *The History of Sexuality*. Vol. 1: An Introduction. Translated by Robert Hurley. New York: Vintage Books, 1990.

———. *Madness and Civilization: A History of Insanity in the Age of Reason*. Translated by Richard Howard. New York: Vintage Books, 1988.

———. "The Subject and Power." In *Michel Foucault: Beyond Structuralism and Hermeneutics*, by Hubert L. Dreyfus and Paul Rabinow, 208-226. 2ⁿᵈ ed. Chicago: University of Chicago Press, 1983.

Gibian, George, and H. W. Tjalsma, eds. *Russian Modernism: Culture and the Avant-garde, 1900-1930*. Ithaca, NY: Cornell University Press, 1976.

Glad, John, ed. *Literature in Exile*. Durham: Duke University Press, 1990.

Grabes, Herbert. "Ethics, Aesthetics, and Alterity." In *Ethics and Aesthetics: The Moral Turn of Postmodernism*, edited by Gerhard Hoffmann and Alfred Hornung, 13-28. Heidelberg: Universitätsverlag C. Winter, 1996.

Grabowicz, George G. "Commentary: Exorcising Ukrainian Modernism." *Harvard Ukrainian Studies* 15 (1991): 273-83.

———. "A Great Literature." In *The Refugee Experience: Ukrainian Displaced Persons after World War II*, edited by Wsewolod W. Isajiw, Yury Boshyk, and Roman Senkus, 240-68. Edmonton: CIUS Press, 1992.

———. "New Directions in Ukrainian Poetry in the United States." In *The Ukrainian Experience in the United States: A Symposium*, edited by Paul R. Magosci, 156-78. Cambridge: Harvard Ukrainian Research Institute, 1979.

Graff, Gerald. *Literature Against Itself: Literary Ideas in Modern Society*. Chicago: University of Chicago Press, 1979.

Gurr, Andrew. *Writers in Exile: The Identity of Home in Modern Literature*. Brighton, UK: Harvester, 1981.

Habermas, Jürgen. "Modernity versus Postmodernity." *New German Critique* 22 (1981): 3-14.

Hans, James S. *The Play of the World*. Amherst: University of Massachusetts Press, 1981.

Hassan, Ihab. *The Dismemberment of Orpheus: Toward a Postmodern Literature*. 2ⁿᵈ ed. Madison: University of Wisconsin, 1982.

———. *The Postmodern Turn: Essays in Postmodern Theory and Culture*. Columbus: Ohio State University Press, 1987.

Hemingway, Ernest. *Death in the Afternoon*. New York: Scribner, 1932.

Hrabovych, Hryhorii [George G. Grabowicz]. "Vid mitiv do krytyky: deshcho pro analizu Rubchaka ta poeziiu Patrytsii Kylyny." *Suchasnist'* 5 (1969): 74-87.

Huizinga, Johan. *Homo Ludens: A Study of the Play-Element in Culture*. Boston: Beacon, 1955.

Hundorova, Tamara. "Dekadans i postmodernizm: pytannia movy." *Svito-vyd* 1 (1995): 64-75.

Hutcheon, Linda. *A Poetics of Postmodernism: History, Theory, Fiction*. New York: Routledge, 1988.

Huyssen, Andreas. *After the Great Divide: Modernism, Mass Culture, Postmodernism*. Bloomington: Indiana University Press, 1986.

Ilie, Paul. *Literature and Inner Exile: Authoritarian Spain, 1939-1975*. Baltimore: Johns Hopkins University Press, 1980.

Il'nyts'kyi, Mykola. "At the Crossroads of the Century." Translated by Olesia Shchur. In *A Hundred Years of Youth: A Bilingual Anthology of the 20th Century Ukrainian Poetry*, edited by Olha Luchuk and Michael M. Naydan, 59-72. Lviv: Litopys, 2000.

Ilnytzkyj, Oleh S. "The Modernist Ideology of Mykola Khvyl'ovyi." *Harvard Ukrainian Studies* 15 (1991): 257-62.

———. "Ukrainian Symbolism and the Problem of Modernism." *Canadian Slavonic Papers* 34 (1992): 113-30.

———. "*Ukrains'ka khata* and the Paradoxes of Ukrainian Modernism." *Journal of Ukrainian Studies* 19.2 (1994): 5-30.

Jameson, Fredric. "Modernity, Modernism, Late Modernism." Lecture, University of Toronto. 20 Mar. 2001.

———. "Postmodernism, or The Cultural Logic of Late Capitalism." *New Left Review* 146 (1984): 53-92.

Knapp, Bettina L. *Exile and the Writer: Exoteric and Esoteric Experiences. A Jungian Approach*. University Park, PA: Pennsylvania State University Press, 1991.

Kostelanetz, Richard, ed. *The Avant-garde Tradition in Literature*. Buffalo: Prometheus, 1982.

Kostets'kyi, Ihor. "Review of *Trahediia dzhmeliv*, by Patrytsiia Kylyna." *Ukraina i svit* 25-27 (1963-65): 113.

Kotyk, Ihor. *Ekzystentsiinyi vymir liudyny v poezii Iuriia Tarnavs'koho*. Lviv: Natsional'na akademiia nauk Ukrainy, L'vivs'ke viddilennia, 2009.

Kristeva, Julia. *The Kristeva Reader*, edited by Toril Moi. New York: Columbia University Press, 1986.

Kylyna, Patrytsiia [Patricia Nell Warren]. *Legendy i sny*. New York: V-vo N'iu-Iorks'koi hrupy, 1964.

———. *Rozhevi mista*. Munich: Suchasnist', 1969.

———. *Trahediia dzhmeliv*. New York: NIH, 1960.

Lavrinenko, Iurii. *Zrub i parosty: Literaturno-krytychni statti, esei, refleksii*. Munich: Suchasnist', 1971.

Lesych, Vadym. "Andiievs'ka, Kylyna, Iurii Tarnavs'kyi." *Lysty do pryiateliv* 9.11-12 (1961): 26-29.

Levinas, Emmanuel. *Alterity and Transcendence*. Translated by Michael B. Smith. London: Athlone, 1999.

———. *Ethics and Infinity: Conversations with Philippe Nemo*. Translated by Richard A. Cohen. Pittsburgh: Duquesne University Press, 1985.

———. *The Levinas Reader*. Edited by Seán Hand. Cambridge, MA: Blackwell, 1989.

———. *Otherwise than Being or Beyond Essence*. Translated by Alphonso Lingis. Pittsburgh: Duquesne University Press, 1998.

———. *Time and the Other*. Translated by Richard A. Cohen. Pittsburgh: Duquesne University Press, 1987.

Lorca, García Federico. *Collected Poems*. Edited by Christopher Maurer. Vol. 2. New York: Farrar, 1991.

———. *Poet in New York*. Translated by Ben Belitt. New York: Grove Press, 1983.

Lutsyshyna, Oksana. "*Winter Letters* Across Time and Space." *The Ukrainian Weekly* 24 (10 June 2012): 10, 13.

Luckyj, George S. N. *Ukrainian Literature in the Twentieth Century: A Reader's Guide*. Toronto: University of Toronto Press, 1992.

Makaryk, Irena R., and Virlana Tkacz, eds. *Modernism in Kyiv: Kiev/Kyïv/Kiev/Kijów/Kiev. Jubilant Experimentation*. Toronto: University of Toronto Press, 2010.

Makhno, Vasyl'. *Cornelia Street Café*. Kyiv: Fakt, 2007.

―――. *Thread and Selected New York Poems*. Translated by Orest Popovych. New York: Meeting Eyes Bindery, 2009.

―――. *38 virshiv pro n'iu-iork i deshcho inshe*. Kyiv: Krytyka, 2004.

Mazzotta, Giuseppe. *Dante, Poet of the Desert: History and Allegory in the Divine Comedy*. Princeton: Princeton University Press, 1979.

Morenets', Volodymyr. Introduction to *Sady Marii*, by Mykhailo Hryhoriv, 5-33. Kyiv: Svito-vyd, 1997.

Motte, Warren. *Playtexts: Ludics in Contemporary Literature*. Lincoln: University of Nebraska Press, 1995.

Murphy, Richard. *Theorizing the Avant-garde: Modernism, Expressionism, and the Problem of Postmodernity*. Cambridge: Cambridge University Press, 1998.

Nicholls, Peter. *Modernism: A Literary Guide*. Berkeley: University of California Press, 1995.

Novi poezii. 1-12/13. New York: V-vo N'iu-Iorks'koi hrupy, 1959-71.

Pana Grigorescu, Irina. *The Tomis Complex: Exile and Eros in Australian Literature*. Berne: Peter Lang, 1996.

Pavel, Thomas. "Exile as Romance and as Tragedy." In *Exile and Creativity: Signposts, Travelers, Outsiders, Backward Glances*, edited by Susan Rubin Suleiman, 25-36. Durham: Duke University Press, 1998.

Pavlychko, Solomiia. *Dyskurs modernizmu v ukrains'kii literaturi*. 2nd ed. Kyiv: Lybid', 1999.

Paz, Octavio. *The Bow and the Lyre: The Poem, the Poetic Revelation, Poetry and History*. Trans. Ruth L. C. Simms. Austin: University of Texas Press, 1973.

―――. *The Double Flame: Love and Eroticism*. Translated by Helen Lane. New York: Harcourt, 1993.

―――. *An Erotic Beyond: Sade*. Translated by Eliot Weinberger. New York: Harcourt, 1993.

Plato. *Lysis, Pheadrus, and Symposium: Plato on Homosexuality*. Translated by Benjamin Jowett. Amherst, NY: Prometheus, 1991.

Poggioli, Renato. *The Theory of the Avant-garde*. Translated by Gerald Fitzgerald. Cambridge: Harvard University Press, 1968.

Pytlowany, Melanie. "Continuity and Innovation in the Poetry of the New York Group." *Journal of Ukrainian Graduate Studies* 2.1 (1977): 3-21.

Rais, Emanuil. "Poezii Emmy Andiievs'koi." *Suchasnist'* 6 (1965): 108-10.

Revakovych, Mariia [Maria G. Rewakowicz]. "Elementy dehumanizatsii v poezii Emmy Andiievs'koi." *Svito-vyd* 3 (1992): 11-17.

Revakovych, Mariia, ed. *Pivstolittia napivtyshi: Antolohiia poezii N'iu-Iorks'koi hrupy.* Kyiv: Fakt, 2005.

Revakovych, Mariia, and Vasyl' Gabor, eds. *N'iu-Iorks'ka hrupa: Antolohiia poezii, prozy ta eseistyky.* Lviv: Piramida, 2012.

Rewakowicz, Maria G. "Introducing Ukrainian Émigré Poets of the New York Group." *Toronto Slavic Quarterly* 1.3 (2003). http://www.utoronto.ca/slavic/tsq/03/rewakowicz.html. Reprinted in *Toronto Slavic Annual* 1 (2003): 34-50.

Riffaterre, Michael. *Semiotics of Poetry.* Bloomington: Indiana University Press, 1978.

Robinson, Marc, ed. *Altogether Elsewhere: Writers on Exile.* Boston: Faber, 1994.

Rubchak, Bohdan. *Divchyni bez krainy.* New York: V-vo N'iu-Iorks'koi hrupy, 1963.

———. "Homes as Shells: Ukrainian Émigré Poetry." In *New Soil—Old Roots: The Ukrainian Experience in Canada,* edited by Jaroslav Rozumnyj, 87-123. Winnipeg: Ukrainian Academy of Arts and Sciences in Canada, 1983.

———. *Kaminnyi sad.* New York: Slovo, 1956.

———. *Krylo Ikarove.* Kyiv: Dnipro, 1991.

———. *Krylo Ikarove: Novi i vybrani poezii.* Munich: Suchasnist', 1983.

———. "Mandrivnyk, inodi ryba." Introduction to *Cornelia Street Café,* by Vasyl' Makhno, 7-22. Kyiv: Fakt, 2007.

———. "Meandramy Viry Vovk." *Suchasnist'* 1 (1981): 32-49.

———. "Mity chuzhynky." *Suchasnist'* 1 (1968): 10-29; 2 (1968): 33-60.

———. *Mity metamorfoz, abo poshuky dobroho svitu: eseï.* Lviv: Piramida, 2012.

———. *Osobysta Klio.* New York: V-vo N'iu-Iorks'koi hrupy, 1967.

———. "Poeziia antypoezii: Zahal'ni obrysy poezii Iuriia Tarnavs'koho." *Suchasnist'* 4 (1968): 44-55.

———. "Probnyi let." In *Ostap Luts'kyi—Molodomuzivets',* edited by Iurii Luts'kyi, 9-43. New York: Slovo, 1968.

———. *Promenysta zrada.* New York: V-vo N'iu-Iorks'koi hrupy, 1960.

———. "Vid 'sviatykh koriv' do tvorchoho myslennia: Ahon z Hryhoriiem Hrabovychem." *Suchasnist'* 9 (1969): 42-76.

Rudman, Mark. "Introduction." In *Memories of Love: The Selected Poems of Bohdan Boychuk*, edited and translated by David Ignatow and Mark Rudman, 7-14. Riverdale-on-Hudson, NY: The Sheep Meadow Press, 1989.

Rudnytzky, Leonid. "A Poetical Voice of the Ukrainian Diaspora: Random Notes on the Poetry of Vasyl Makhno." *The Ukrainian Quarterly* 67 (2011): 158-64.

Russell, Charles. *Poets, Prophets, and Revolutionaries: The Literary Avant-garde from Rimbaud through Postmodernism*. New York: Oxford University Press, 1985.

Said, Edward. "Reflections on Exile." *Granta* 13 (1984): 159-72.

Sherekh, Iurii [George Shevelov]. *Tretia storozha*. Baltimore: Smoloskyp, 1991.

———. "V oboroni velykykh." *MUR Zbirnyk* 2 (1946): 11-26.

Shevelov, Iurii [George]. "Troie proshchan' i pro te, shcho take istoriia literatury." *Slovo* 3 (1968): 476-84.

Solovei, Eleonora. "Shche trokhy pro misiachni zatemnennia." *Krytyka* 5.1-2 (2001): 27-28.

Struk, Danylo Husar. "Emma Andiievs'ka: 'vershyvannia—virshuvannia.'" *Smoloskyp* 19.5 (1967): 7-8.

———. "The Journal *Svit*: A Barometer of Modernism." *Harvard Ukrainian Studies* 15 (1991): 245-56.

———. "Organizational Aspects of DP Literary Activity." In *The Refugee Experience: Ukrainian Displaced Persons After World War II*, edited by Wsewolod W. Isajiw, Yury Boshyk, and Roman Senkus, 223-39. Edmonton: CIUS Press, 1992.

Suleiman, Susan Rubin, ed. *Exile and Creativity: Signposts, Travelers, Outsiders, Backward Glances*. Durham: Duke University Press, 1998.

Tarnavs'kyi, Iurii. *Bez Espanii*. Munich: Suchasnist', 1969.

———. "Bez Espanii, chy bez znachennia?" *Suchasnist'* 12 (1969): 13-29.

———. *Bez nichoho*. Kyiv: Dnipro, 1991.

———. *Idealizovana biohrafiia*. Munich: Suchasnist', 1964.

———. *Ikh nemaie: Poezii, 1970-1999*. Kyiv: Rodovid, 1999.

———. *Os', iak ia vyduzhuiu*. Munich: Suchasnist', 1978.

———. *Poezii pro nishcho i inshi poezii na tsiu samu temu: Poezii, 1955-1970*. New York: V-vo N'iu-Iorks'koi hrupy, 1970.

———. *Popoludni v Pokipsi.* New York: V-vo N'iu-Iorks'koi hrupy, 1960.

———. *Spomyny.* Munich: Suchasnist', 1964.

———. "Temna storona misiatsia." *Krytyka* 4.7-8 (2000): 4-10.

———. *U ra na.* Kharkiv: Kots, 1993.

———. *Zhyttia v misti.* New York: Slovo, 1956.

Tarnawsky, Maxim. "Modernism in Ukrainian Prose." *Harvard Ukrainian Studies* 15 (1991): 263-72.

Terras, Victor, ed. *Handbook of Russian Literature.* New Haven: Yale University Press, 1985.

Tsarynnyk, Marko. "Mitotvorcha spadshchyna." Rev. of *Legendy i sny.* By Patrytsiia Kylyna. *Suchasnist'* 12 (1965): 106-9.

Turner, Victor. *The Ritual Process: Structure and Anti-Structure.* Chicago: Aldine, 1969.

Vasyl'kivs'ka, Zhenia. *Korotki viddali.* New York: Slovo, 1959.

Vovk, Vira. *Chorni akatsii.* Munich: Na hori, 1961.

———. *Elehii.* Munich: Ukrains'ke V-vo, 1956.

———. *Iunist'.* Munich: Molode zhyttia, 1954.

———. *Kappa khresta.* Munich: Suchasnist', 1969.

———. *Liubovni lysty kniazhny Veroniky do kardynala Dzhovannibattisty.* Munich: Na hori, 1967.

———. *Mandalia.* Rio de Janeiro: Artes Gráficas, 1980.

———. *Meandry.* Rio de Janeiro: Artes Gráficas, 1979.

———. *Poezii.* Kyiv: Rodovid, 2000.

———. "Pro tekhnolohichnyi i metafizychnyi kshtalt myslennia." *Suchasnist'* 12 (1970): 81-86.

———. *Zoria providna.* Munich: Molode zhyttia, 1955.

Warren, Patricia Nell [Kylyna]. *The Beauty Queen.* New York: Morrow, 1978.

———. *Billy's Boy.* Beverly Hills: Wildcat Press, 1997.

———. *The Fancy Dancer.* New York: Morrow, 1976.

———. "From Beginning to New Beginning: A Cycle of Poetry." *Lodestar Quarterly* 6 (2003). Web. http://lodestarquarterly.com/work/113/ (accessed 25 Nov. 2013).

———. *The Front Runner.* New York: Morrow, 1974.

———. *Harlan's Race.* Beverly Hills: Wildcat Press, 1994.

———. *The Last Centennial.* New York: Dial Press, 1971.

242 Selected Bibliography

———. "A Tragedy of Bees: My Years as a Poet in Exile, 1957 to 1973." *The Harvard Gay & Lesbian Review* 2.4 (1995): 17-21.

———. *The Wild Man.* Beverly Hills: Wildcat Press, 2001.

Weightman, John. *The Concept of the Avant-garde: Explorations in Modernism.* London: Alcove, 1973.

Wellek, René. *Discriminations: Further Concepts of Criticism.* New Haven: Yale University Press, 1970.

Index